THE NUMBERS GAME

To Steve —

   It's been wonderful getting
to know you (and your staff!) the
past three years. Thank you for
making us feel so welcome. We're
looking forward to many more great
evenings at Ivy's —

                    Best Always,

THE NUMBERS GAME

Baseball's Lifelong Fascination with Statistics

Alan Schwarz

Thomas Dunne Books

St. Martin's Press New York

THOMAS DUNNE BOOKS.
An imprint of St. Martin's Press.

www.stmartins.com

Design by Nancy Singer Olaguera

Library of Congress Cataloging-in-Publication Data
Schwarz, Alan.
    The numbers game : baseball's lifelong fascination with statistics / Alan Schwarz.
        p. cm.
    ISBN 0-312-32222-4
    EAN 978-0312-32222-9
    I. Baseball—United States—Statistics—History. 2. Baseball statisticians—United States—History. I. Title.

GV877.S385 2004
796.357'021—dc22

2004042755

10 9 8 7 6 5 4 3 2

To everyone who taught me well

Contents

Foreword

By Peter Gammons

Grady Little called it "his gut." It cost him his job.

Last October, Little, then manager of the Boston Red Sox, found his team perilously clinging to a 5–2 lead over the New York Yankees in the decisive seventh game of the American League Championship Series. With one out in the eighth, Boston just five outs from its first World Series since 1986, New York began to rally against the Red Sox ace, Pedro Martinez. Little decided to keep Martinez in—and the move immediately backfired. The Yankees pounded Martinez for three runs to tie the score and went on to win the game and the series, while Little—Boston's new Bill Buckner—was left with a decision to defend.

Little said he was simply holding fast to his instinct, that this was *Pedro Martinez*, after all, the best pitcher on the team. But his bosses knew better. Boston's general manager, Theo Epstein, knew that all season, after passing the 100-pitch mark, Martinez was a ticking bomb. Before that point his statistics confirmed him as one of the best pitchers in the history of baseball; afterward, nothing close. The Red Sox owner, John Henry, knew this, too. He didn't become a billionaire hedge fund operator without knowing a little something about data and predictability. Little had chosen to go with his gut over what the numbers unequivocally demanded. He lost his job soon thereafter.

It wasn't long before columnists who canoe in the mainstream lampooned the Boston front office—which also includes the high priest of statistical analysis, Bill James—as leaders of the Stat Freak Era. Epstein didn't play college or professional baseball, graduated from Yale, has a law degree, and respects statistics, so he is (in the words of one New York columnist) a "geek." This went beyond Boston: Scouts, writers, and other traditionalists have chafed at Michael Lewis's 2003 bestseller, *Moneyball*, which examined the way Billy Beane and his two Harvard-educated assistants, Paul DePodesta and David Forst, used statistics and predictability studies to run the Oakland Athletics.

These folks have it all so wrong. When will they realize this is anything but new?

Critics didn't want to hear that the A's philosophy was ushered in two decades ago by Sandy Alderson, a Dartmouth and Harvard Law School grad who rebuilt the Oakland operation around on-base percentage. Or that two future general managers (Danny Evans of the Dodgers and Doug Melvin of the Brewers) cut their front-office teeth on statistical computer systems in the early 1980s. The Chicken Littles who complained that baseball's sky was falling conveniently forgot that Earl Weaver kept batter–pitcher breakdowns on index cards, and that Whitey Herzog, who believed that defense won more games than statistics showed, used to sit in his office every day and chart every ball hit during his games. Or that the brilliant Branch Rickey used a Canadian statistician, Allan Roth, in the 1940s to help run the Brooklyn Dodgers. Or that all the way back to the 1860s, writers such as Henry Chadwick were fiddling around with new-fangled defensive statistics.

Then again, chances are that the people complaining haven't *forgotten* about this stuff. They never knew it in the first place. That's what makes the book you're holding so important.

Alan Schwarz has written one of the most original and engrossing histories of baseball you could ever read. He traces the evolution of America's pastime through its obsession with statistics, which has bubbled over since day one—from Henry Chadwick to the Bill James generation and beyond, with all sorts of captivating stops in between. The nasty fights over Ty Cobb's batting averages. The birth of statistics houses like the Elias Sports Bureau and STATS Inc. The unending debates over which statistical widgets work best. If you read today that batting averages are "worse than worthless," you'd assume it came out of the mouth of James, Epstein, or some other modern stathead, right? Nope. It was F. C. Lane of *Baseball Magazine*, almost a hundred years ago, before he launched into a two-part series that invented a whole new set of illuminating statistics. If they'd had salary arbitration cases at the turn of the century, Lane would have been right there, banging on the numbers just like the geeks do today.

Whether professionals or not, so many of us fans grew up playing with baseball statistics, so much so that we got higher SAT scores because they taught us to think mathematically before the third grade. We played those wonderful tabletop statistics games like All-Star Baseball (invented by my cousin, Ethan Allen) and Strat-O-Matic. An entire generation grew up on Bill James's *Baseball Abstract* series and the *Elias Baseball Analysts*. These folks aren't all geeks, by the way; John F. Kennedy kept the 1961 *Baseball Register* in his White House desk drawer his entire presidency.

Statistics have been an integral part of baseball for more than 150 years, studied and sanctified in ways few fans (and industry insiders) have ever known. This book should change that.

Henry Chadwick would have loved it. He would have fired Grady Little, too.

◇ Introduction

When you get right down to it, no corner of American culture is more precisely counted, more passionately quantified, than the performance of baseball players. Television advertisers decide how to spend $30 billion a year based on information from just 5,000 Nielsen boxes. The U.S. Census aims only to be a pretty good estimate. Even the counting of presidential votes has been unmasked as shockingly murky. But baseball statistics? They are recorded, analyzed, and memorized with an exactitude that humans summon only for matters so, well, so *important*.

We know that in 2003 Alex Rodriguez slugged .555 with men on base, hit 3 doubles on 2–1 counts, and had a .859 "zone rating" at shortstop. We can look up that Nolan Ryan had 1.78 groundball-to-flyball ratio in 1974, and yielded batters a .295 on-base percentage with the bases loaded. Dozens of these and other categories appear in newspapers and on Web sites every single day of the baseball season, updated to the instant, for every one of a thousand players. Eventually, the best of these numbers ascend to a meaning well above the simple digits that comprise them: The number .406 *is* Ted Williams's 1941 batting average, 56 the length of Joe DiMaggio's hitting streak. The list goes on: 61 . . . 4,256 . . . 1.12 . . . 755. These numbers tell the stories of players and pennant races in a manner that words, photographs, and videotape never do. Baseball and its statistics are inseparable, as lovingly intertwined as the swirls of a candy cane.

And the funny thing is, they always have been. Most fans assume that baseball's infatuation with statistics is a modern phenomenon, a product of the computer age. But it is not, not by a longshot. Arguments over the relative merits of batting average and fielding percentage, runs scored and runs driven in, date back to the game's earliest days in the nineteenth century, with annual scrambles to invent new measures. (One writer back then feared that baseball "will be brought down almost to a mathematical calculation.") And while many people believe that the serious study of baseball statistics was invented by Bill James in the 1980s, the science he made famous has consumed people from chemists to crackpots for more than a century. I wanted to read a book about all this, about baseball's lifelong passion for its numbers, but it didn't exist. So I decided to write it.

This book is not about the statistics themselves. It is about the *people* obsessed with baseball's statistics ever since the box score started it all in 1845: The zealots who keep them, the fans who devise them, the scientists—some of them Nobel laureates—who pursue a grand unifying theory for them. I want you to feel as if you're meeting Henry Chadwick, who built the game's early statistical skeleton with his customized box score and a slew of early categories. Or George Lindsey, a Canadian military officer in the 1950s who blew off his command to figure out, once and for all, how many runners score from second base on a single. Or Dan Okrent, the writer who both discovered Bill James, of which he is proud, and invented Rotisserie league baseball, of which he is considerably less so.

You should feel the passion of the dozens of researchers and college students in the late 1960s who spent years crisscrossing the United States, cobbling together statistical minutae and other factoids, to finally unveil *The Baseball Encyclopedia.* You should sense the hatred between Bill James and Seymour Siwoff of the Elias Sports Bureau, and watch how that enmity led to the rise of STATS Inc., the behemoth company that today spits out more statistics than anyone. Along the journey you will run into Allan Roth, Branch Rickey's right-hand stats whiz who helped devise strategies for the Jackie Robinson Brooklyn Dodgers; Hal Richman, who invented the Strat-O-Matic Baseball dice game when he was only 11; and Eric Walker, the NPR radio voice whose statistical reports for the Oakland A's spawned the major leagues' modern on-base percentage craze. There are so many more, all of them playing his (or her) role in the history of baseball statistics, a time line that has always run parallel to that of the pastime itself.

No other sport has anywhere near such reverence for its statistics. Few fans or journalists, if any, could name last year's basketball assist leader or Walter Payton's lifetime rushing total. Baseball's reams of numbers, meanwhile, form a captivating universe that has spawned a science all its own: sabermetrics, named after the Society for American Baseball

Research, whose members study statistics like solar systems in baseball's sky. Do doubles or walks revolve around runs scored? Which model best accounts for luck's everpresent gravity? The pursuit is as aesthetic as it is intellectual. A hitter with a .300 batting average, .400 on-base percentage, and .500 slugging percentage is as beautiful to a sabermetrician as the 3-4-5 triangle was to Pythagoras.

Every fan, for 150 years, has connected to baseball through statistics in a different way, whether from newspaper box scores, the backs of Topps baseball cards, or modern fantasy leagues. This is the story of that rich and eternal attraction through the stories of the people who felt it most. I hope you enjoy meeting them as much as I did.

THE
NUMBERS
GAME

Henry Chadwick. *(National Baseball Hall of Fame Library, Cooperstown, N.Y.)*

1

Bless Them, Father

The tobacconist turned the corner from Bond Street onto Lafayette and keyed open his store at the usual time, 7 A.M. He sat down with his tea and unfolded his two-penny paper, the *New York Herald*. The date: August 18, 1858.

The front page retold yesterday's incredible news. The new transatlantic telegraph cable, a 2,200-mile piece of copper wire that took a year to string under the ocean, had allowed a ninety-eight-word message from Queen Victoria to President Buchanan to flash across the water in a mere 17 hours. To think—information that once took a fortnight to reach the other continent now took less than a day. Fireworks exploded around City Hall; the United States and England felt closer to one another than they had since, well, that little tiff at Lexington and Concord.

The merchant turned the page to his steady interest, the business section. As usual, numbers buzzed about like bees in a honeycomb: From the loan and deposit totals of 40 New York banks, earnings breakdowns of the Erie Railroad, dozens of stock fluctuations, and the prices of flour, coffee, cotton, iron, and molasses, numerical charts carried with them a fascinating immediacy and exactitude. After soaking it all in, he flipped to page four, where midway down the right-hand column he found yet another chart. This one was different from the others.

BROOKLYN			NEW YORK		
Names.	**H.L.**	**R's**	**Names.**	**H.L.**	**R's**
Masten, catcher	3	4	Van Cott, pitcher	2	1
Pidgeon, pitcher	5	3	De Bost, catcher	3	0
Oliver, second base	3	3	Gelston, short	2	3
M. O'Brien, third base	4	2	Bixby, first base	4	0
Pearce, short	2	4	Pinckney, sec'nd base	3	1
P. O'Brien, left field	2	3	Davis, centre field	4	0
Grum, right field	1	6	Marsh, third base	3	1
Manolt, centre field	4	2	Tooker, left field	3	1
Price, first base	3	2	Hoyt, right field	3	1
Total		29	Total		8

Runs Made in each Inning.

	1st.	2d.	3rd.	4th.	5th.	6th.	7th.	8th.	9th.		
Brooklyn	6	0	5	6	2	3	4	2	1	—Total	29
New York	2	0	1	0	0	0	1	0	4	—Total	8

THE GREAT BASE BALL MATCH—ALL NEW YORK VS. ALL BROOKLYN, the headline above it read, followed by two long paragraphs recounting the event. The best ballplayers of New York and Brooklyn, representing then-separate cities eager to prove their mettle against each other, had staged an exhibition of baseball, a new sport descendant of cricket, that attracted thousands of spectators—even the "fair sex," the article claimed—to the Fashion Race Course in upper Queens. The tobacconist had in fact heard of this series, now tied at one win apiece. The first game, back in July, had attracted more than 10,000 spectators, jamming the roads with horse-drawn buses and carriages. People taking the Flushing Railroad were met at the station by a carnival atmosphere, complete with guess-your-weight booths and shysters playing three-card monte. *All for adults playing a child's game?* he wondered. The fellow would have turned the page dismissively, but the numbers in "the score," the accompanying array of dots and digits, testified to something more significant, more scientific. More *legitimate*.

Brooklyn had won, 29 runs to 8, but the little chart told stories of Brooklyn's 29–8 victory and offered explanations as succinctly as his stock listings. Grum, Brooklyn's right fielder, clearly had led his team to victory, having scored 6 runs with just 1 "hand lost," or out. New York's shortstop, Gelston, scored 3 runs with 2 hands lost, while several of his mates—De Bost, Bixby, and Davis—scored nary one run among them. It was all very clear; responsibility for the win or loss was identified, codified, and solidified, fired in the dispassionate kiln of numbers. Perhaps this baseball held more than at first glance . . .

Several weeks later, on September 10, the tobacconist decided to close shop early and check out the third and final game of the New York–Brooklyn series in person. He caught a small steamer from the Fulton Ferry, disembarked at Hunter's Point, and took the Flushing Railroad to the Fashion Course, where he paid 50 cents admission—a decidedly new custom of the day. He watched the New Yorkers mount an early 7–2 lead and hold off the Brooklynites 29–18, with groups of partisans vociferously rooting and clapping for fine plays from their side.

The next day, perusing his morning *Herald*, he found the box score, a perfect little encapsulation of the afternoon's events. There was Gelston, scoring five runs for the New Yorks. Tooker, who also made a splendid catch in left field, made three runs of his own. And De Bost! A fine catcher indeed. The numbers confirmed what he had seen. They let him relive it, measure it, analyze it. A baseball fan was born.

The scene repeated itself with countless bank clerks, teachers, dry-goods dealers, and more in the late 1850s throughout New York, baseball's primordial petri dish. The new sport's statistics carried an unexpected purposefulness. After the last out had been made and the sun had set on the ball field, the numbers emerged to glow like gas lamps, lighting the way to a new appreciation for the game.

Humans' compulsion to count, to quantify the world around them, has been around almost as long as their 10 fingers. Ancient civilizations would keep tallies by etching notches on bones or wooden sticks. (This led to today's double meaning of the word *score*.) The Domesday Book of 1086 statistically surveyed William the Conqueror's England to determine land revenues due the crown. Almanacs from 1500 on evolved from navigational charts to agricultural databanks, becoming some of the world's most widely selling books. The mid-nineteenth century in particular saw a sharp spike in the keeping of statistics: Insurance men waded through mortality rate ledgers and accountants mastered double-entry bookkeeping while social reformers debated issues of prisons, schools, and drunkenness with ever more sophisticated numerical information. "When you can't express it in numbers," the scientist Lord Kelvin (1824–1907) once said, "your knowledge is of a meager and unsatisfactory kind." Statistics were becoming cold and incontrovertible tools of a new generation. How fitting, then, that they be married with its new game: baseball.

Despite later efforts to award the genesis of baseball to Abner Doubleday and his merry men of Cooperstown in 1839—a stubborn myth since picked apart like a Thanksgiving turkey—the sport in fact evolved from the English games of cricket and rounders, ball games that bequeathed to it their zeal for quantifying the goings-on in charts of numbers. In 1837, the Constitution of the Olympic Ball Club of Philadelphia, which played a variety called town ball, mandated that a scorer must record in a book "an accurate account of all the games played on Club days, date of the same, names of the players, the number of points made by each . . ." Eight years later, Alexander Cartwright and his New York Knickerbockers codified the first set of modern baseball rules: Bases were set 42 paces (approximately today's 90 feet) apart, batters got three strikes and teams three outs, and the game ended when one team scored its 21st "ace," or run. It took mere weeks before the first primitive box score—initially termed an "abstract"—appeared in the New York *Morning News* on October 22, 1845.

The chart clearly demonstrated baseball's recent roots in cricket. That sport's batters have but two fates: either being put out or scoring a point by reaching the opposite wicket. With those sensibilities in mind, the first baseball box score listed each New York and Brooklyn player beside his two totals of runs and "hands out"; hits that placed a batter on base without ultimately helping him score a run went wholly unrecorded. But as the game grew more popular, spreading to more than a dozen teams in the New York area and many others outside the city, baseball's record keepers quickly recognized how complicated, and scientific, the new sport already was becoming.

Baseball was a pastoral game, to be sure. Games at Hoboken, New Jersey's Elysian Fields, one of the most popular grounds, sat atop a cliff and overlooked the Hudson River with a gorgeous view of lower Manhattan island. (The longest drives to right field could plop into the water.) In 1856, a young cricket reporter happened upon a ball game there between New York's Eagle and Gotham clubs and was transfixed by the intricacy of the contest, the dance among batters, fielders, and base runners. "The game was being sharply played on both sides and I watched it with deeper interest than any previous base ball match that I had seen," the man recalled some years later. His name was Henry Chadwick, and he soon decided to become baseball's greatest evangelist, a preacher from the pulpit of numbers. "The Father of Baseball," as he came to be known, Chadwick spent the next half-century designing new scoring methods, box scores and statistics, all formulated not just to capture the events of the game but to encourage a value system he held desperately dear.

Chadwick came from a long line of social reformers. Born on October 5, 1824, in Exeter, England, he counted among his relatives a grandfather who, according to the historian Jules Tygiel, dedicated his days to promoting "measures for the improvement of the condition of the population," as well as a half-brother, Edwin, who designed Britain's public health and poor laws throughout the mid-1800s, often relying upon statistics to prove his points. (Edwin was later knighted for this.) Henry, who moved with his family to Brooklyn when he was 12, soon enjoyed playing ball games such as rounders, though he detested the custom of getting "soaked" with the ball—hit with it, often square in the ribs—to be retired while running the bases. By his early twenties Chadwick had begun stringing for the Long Island *Star* and soon was covering cricket for several local newspapers. It was after joining the New York *Clipper*, a weekly devoted mostly to cricket and the theater, in 1857 that he focused his attention chiefly on baseball.

The game to which Chadwick was attracted bore scant resemblance to the one we know today. The bases did sit 90 feet apart, with nine men to a side and nine innings to a game, but the competition mainly pitted the batters and base runners against the fielders; the pitcher was a mere convenience. The early rules of the National Association of Base Ball Players (the sport's first formal organizational body) mandated that the pitcher, standing 45 feet from the batter and tossing underhand, "deliver the ball as near as possible over the center of the home base, and for the striker . . . The ball must be pitched, not jerked or thrown to the bat." He was a *pitcher*, not a *thrower*, and was considered simply an enabler to getting the ball put in play, after which the true game took place. Fielders wore no gloves, making catches of ground balls, line drives, and even pop flies displays of skill nowhere near as routine as today. Master bunters such as Dickey Pearce vexed the defense; base runners took extra bases with abandon. Whereas now much of baseball boils down to the 60-foot tunnel between pitcher and batter, intrigue in the early game lay everywhere but.

Reports of games captured this dynamic in staggeringly detailed statistics. One box score from 1858 listed runs and outs, as usual, but for each player presented nine more columns: for his defense, his total of fly catches, bound catches (balls caught on one bounce, which then counted as outs), and times putting out a runner on the bases; for his batting, times put out on flies, bounds, and foul balls; and for his base running, how often he was put out at first, second, and third bases (not home, curiously). These tallies gave a reader a vivid snapshot of how every player's bat, legs, and glove impacted a win or loss.

Chadwick considered the generation of such statistics vital to the young game. Grey-bearded, tall and sourly austere, the Englishman wrote hundreds of thousands of paragraphs on baseball over the next 50 years, railing against gambling, alcohol, and profanity as the game evolved from gentleman's sport to serious industry. Yet he pounded his rhetorical fist hardest while discussing the importance of statistics. As early as 1861, he wrote in Beadle's *Dime Base-Ball Player,* his annual guide to the game, "In order to obtain an accurate estimate of a player's skill, an analysis, both of his play at the bat and in the field, should be made, inclusive of the way in which he was put out; and that this may be done, it is requisite that all . . . contests should be recorded in a uniform manner."

To spread the gospel, Chadwick invented his own personal scoring form in the hope that it would become standard. The grid extended nine players deep and nine innings wide, each box housing a player's at-bat as he came up in turn. Each outcome was coded with either numbers, for the fielder who handled the ball, or letters, to denote a fly ball or the like. (Many of those letters were chosen as the last of the events they connoted, such as "D" for catch on bound, "L" for foul ball and "K" for struck out, the last of which has survived to delight generations of kids as they first learn to score.) Chadwick's grid, which remains virtually unchanged to this day, then could be distilled into a detailed box score like this one, from an 1861 game between the Atlantic and Eckford clubs:

			BATTING			
ATLANTIC.	**H.L.**	**R'NS.**	**ECKFORD.**	**H.L.**	**R'NS.**
Pearce, ss	4	2	Manolt, lf	4	0
Smith, 3d b	2	3	Grum, p	3	2
Oliver, 2d b	2	4	Beach, c	1	3
Price, 1st b	1	4	Pidgeon, 2d b	5	0
Joe Oliver, cf	2	1	Campbell, 1st b	2	2
Boerum, c	6	0	J. Snyder, cf	4	0
P. O'Brien, lf	1	5	Mills, 3d b	3	1

BATTING

ATLANTIC.	H.L.	R'NS.	ECKFORD.	H.L.	R'NS.
Hawxhurst, rf	3	1	Josh Snyder, ss	3	1
M. O'Brien, p	6	0	Woods, rf	2	2
Total	27	20	Total	27	11

RUNS MADE EACH INNING

CLUBS	1	2	3	4	5	6	7	8	9	TOTALS
Eckford	2	1	0	1	1	2	0	1	3	11
Atlantic	0	2	0	1	2	6	5	4	0	20

FIELDING

ATLANTIC.	Fl	Bnd	Ba	Tot	ECKFORD.	Fl	Bnd	Ba	Tot
Pearce	0	0	1	1	Manolt	1	1	0	2
Smith	0	0	0	0	Grum	1	0	2	3
Oliver	0	0	2	2	Beach	2	1	0	3
Price	1	0	15	16	Pidgeon	0	0	0	0
Joe Oliver	0	0	0	0	Campbell	1	0	7	8
Boerum	0	3	0	3	J. Snyder	4	0	0	4
P. O'Brien	1	2	0	3	Mills	1	1	0	2
Hawxhurst	0	1	0	1	Josh Snyder	0	0	0	0
M. O'Brien	0	0	0	0	Woods	4	1	0	5
Total	2	6	18	26	Total	14	4	9	27

HOW PUT OUT

ATLANTIC.	BASES						ECKFORD.	BASES					
	Fly	Bnd	1	2	3	Fo		Fly	Bnd	1	2	3	Fo
Pearce	1	0	3	0	0	0	Manolt	0	0	2	1	0	1
Smith	0	1	1	0	0	0	Grum	0	1	1	1	0	0
Oliver	1	1	0	0	0	0	Beach	0	0	0	1	0	0
Price	0	1	0	0	0	0	Pidgeon	0	0	5	0	0	0
Joe Oliver	1	0	1	0	0	0	Campbell	1	0	1	0	0	0
Boerum	3	0	1	0	0	2	J. Snyder	1	1	2	0	0	0
P. O'Brien	1	0	0	0	0	0	Mills	0	1	2	0	0	0
Hawxhurst	2	0	1	0	0	0	Josh Snyder	1	1	2	0	0	2
M. O'Brien	3	0	2	0	0	1	Woods	0	0	1	0	0	0
Total	12	3	9	0	0	3	Total	3	4	16	3	0	3

Passed balls, on which bases were run—Beach 6, Boerum 4.

Struck out—Woods 1.

Catches missed on the fly—Boerum 1, Mills 2, Josh Snyder 2, Grum 2, Manolt 1, Woods 1.

Catches missed on the bound—Beach 1, Grum 1.

Times left on bases—Smith 1, Price 1, Joe Oliver 3, Hawkshurst 2, Manolt 1, Beach 1.

Time of game—two hours and forty-five minutes.

Umpire—Mr. A. L. Brainard, of the Excelsior Club.

Scorer for the Atlantic—Mr. G. W. Moore.

Scorer for the Eckford—Mr. McAuslan.

Note how fielding and base running were quantified in considerably more detail than batting, and that pitching was ignored altogether. Hits made by batters appeared nowhere—just runs and outs, the only items that ultimately mattered to the team. Chadwick did sense some unfairness to individual players who reached base with a hit but didn't score a run—hence the Times Left on Bases category, then used for individuals rather than teams. But just like today, the box score was a perfect illustration of double-entry bookkeeping, yielding a self-contained universe as busy and balanced as a carbon atom. Positives (fielding plays) and negatives (batting outs) canceled each other out with no stragglers to upset the equilibrium. Everything was divvied up among those responsible. From the very start baseball's box score was, as Roger Angell would note a century later, "a precisely etched miniature of the sport itself."

Chadwick had grander plans for his box scores than to provide breakfast fare in morning papers. The system would allow him to compile cumulative statistics at the end of the season to assess which players were the true stars. Chadwick had his own opinions—more than hairs on his chinny-chin-chin, it turned out—but he strived to formulate a set of measures that would reveal cold, hard evidence of who helped his team win and who didn't. In his 1861 *Beadle* guide, he presented the totals of games played, outs, runs, home runs, and strikeouts for the hitters on five prominent clubs. Since teams and batters did not all play the same number of games, Chadwick, all but obsessed with issues of fairness, introduced a new method to even the scale: dividing runs and outs by games played. (These were presented not with decimals but through the average-and-over method of the time, whereby seven hits in 19 games would yield an average of two with five "over.") The best hitters, Chadwick declared, were those with the highest average of runs per game. Burtis of the Gotham club fared best, at three and two over.

These were the first tracks on which baseball statistics began their long journey to the modern day. The sport was just taking shape, malleable as wet clay, as dozens of new clubs emerged all over the Northeast. Rules changed almost every season for the next 20 to 30 years in a lurching attempt to achieve a balance between the offense and defense. Pitchers slowly gained the right to throw hard, develop curveballs, and pitch overhand. Hitters would gain the right to call for a high or low pitch, but lose some bunting privileges, as baseball sought a pleasing equilibrium.

To Chadwick, the game's station would always be found through the statistics it generated; runs and outs were its latitude and longitude. And more than anyone else, as he wrote for the *Clipper* and edited various annual guides, Chadwick would stand behind the nautical steering wheel, using those ever-changing coordinates—and devising new and improved methods to interpret them—to guide baseball where he wanted it to go.

I t's almost impossible for a modern baseball fan, conditioned to focus on the battle between pitcher and batter, to appreciate how important fielding was in the early game. Whereas we now often think of baseball as one (pitcher) versus nine (batters), it began more as one hitter versus nine fielders trying to keep him off base. Even as fielding gloves became more common after the sketchy National Association gave way to the more formalized National League in 1876, the mitts were small and had no padding, nothing like today's comfy fishnets. Particularly after bound catches (fair balls caught on one bounce) were no longer considered outs, starting in 1864, stopping a ball required a dexterity (and tolerance for pain) that only the best demonstrated with any consistency. Balls were muffed all over the place, even 10 times in a game or more. As baseball historian John Thorn has noted, "Fielding skill was still the most highly sought after attribute of a ball player."

Statistics of the time reflected this. They counted how many outs a fielder recorded four different ways: by catching balls on the fly or bound, and by tagging either runners or bases. A box score in New York's *Sunday Mercury* in 1863 decided to highlight the *failure* to make a play, noting players' Catches Missed (there were 21 between the two clubs); the term evolved into Errors of Fielding before its inevitable shortening to Errors. Chadwick, wanting to distinguish between runs scored because of offensive skill (clean hits) rather than defensive ineptitude (errors), in 1867 called runs untainted by miscues "earned" runs. Yes, roots of the statistic we now call Earned Run Average lie in an effort not to evaluate pitching, but batting and fielding.

Around 1870, fielders began to be rated as they are today, getting a putout for directly registering an out, and an assist when a throw resulted in one. But errors took center stage, to Chadwick's consternation. "The best player in a nine is he who makes the most good plays in a match," he wrote, "not the one who commits the fewest errors." In other words Chadwick preferred range—the ability to field more balls overall—to avoiding the occasional error. His approach was shared by a Mr. Reed of the Philadelphia Athletics, presumably the club score-keeper, who after the 1872 season prepared for Chadwick's *Beadle* guide tables of fielding statistics that listed average putouts per game, assists per game, and the sum of the two, effectively chances per game; errors were not included at all.

Alas, this did not catch on. When the National League formed in 1876, it adopted as its official fielding measure successful plays (putouts plus assists) divided by total chances (putouts plus assists plus errors), thenceforth known as fielding percentage. That statistic lived virtually uncontested for more than 100 years, before a Kansan named Bill James introduced something he called Range Factor—the number of plays a fielder made per game. Many hooted this as some newfangled widget, unaware that, thanks to Philadelphia's Mr. Reed, it predated almost every statistic there was.

As integral as fielding was to early baseball, the game's statistics found even stronger footing in the batter's box. Newspapers as early as 1860 printed column upon column of numbers—tables that would all but suffocate even today's stat heads—most of them in the elemental and ceaseless quest to compare one hitter to another.

As noted earlier, with the first box scores counting only runs and outs, those were the only statistics consistently available. But the numbers mavens still kneaded them in all sorts of ways: It was not uncommon for newspapers to present every player's games played, total runs and outs, average runs and outs per game, most runs in a game, games with no runs, most outs in a game, fewest outs in a game, and more. (Before some *dozen* fielding columns.) Chadwick insisted that only through statistics could the truly special players be recognized. "Many a dashing general player, who carries off a great deal of éclat in prominent matches, has all 'the gilt taken off the gingerbread,' as the saying is, by these matter-of-fact figures," he puffed in 1864. "And we are frequently surprised to find that the modest but efficient worker, who has played earnestly and steadily through the season, apparently unnoticed, has come in, at the close of the race, the real victor." The batting champion, Chadwick decreed, was the player who scored the most runs per game.

As he would for half a century, writing for the *Clipper,* editing various annual guides, serving on the National League's rules committee and generally assuming the stature of baseball's moral compass, Chadwick claimed that his categories were the best ways to rate players—until he thought of new ones, which would quantify (and therefore encourage respect for) what he considered important. His most critical early addition, in 1867, was to note how many times batters reached base on a hit. Until then, a batter could rap out a single and be stranded by succeeding hitters and get no credit for this temporary success. Chadwick also measured the Total Bases secured by such hits: one for a single, two for a double, three for a triple, and so on, to suggest the importance of extra-base power. (As we will learn, he came to sorely rue that.)

Hits Per Game and Total Bases Per Game became popular statistics, but soon it was recognized that players higher in a team's batting order got more chances to hit; in 1870 the *Clipper* started recording times at-bat. Within two years an H. A. Dobson of Washington wrote Chadwick and presented his new way to rate hitters: hits divided by *at-bats.* Chadwick heralded Dobson's plan in the 1872 *Beadle* guide. "According to man's chance, so should his record be," he pontificated. "Then what is true of one player is true of all." Chadwick declared that this new measure immediately trumped all others. "One is erroneous, one is right," he nodded. Ironically, this Batting Average, one of the few early statistics *not* invented by Henry Chadwick, remains to this day baseball's most famous.

Baseball's statistical skeleton was forming as the game grew outward and strong. New York had been the primary incubator of the sport throughout the 1850s, with the Knickerbockers, Gothams, Eagles, and Empires based in Manhattan, and the Excelsiors, Putnams, Eckfords, and Atlantics across the East River in Brooklyn. Beyond those, 50 less formal groups, often representing occupations like firefighters and schoolteachers, were playing baseball by 1858. The sport spread northward throughout New York State, south to Washington, and westward through Pennsylvania—and even to California—by the end of the decade. The National Association of Base Ball Players was formed in 1858 to regulate rules through an annual convention; the NA would grow to include more than 300 clubs by 1868, when crowds of 5,000 and even 10,000 fans would come out to watch the top teams.

Those fans craved news about baseball. Every New York newspaper, starting with the weekly *Mercury* (served by writer William Cauldwell) and several that employed Chadwick, offered frequent reports on the game, as did many others in cities beginning to embrace the sport. William Porter's *Spirit of the Times*, the nation's leading sports weekly, began covering baseball regularly in the mid-1850s, while the *Clipper* was another popular read among fans throughout the United States. (Even when not so united. After South Carolina seceded in 1860, base-ball historian Harold Seymour noted, many *Clipper* readers proudly kept up their subscriptions.) Chadwick's *Beadle* guide appeared that same year and came to sell 50,000 copies annually, encouraging several competitors to print annual information books of their own. Betting on games be-came popular around this time, too, with enthusiasts thirsting for more news than ever, especially numbers. Statistics became part of the game's daily fare. This trend mirrored that of the rest of America, which was bustling more than ever with the growth of railroads and urban popula-tions. Seymour wrote, "Each decade saw the pace accelerated so furiously that 'a new vocabulary and almost a new arithmetic' were required to de-scribe it."

Baseball's rising popularity led to the charging of admission prices, clubs bidding for the best players and, ultimately, outright professional-ism. The Cincinnati Red Stockings were the first team to make such a move. Managed by Harry Wright, an English-born former cricket star who abandoned that sport for baseball, the club toured the young nation from 1869 to 1870 and went undefeated in all 57 of its games, some by the most unseemly scores of 80–5 and 103–8. Wright is credited with sev-eral baseball innovations, such as fielders backing up each other and the double steal, but he also was a devotee of statistics, poring over box scores to assess players' skills. The Reds were such a sensation that Chadwick printed a staggering statistical portrait of the club, listing the totals for the Reds and their opponents in 42 different categories, from the routine (runs and total innings played) to the hopelessly esoteric (Times Forced Out on the Bases, and Number of Games in Which One Innings [sic] Equaled Opponents' Total Score). That wasn't all. Chadwick broke down each player's performance as well:

	G. Wright	Gould	Waterman	Allison	H. Wright	Leonard	Brainard	Sweasy	McVey
Games	57	57	57	53	57	54	55	57	57
Outs—Total	116	191	156	140	186	146	159	155	146
Outs—Average	2-02	3-20	2-42	2-34	3-15	2-38	2-49	2-41	2-32
Runs	339	258	293	246	232	247	233	248	262
Average	5-54	4-30	5-08	4-34	4-04	4-31	4-13	4-20	4-34
First Base	304	217	226	210	221	211	195	219	217
Average	5-19	3-46	3-55	3-51	3-50	3-49	3-30	3-48	3-46
Bases	614	363	377	331	332	358	278	422	348
Average	10-44	6-21	6-35	6-13	5-47	6-34	5-03	7-23	6-06
Times to Bat	483	479	470	426	456	429	427	438	436
Average	8-27	8-23	8-14	8-02	8-00	7-51	7-42	7-39	7-37
Bases on Called Balls	3	4	6	9	8	1	6	2	4
Left on Bases	28	29	20	40	37	35	35	34	26
Home Runs	49	21	11	11	9	23	5	30	10
Out on Files	44	64	50	46	54	45	65	54	51
Out on Fouls	7	49	48	36	29	35	36	36	25
Out on Bases	56	72	55	55	99	62	52	60	70
Run Out	8	5	4	2	3	4	3	3	0
Struck Out	0	1	1	1	1	0	2	2	0
Forced Out	2	7	6	3	14	2	8	9	7
Flies Caught	82	25	25	17	66	51	21	86	60
Fouls Caught	16	26	42	161	0	13	21	0	3
Number Put Out on Bases	19	456	49	13	0	1	1	107	0
Assisting	179	11	106	38	28	9	48	139	4
Catches on Strikes	0	0	0	38	0	0	0	0	0
Flies Missed	4	16	5	8	7	16	7	5	11

The chart described to readers, many of whom had never laid eyes on the Red Stockings more than once or twice, if at all, the players' various talents. And it did so in ways that words could not. George Wright clearly was the master batsman, scoring almost six runs per game. (He reached first base on clean hits a whopping 304 times in 483 times to the plate, for what we now call a batting average of .629; unfortunately for him, as we've seen, that statistic wasn't invented for another three years.) Wright also was the top power hitter with 49 home runs, followed by Sweasy, a fine defensive infielder with just five missed flies against 139 assists. And Gould! Clearly the first baseman—look at the putouts—he didn't appear to pull his weight much at all, making a slew of outs at the plate, many on fouls, and muffing 16 flies.

Pitching statistics, as usual, were of no particular consequence. For a matter of record only, Chadwick wrote at the end of the chart: "Brainard has pitched in 338 innings, for a total of 403 runs, an average of 1-65 to an inning . . ." Asa Brainard indeed was a valuable pitcher. For the large sum (at the time) of $1,100 for the season he threw virtually every inning of every game, which was customary for pitchers of that era. (Some believe that his first name was occasionally shortened to "Ace," leading to today's title for star hurlers.) As for statistics to describe his work, though, nothing existed. Chadwick's mention of Brainard is one of the first numerical suggestions that the pitcher had anything to do with the outcome of the game. That would change, because the entire concept of the pitcher was shifting as well, and rapidly.

Pitchers, as mentioned earlier, originally were to serve the ball over the plate so that it could be put in play, with no intent to make matters difficult for the batter—a rather odd function of a member of the defensive team, but such was gentlemanly custom. Throwing was to be done underhand, with wrist stiff and pointing upward, as if pitching a horseshoe. Batters waited as long as they wanted for a pitch to their liking. As games became more serious competition, though, the evolution began: Pitchers would offer tosses that were good but not too good; as batters became too selective, umpires in 1858 were allowed to call a strike if the pitch was "within fair reach of the batter"; and in 1863, the concept of the base on balls was introduced, punishing the pitcher for missing with too many wild offerings. As significant as these changes sound today, though, they didn't compare with the arrival of the hurricane of pitching reform, a New York–born teenager named Jim Creighton.

Just 18 years old when he joined the Brooklyn Excelsiors in 1860,

Creighton effectively cheated his way to national celebrity. He would employ a late wrist snap on his pitches that was barely perceptible until the ball came zooming out of his hand, leaving batters all but helpless. This maneuver, completely against both written and unwritten rules, would have been roundly decried if it hadn't been so darned thrilling. Crowds flocked to see Creighton pitch. Younger players imitated him. The game became faster and a clearer competition between one side and the other. Purists called for Creighton's punishment, but they were steamrolled by public sentiment (and dollars) to the point where reform was inevitable. By 1872 the wrist snap was entirely legal. Pitchers could attempt to outmuscle hitters with speed or outwit them with strategy. Baseball's long, delicate balancing act between batting and pitching—the yin-and-yang tango that would characterize it forevermore—had begun.

One of the pitchers to benefit from the new freedom was a righthander in his twenties named Albert Spalding, the star of the Boston Red Stockings as they rampaged through the National Association during its short life as the first quasi-major league, from 1871 to 1875. But Spalding had grander plans. He helped formulate the new National League in 1876 and became the Chicago White Stockings' first manager and pitching star. During this time he also began his own sporting goods company, A.G. Spalding & Bros., which marketed the likes of bicycles and fencing sabres but particularly baseball equipment, including the official National League baseball. Beyond this he published the National League's inaugural "Official League Book," page four of which presented this Publisher's Notice:

> We have paid the National League of Professional Base Ball Clubs very liberally for the exclusive privilege of publishing the official Book of the League, containing the Constitution, Playing Rules, Averages, etc., and have gone to great expense and labor in securing and tabulating the batting and fielding averages of every prominent professional ball player in America. We hereby warn all parties that the Book is copyrighted . . .

Those averages became one of the book's most popular features, as fans of that era gobbled up just about any statistic put before them. Most daily newspapers were printing daily box scores as the National League began, distilling games into rows and columns that vexed typesetters but captured readers. The *Philadelphia Record* instructed its writers before spring training, "The games you play in the South mean nothing, but the [box] score of even a five-inning practice game will be greedily scanned by the enthusiasts here." Up-to-date statistics of the local team would appear from time to time during the season. Annual guides from Beadle, Spalding, Reach, and DeWitt crowed that their statistics were the most complete and reliable. "As to the truth of that statement," one puffed, "the publishers invite an investigation."

New stats cropped up everywhere. Some scorers, trying to quantify base running ability, figured out the percentage of each player's runs scored per time he reached first base. One newspaper in Lowell, Massachusetts, suggested someone keep track of Earned Hits, the definition of which was left tantalizingly murky, while a New York writer demanded a column for hitting to right field with a man on third with one out. The *Clipper* in 1875 printed a humongous chart of each batter's full record against every pitcher in the National Association. In 1880, the National League recorded each hitter's Bases Touched, a one-year category led by the 501 of the one-and-only Abner Dalrymple, left fielder for the Chicagos. Soon, the influence of a pitcher publishing the National League guide was unmistakable: While batters and fielders were rated in six categories apiece, hurlers got 11, including earned runs per at-bat and opponents' batting average. One journalist threw up his hands and complained, "For some years past there has been a decided waste of figuring indulged in recording the scores of base ball matches . . . The present method of scoring the game and preparing scores for publication is faulty to the extreme, and it is calculated to drive players into playing for their records rather than for their side."

That journalist was Henry Chadwick, baseball's Dr. Frankenstein, who was finding his science of rating players with statistics now widespread and completely out of control. Writing for the *Clipper* and several annual guides, he grew ever more imperious as he aged. Every few weeks he would claim that earned runs were useless, because bases stolen off the defense counted toward them; far better to rate pitchers by hits or runs allowed. When he decided that runs scored were a misleading statistic for batters, he simply didn't print them. *So there*, Henry Chadwick said.

As Chadwick's writings, in Tygiel's words, "reverberated with the rhetoric of American reform," he grew no more indignant than when he realized that statistics were actually changing the game. Chadwick's model game was a taut, 1–0, scientific chess match. But as player salaries began to be influenced by run and hit totals, batters became less inter-

Albert Spalding and Cap Anson. *(National Baseball Hall of Fame Library, Cooperstown, N.Y.)*

ested in bunting and moving runners over, teamwork-oriented acts, and instead swung for home runs. Chadwick was aghast. One bizarre argument, which Chadwick repeated ad nauseam, was that hitters (many of whom batted in parks that did not yet include outfield fences) shouldn't go for home runs because, "If the batsman hits the ball over the heads of the outfielders he gets his run at once, but at what cost? Why, at the expense of running one hundred and twenty yards at his utmost speed . . . which involves an expenditure of muscular power needing a half-hour rest to recuperate from."

Chadwick harrumphed that players no longer played "for the side" but "for their record," with "base-hits having a certain market value." He wasn't alone. One Boston newspaper went so far as to suggest, "It is high time that a protest was entered against the growing and prevalent custom of papers in printing the averages of the players." It was roundly suspected that some players were in cahoots with official scorers to have a hit or two added to their record; owners finagled with them as well, to boost the trade and sale values of their players. Such shenanigans reached all the way to the National League office: When Cap Anson, Chicago's first baseman and manager, was credited with a .407 batting average by league secretary Nick Young (an Anson fan), Chadwick responded in the next *DeWitt* guide by printing not Young's official records, but those of the *Boston Herald*'s William Stevens, calling those "the fairest statement published." Anson, Stevens's numbers revealed, had actually hit just .318.

The National League spent its first decade trying to achieve a comfortable balance between offense and defense. After its inaugural season of 1876 it outlawed the "fair-foul" hit, a bunt that once fair was always fair, even if it rolled foul after 10 feet. The pitcher's box (the mound didn't arrive until 1893) moved back from 45 to 50 feet in 1881. In 1884, pitchers were allowed to throw overhand with any motion, which freed fastball pitchers like John Clarkson of the White Stockings to win 53 games; but batters were compensated by earning walks on just six balls, rather than the seven, eight or nine of previous years. Offense began to slump. Leaguewide batting averages dropped from .262 to .241 by 1885, and the next year pitcher Matt Kilroy of the American Association's Baltimore club struck out a staggering 513 batters.

This was alarming enough for the 1887 rules to adopt several sweeping changes: pitchers could no longer take a running start (just one step before delivering the ball) while batters got four strikes rather than three, among other tweaks. Offense shot back up, and by 1889, the backbone of four balls and three strikes that we know today was instituted for good. (One other wrinkle in the 1887 rules called for batters to receive first base when hit by one of these faster pitches. This spawned the now-standard Hit-by-Pitch category in statistics rather than more improvisational methods, such as this early one from a *Utica Herald* box score: "Apologies by pitchers for hitting batsmen, Morgan 4, Neale 3.")

Rulemakers tinkered with the stat-keeping, too. As baseball grew more popular its star power was measured by its number of .300 hitters. Along with the other changes in 1887, the league instituted one whopper with regard to statistics: Box scores, and therefore batting averages, would recognize walks as full-fledged hits. This predictably shot averages upward to unprecedented heights. Almost every batter in both the National League and American Association hit at least .300; 17 reached .400, topped by St. Louis left fielder Tip O'Neill, who batted .492. Some batters went to the plate *looking* for walks to boost their averages, causing games to drag horribly and fans to leave early. The rules were scrapped after one season. But Tip O'Neill's .492 would live forever as a sign of that era's infatuation with batting average, and cause controversy in record keeping for more than 100 years.

Chadwick seemed content by the early 1890s. The game he extolled had returned—thanks to pitchers' growing skills, slugging was down, bunting was up. Some stars such as batting champion Cap Anson loathed this latter practice of "baby hitting"—even calling for its expulsion—but Chadwick's preference for station-to-station ball was finding traction, evidence for which could be seen in evolving statistical categories. Stolen Bases began being recorded in 1886, though at first they were given to any runner who advanced an extra base on his own volition, such as going from first to third on a single; this led to wildly high totals through the 1890s, such as Harry Stovey's 156 steals for the Philadelphia Athletics in 1888. (The modern definition of stolen bases came a decade later.) One of Chadwick's proudest moments arrived when batters who bunted to advance a teammate began to be rewarded with a Sacrifice in 1889 box scores, dignifying it as smart play. The reward was only sweetened in 1893, when batters who sacrificed were not charged with an official at-bat.

From the 1893 *Reach* guide:

> To sacrifice, or not to sacrifice, that is the question.
> Whether 'tis better to the average to suffer
> The absence and lack of base hits,
> Or take chances against a lot of fielders
> And by slugging make them. To find—to fan
> No more, and by a drive, to say we end
> The strike out, and the thousand natural slips
> This flesh is heir to: 'tis a consummation
> Devoutly to be wished. To find—to fan—
> To fan! perchance to touch—ay, there's the rub

The *New York Times* explained that sacrifices were put in box scores "with a view of promoting more team work among players. Some of the record seekers always claimed that they could not sacrifice to advantage. In reality they did not care to, as it impaired their batting record." Chadwick's preference for celebrating all-for-one sportsmen who played "little ball" was being followed. Imagine his ecstasy when Wee Willie Keeler, a five-foot-four, 140-pound waterbug for the Baltimore Orioles, entered the league, choked up on his tiny bat and began to "hit 'em where they ain't."

It wouldn't last. By 1892, offenses had withered to the point where the National League as a whole hit a soporific .245, down 19 points from three years before. Stars such as Pete Browning of Louisville and Mike Tiernan of New York failed to hit .300. "There should be fifty or seventy-five batters in the .300 class, not eight or ten," Elmer E. Bates of the Cleveland *World* wrote. Although two top young pitchers, Jake Stivetts of the Boston Beaneaters and Denton "Cy" Young of the Cleveland Spiders, battled to a thrilling 0–0 tie in the opening game of the National League's 1892 championship series, league powers decided that pitching indeed had gained too much of an advantage. The front of the pitcher's box— then 50 feet from home plate—would have to move back.

The debates ensued. Some delegates at the annual meeting of the NL's Playing Rules Committee argued for five more feet, some eight, some even more. (Frank Robison of Cleveland, opposed to all this, carped that the Brooklyn delegate "if he had his way, would place the pitcher at second base.") Amazingly, the conservative Chadwick supported moving the pitcher back to almost 66 feet and increasing the basepaths to 93 feet apiece; he thought those changes would foster more bunting. In the end, a more straightforward compromise was reached: the pitcher would no longer deliver the ball with his front foot 50 feet from the batter, but his back foot on a plate that sat atop a small mound, 60 feet 6 inches away.

Statistics immediately heralded a new game. Offense sizzled as pitchers struggled with the new distance: After two seasons, National League contests were seeing close to 15 runs scored per game, up 44 percent and by far the most ever. Dozens of players batted .300 in 1894, led by the staggering .438 of five-foot-seven Boston center fielder Hugh Duffy. The Philadelphia Phillies' outfield of Ed Delahanty, Billy Hamilton and Sam Thompson hit .400 combined.* Pitchers of course took a statistical beating. Kid Nichols, star righthander for the Beaneaters, saw his earned runs per game (the most popular of pitching statistics) zoom up to an unheard-of 3.56. But the rules were deemed an unqualified success. "The public interest in the game was thereby most certainly stimulated," the 1895 *Reach* guide reported. "The more uncertain quality in games under the increased batting gave fascination to the sport, and crowds which filled the grounds of the various clubs attested to the popularity of the new rule and its workings."

After a half century of constant tinkering and evolution, baseball in the late 1890s had, in many respects, taken on much of the rules structure it retains today—pitchers throwing hard from 60 feet 6 inches, four balls and three strikes, and so on. And statistics, having started as mere runs and outs, had exploded into page upon page of newspaper data that fans

---

*Statistics cited throughout this chapter are those reported at the time, not versions that have been adjusted by subsequent research.

grazed on every morning in preparation for that afternoon's games. The sport had stumbled upon some of the most fortuitous free advertising in the history of American business: a self-sustaining cycle whereby games generated statistics that only attracted more customers. It wasn't long before the statistics would become a business all their own.

2

The Second Generation

Ernie Lanigan could barely breathe. The young Philadelphia bank clerk had been frail since childhood, with lungs like damp balloons. But when pneumonia finally set in, he had to retreat to the clean, thin air of a sanatorium in the Adirondacks, separating himself from his greatest love, professional baseball. Oh, what he missed during those two years! The American League was born in 1901, with Napoleon Lajoie, the great second baseman for Philadelphia's Athletics, batting a staggering .422. The next season Pittsburgh of the National League won 103 games, more than any team in the circuit's 27-year history. But even cooped up in the hospital, Lanigan still felt connected to baseball—through the box scores of his weekly *Sporting News*. The little ledgers even nursed him back to health. He begged his caretakers to allow him three hours a day sit at a desk and compile his own statistics for fun. "That," Lanigan later recalled, "kept me going." It also set him on course to become one of baseball's most influential early numbers men.

Lanigan was the first second-generation statistics buff. Whereas grown men like Henry Chadwick took to compiling baseball's numbers in the game's early days, Lanigan was one of thousands of kids who weaned themselves on the sports pages' stat sections, their passion for box scores and batting averages baked in from the start. An alarmingly sickly boy, Ernie could never play the game competitively, but it came alive through the numbers in the newspapers. He was 11 when Ned Williamson of the 1884 Chicago White Stockings slammed 27 home runs, the most ever in a regular season. He was 14 when Tip O'Neill batted his .492. Amazing! Ernie's family took delight in these things as well, so much so that in 1886, his uncles, Alfred and Charles Spink, started a new weekly called *The Sporting News*. Soon 15-year-old Ernie was sent to the Spinks' office in St. Louis to become a copy boy and help compile the paper's baseball statistics. The boy was in heaven. It wasn't long before Ernie got to meet the great St. Louis Browns first baseman Charles Comiskey, and shake hands with him. Ernie didn't wash his hand for two days.

Lanigan's rise had begun. He cut his teeth at *The Sporting News* for three years and even after leaving continued keeping statistics for himself, occasionally selling some notes and tidbits to various publications. In 1907, the *New York Press* was looking for a baseball editor. The paper first offered the job to a young writer in Atlanta named Grantland Rice, but Lanigan eventually won out. So did the field of baseball statistics, because Ernie Lanigan, who quite seriously credited them with having seen him through pneumonia back in the Adirondacks, soon became their primary innovator and exponent for the next 20 years. "I really don't care much about baseball, or looking at ball games," he admitted. "All my interest in baseball is in its statistics."

Those statistics reflected a game that pitchers were dominating like never before. While the 1893 decision to move the pitcher back to 60 feet 6 inches quickly helped teams score a whopping 15 total runs per game, within four years pitchers had reasserted themselves and brought scoring back down to a more normal 10. Then they proceeded to whittle bats down to matchsticks—by 1908 major league teams were batting just .239 and scoring only 6.6 runs per game. Making life even tougher for batters was the National League's 1901 adoption of the "foul-strike rule," which by making foul balls count as strikes put hitters even more on the defensive. (The AL didn't follow suit for two years, which helps explain Lajoie's .422 average in 1901, still the AL record.*) Home runs became virtually extinct: No National League batter from 1902 to 1905 hit more than nine in a season. The 1906 White Sox won the World Series despite batting just .230 and went down forever as the "Hitless Wonders." Offenses all over were highlighted by high-average hitters who could steal bases, such as Pittsburgh's Honus Wagner and a precocious Detroit outfielder just breaking in, Ty Cobb.

With one run often deciding these increasingly tight games, Lanigan

---

*Subsequent research has revised that number to its present recognized value of .426.

Ernie Lanigan. (*National Baseball Hall of Fame Library, Cooperstown, N.Y.*)

wanted to know not just who was *scoring* runs—tabulations kept since Alexander Cartwright's game broke away from cricket—but which players were *driving them in*. His curiosity in this area was not entirely new. Thirty years earlier, in 1879, a Buffalo newspaper counted Runs Batted In for its Bisons, then in the National League. The next season the *Chicago Tribune* did the same for the local White Stockings. This caused quite a furor. Increasingly savvy readers complained that while Cap Anson and Mike "King" Kelly drove in many runs, Chicago's leadoff hitter, Abner Dalrymple, had considerably fewer chances to do the same. The *Tribune* wound up banishing RBIs from its box scores, in one historian's words "almost apologizing for the computation."

Henry Chadwick, never one to remain silent on such matters, took up the cause of the RBI and even preferred it to the keeping of hits and runs scored, which he decided were "useless and deceiving." "Look at the score of a game as recorded in the papers," he yelped. "What do we see? Is there the slightest record of the efforts made by batsmen to bring in runs? None at all." Chadwick got his way in 1891, when the National League instructed all its official scorers to record RBIs as a column in the box score; the league even decreed that-batting average, and the year-end batting championship, would thenceforth be figured by the number of runs batted in per game. But this guideline met with such outcry for its shortchanging of leadoff men—by May 4 the *New York Sun* was calling it "laughable"— that league officials soon told scorers not to bother with it anymore. The RBI retreated into its hole once again.

Lanigan liked the statistic, however, and after taking over at the *New York Press* in 1907 added it to his paper's box scores. (Lanigan often referred to himself as "the fearless writer," no doubt for staring down any and all RBI detractors.) He personally tracked RBIs for every player in baseball until 1920, when the leagues began recording them officially again, this time for good. But Lanigan wasn't through. With base running during that era so vital to offenses, he added two more categories, Caught Stealing for runners and Thrown Out by Catcher for the backstops who nailed them. Under Lanigan's direction the *Press* devoted more space to baseball than any other New York daily. He even came up with another tidbit that lives on a century later: This Day in Baseball.

L anigan might have carried on as just a quirky zealot, but he found in his audience a vital ally—John Heydler, the National League secretary, who was just as fanatical about statistics. Heck, it was Heydler's job to be. Every morning, after arriving at the National League offices in New York's Metropolitan Tower, 13 stories above Madison Square, Heydler's charge was to paste in a scrapbook every box score from the previous day and check each for accuracy. Then he would record every player's statistics into a ledger, 18 categories for hitters and 17 more for pitchers; he took this job so seriously he went so far as to use black ink for home games and red for away. "It's the most important work I know anything about," Heydler later commented. "Without records, we would have merely a series of exhibitions, meaningless after the game was over . . . They give a permanency to the game which it could never otherwise enjoy." The records, he went on, "are the whole thing in baseball."

Heydler had stumbled into stat-keeping as a career. He began in the 1890s as a printer at the Bureau of Engraving in Washington, where he rooted passionately for his city's baseball Senators. (One day he was sent to the White House with proofs of a document for president Grover Cleveland, who struck up a conversation about baseball; Heydler wound up reciting to the president Ernest Lawrence Thayer's "Casey at the Bat" from memory.) He later went to work at the printing office of the *Washington Star*, was called upon to cover a few Senators games (sports departments being in their infancy at the time) and eventually became the paper's full-time baseball writer. He spent the 1898 season as a National League umpire, of all things, before going back to the *Star*, where he began compiling his own batting and fielding averages to dress up his reports. In 1903, new NL president Harry Pulliam, concerned about the "tangled mass of accumulated records from the official scorers' reports," asked Heydler to proof the previous season's statistics. Before long Heydler was hired as league secretary, where he became renowned for getting the players' averages, in the words of one enthusiastic onlooker, "complete in every detail to absolute mathematical perfection."

John Heydler. (*National Baseball Hall of Fame Library, Cooperstown, N.Y.*)

Heydler took particular interest in pitching statistics. Although moundsmen of the early twentieth century were controlling games more than ever, the numbers to describe their work were still a hodge-podge of measures, none assuming the meaning and general acceptance of batting average. *Spalding* guides at various junctures listed pitchers by games, opponents' at-bats, hits, runs, runs per game, runs per at-bat, hits per game, opponents' batting average, earned runs, earned runs per game, and—get this—earned runs per at-bat. (The 1884 *Reach* guide declared Tim Keefe of the New York Metropolitans the 1883 American Association pitching champion for having a .0362 earned run–at-bat ratio. And people think today's stats are weird.) Later introductions included walks allowed and strikeouts, averages of those per game, total base runners, opponents' total bases, wild pitches, and hit batsmen. An American Association box score from 1884 even shows each pitcher's number of called strikes.

Through this thicket, however, pitchers were generally judged on their earned runs allowed. Chadwick hated this, and judging from his frequent diatribes against them undoubtedly suffered several aneurysms a month. (Now *there's* a statistic.) Chadwick argued that runs should be earned only if they scored via base hits, not through stolen bases, which he considered the result of subpar fielding. He wound up refusing to print earned runs at all in any of the guides he edited. Instead he lobbied to have pitchers rated by whether their teams won or lost.

Pitchers' jobs were changing, and statistics changed with them. They were entrusted with more and more responsibility, so by the early 1890s some box scores began to include a separate Pitching Score, listing each hurler's innings pitched, hits, earned runs, walks, and strikeouts, same as today. As starting pitchers began to leave games for relievers (then called "change pitchers") the *Reach* guide decided in 1905 to count Times Taken Out, the opposite of the modern Complete Games. That guide did not list earned runs—Chadwick, a grey-bearded, Buddha-like figure in his 80s, had tremendous influence—while others flailed to find a suitable statistic for pitchers. Matters got so out of control by 1910 that one unofficial measure added pitchers' won-lost percentage, batting average, and fielding average together. The New York Giants' Otis Crandall won out at 2.136.

Heydler kept his head throughout this silliness. Forty-five years younger than Chadwick and no doubt chuckling at the old man's ravings, Heydler understood that baseball had changed enough to embrace the simple concept of earned runs. Thanks in large part to better gloves, fielders were making just five errors per game, half of what they had before, making it easier to untangle which runs were the responsibility of the pitcher. Stolen bases were at least part of pitchers' responsibility, too, weren't they?

By the time Heydler was ready to act, earned runs' main opponent had departed the scene. In April 1908, at the age of 83, Henry Chadwick went out into a cold wind to watch the home opener of the Brooklyn Superbas (later the Dodgers) at Washington Park. He caught a severe cold that later turned into pneumonia, and died six days later. *The Sporting News* eulogized him in an immense obituary, and he was buried in the Greenwood Cemetery in Brooklyn under a large concrete memorial topped by a giant baseball. Fans stopping through New York still visit the site today to remember Father Chadwick.

His death, however, left the landscape clear for Heydler to bring back the average of earned runs as an official National League statistic. But Heydler made a significant concession to the increasing use of relievers. Rather than determine pitchers' earned runs per game, starting in 1912 he would figure their average per *inning* and then multiply by nine, locking everyone to a complete-game baseline. The modern Earned Run Average was born.

Whatever advance earned run average might have represented—it was met with immediate favor by most sports writers—no statistic could compete with the devotion inspired by batting average. Ever since the National League decided in 1876 that hits divided by at-bats would determine the circuit's seasonal batting championship, batting average had become by far the sport's most relied upon statistic. It entered the lexicon; even nonfans knew that being a ".300 hitter" confirmed unassailable talent. "There is a certain charm about .300," said Gavvy "Cactus" Cravath, the slugging right fielder for the Philadelphia Phillies from 1912 to 1920. "If a man hits it he is a star, if he doesn't he isn't." Added Boston Red Sox standout Tris Speaker, "You will find players who are hitting somewhere near .300 fighting tooth and nail to boost their average above that mark, knowing that if they succeed their names will be inscribed with honorable mention in the records."

In 1910, batting average became the focus of one of the early century's greatest controversies. That season, Hugh Chalmers, president of the Chalmers Motor Company, promised a new Chalmers "30" automobile to the top hitter in the major leagues—by batting average, of course. (Statistics-based bounties were not uncommon; after striking out 313 men that same season, Walter Johnson received $500 from appreciative Washington fans.) By September, the Chalmers batting derby had become a clear two-man race between Detroit's tempestuous and generally loathsome outfielder, Ty Cobb, and Napoleon "Larry" Lajoie, the gentlemanly and immensely popular second baseman from Cleveland. It became a battle of good versus evil. Writers and fans kept up daily with each man's hits and at-bats, rooting for one or the other as one would Jesus or Judas.

But no one knew who was truly ahead. The leagues didn't release official statistics until after the season, and tallies kept by others differed wildly. Late in the season one source had Cobb ahead by eight points. Another said Lajoie led by one. Cobb believed he had the title wrapped up with two days left in the season; never one to pass up the chance for increased wealth, he decided to sit those games out. (Cobb biographer Charles Alexander notes the *Cleveland Plain Dealer* accused Cobb of having the "congealed condition of the pedal extremities," otherwise known as cold feet.) Yet Cobb's sneaky maneuver paled against what transpired when Lajoie played a doubleheader at St. Louis on the final day of the

season: Browns manager Jack O'Connor so badly wanted the dapper Lajoie to win the batting championship that he directed his rookie third
baseman, Red Corriden, to play so deep that Lajoie could bunt for base
hits almost at will. This he did—seven times. Along with one legitimate
triple and one fielder's choice, Lajoie finished the day 8-for-9.

Did this give Lajoie the batting title? Amazingly, no one would know
for sure until the league released its official averages. But there were
plenty of guesses. Newspapers presented their own figuring of the final totals. The *Chicago Tribune* said that Lajoie won, .385 to .382. The *Cleveland Leader* favored Lajoie .382 to .381, while *The Sporting News* credited
Cobb with the title, .38415 to .38411. A debacle on his hands, American
League president Ban Johnson hurried to figure out the final statistics and
got them done within a week—Cobb had won, .385 to .384.

Chalmers extricated himself from the mess by awarding a car to both
Cobb and Lajoie, and the following year decided to give one to the best
player in each league not based on batting average but through a vote
among sportswriters. (This is the forerunner of today's Most Valuable
Player award.) But the Browns' laying down to boost Lajoie's average created ill feeling all over the country. The *St. Louis Post* noted the irony of
the Browns' field being named "Sportsman's Park." *The Detroit Free Press*
called it a fix "which should be investigated by the highest authorities."

Could baseball statistics be so important as to threaten the integrity
of the contests themselves? The *Chicago Tribune* was moved to write this
poem, which presaged more serious trouble the city would encounter at
the end of that decade with its 1919 Black Sox:

> *When Larry faced the St. Louis fire*
> *He'd eight to go to be secure*
> *And what they thought he might require*
> *They slipped it to him, that's pretty sure . . .*
>
> *What must a meek outsider think*
> *When tricks like that they put across?*
> *When at one frameup they will wink*
> *How do we know what games they toss?*

While John Heydler figured his ERA in the National League, and Ernie
Lanigan kept RBIs for the *Press*, those outside the baseball establishment
were quietly keeping their own statistics. And occasionally not so quietly.

One day in 1912, a tall, slender, diffident man around 40 years old strode into the Manhattan office of Baseball Magazine. Under his arm was an enormous book, a ledger of some sort, and the reception clerk, figuring him for a salesman or crackpot or both, tried to shoo him away. But he wanted to see an editor. He demanded to see an editor. He finally talked his way into an audience with some staff members, and informed them of his dream.

For the past 20 years, John Lawres had collected the records of every player in Organized Baseball, from the major leagues to the lowest minors. One season, he managed to record the statistics of some twenty thousand players. Why? His obsession began in his twenties in upstate New York, when some friends questioned his high opinion of the 1889 New York Giants. He decided to compile, and keep in his vest pocket, a little book of what he called "argument settlers"—every player's team, position, games played and batting average for the previous season. He spent two to four hours a day scribbling down all these numbers. This annual compendium grew from 80 pages to 180 to 220 and finally to 500, when he graduated to a full-sized ledger book. "The labor that was begun as a diversion," he said, "has become little short of slavery."

What would compel someone to do this? Lawres had no choice— players' lifetime records were not available anywhere. Even with baseball more popular than ever in the teens, the National and American leagues printed no statistical volumes of their own; there was no such thing as the Baseball Encyclopedia modern fans take for granted. Unless you had back copies of the annual Spalding and Reach guides, there was no way to look up seasonal numbers for current or past stars. What did Tris Speaker, the great Boston center fielder, hit during his first full season of 1909? Who had the highest batting average for the 1908 World Series-champion Cubs: Joe Tinker, Johnny Evers, or Frank Chance? These were questions that would go unanswered, until John Lawres convinced the Baseball Magazine editors that his statistics should be published as a book. They called it Who's Who in Baseball.

The first edition of 1912 listed only three statistics: games, batting average, and fielding average, and nothing for pitchers. But after a three-year hiatus, Who's Who returned with a beefed-up volume that became vital to the serious baseball enthusiast. Hitter listings now added at-bats, runs, hits, and steals to the previous scant three columns, and pitchers got games, innings pitched, wins, losses, won-lost percentage, strikeouts, walks, hits, and John Heydler's recent invention, ERA. Finally, fans and writers alike could answer questions about players' careers not just with their fuzzy and malleable memories, but with hard and fast statistics. "In my own little way," Lawres said, "it is a pleasure to accomplish unknown a work that, in its creation, may please thousands who know neither my face, name, nor even existence." They knew his work, though. *Who's Who in Baseball* became the game's most popular statistics book for decades thereafter, and though long since surpassed in breadth and scope, still is published today.

Others joined Lawres in the stat-keeping biz. In 1914 a writer from Pittsburgh named George Moreland, who for several years had contributed statistical tidbits to various newspapers, wrote a 300-page book titled *Balldom: The Britannica of Baseball*. It cost a dollar, and beyond recounting the history of the game cast Moreland as a most approachable guru of baseball statistics. Its first page declared: "Every purchaser of a copy of BALLDOM is entitled to a membership in the 'BALLDOM BUREAU OF INFORMATION AND STATISTICS' for a period of one year, during which time queries addressed in good faith, with a self-addressed stamped envelope to the main office, 810 United States Rubber Company Building, New York City, N.Y., will receive careful consideration and a prompt, accurate, and authoritative answer. Guaranteed to be backed by official statistics and the opinion of baseball experts."

Balldom presented enough historical statistics to sate even the most voracious fan. This was baseball's first attempt at a true record book. Lists included club rosters and records for each of the 16 clubs and team statistics for every season from 1876 through 1913. Seasonal leaders in batting average, hits, runs, and stolen bases were finally collected in one source. But Moreland went far deeper, unveiling lists of all-time no-hitters, three-homer games, .400 hitters, and dozens of weirder categories, including the vital Eight Games in Which First Basemen Made No Putouts. Readers got their first look at full, lifetime statistics for stars such as Lajoie, Cobb, Cap Anson, Cy Young, and Christy Mathewson. Moreland even became one of the first statistorians to correct a major record: While many newspapers in 1910 reported that Washington Senators fireballer Walter Johnson had set a modern mark with 313 strikeouts, Moreland's subsequent game-by-game research revealed that Rube Waddell—the oft-inebriated lefthander *The Sporting News* gleefully called a "sousepaw"—had actually whiffed 343 for the Philadelphia Athletics six years before. (This uncertainty was not uncommon back then. Two years later, when the Pittsburgh Pirates' Owen Wilson hit 36 triples, no one knew for sure if it was an all-time record;

some contended that Napoleon Lajoie had gone for 43 triples in 1903. That turned out, however, to be merely a typographical error in the *Reach* guide. He actually had just 11.)

All this hand-wringing over statistics began to grate upon more traditional reporters of the game. As Ernie Lanigan of the *New York Press* printed more and more numbers and influenced his competitors to do the same, some writers felt their jobs slipping away from them. Damon Runyon of the *New York American* eventually vented his distaste for baseball's growing preference for statistics over words in this poem:

> *The Sporting Ed. says,*
> *"Cut 'er short!*
> *There's not much space to-day for sport.*
>
> *"Between the ads,*
> *Between the news.*
> *All excess words I must refuse."*
>
> *So short it is.*
> *Quite short you see.*
> *Two ball games at the old P.G.*
>
> *The Pirates won.*
> *The Giants won.*
> *Scores: Three to one, and four to none.*
>
> *The Sporting Ed. says:*
> *"That'll do."*
> *The box scores tell the rest to you.*

Despite the derision, Lanigan still gained a degree of fame for examining baseball statistics. In 1916, while baseball editor of the *Cleveland Leader*, he boldly predicted that Tris Speaker, the Indians' star center fielder recently traded from Boston, would finally unseat Ty Cobb as the American League batting champion. Even though Cobb had won the previous nine titles, Lanigan looked at each team's lineups and determined that since Cobb's Tigers were—like him—mostly lefthanded, he would see a steady diet of lefthanded pitchers who would make life more difficult. Speaker, meanwhile, was a lefthanded batter in a lineup mostly of righties and therefore would feast on more righthanders. Lanigan was ridiculed for this analysis but was proven correct: Speaker won the championship, .386 to .371. It was the only batting title that Cobb would lose in a 13-year period.

Lanigan enjoyed a long career in baseball, influencing the game from an assortment of angles. He brought his statistical bent to the minor leagues, serving as numbers man for several loops well into his sixties. He was an early proponent and longtime member of the Base Ball Writers Association of America, which will soon enter its second century of influencing scoring rules, voting for major awards such as the Most Valuable Player, and electing the most stat-worthy to baseball's Hall of Fame. In fact, Cooperstown is where Lanigan eventually wound up: Brought in as the Hall's first official historian in 1946, at the age of 73, he spent 12 years there as the shrine's gruff but lovable Answer Man, helping callers with statistical questions, usually summoning accurate minutiae straight off the top of his own graying head. Just as they had back in the sanatorium, the numbers kept Lanigan alive until the age of 89, when his lungs finally gave out in a Philadelphia nursing home.

Lanigan's most enduring legacy came early, when he forced the RBI and caught-stealing measures into early-century box scores and generally impressed upon his audience that baseball statistics had an enduring meaning—even higher than the ephemeral players they belonged to. Though Henry Chadwick was gone, Lanigan and his younger followers kept the old man's fascination with baseball's numbers alive and kicking. Not one of them—it wasn't even close—kicked harder than a former biologist named F. C. Lane.

From the beginning, Ferdinand Cole Lane wanted to be a scientist. Born on a Minnesota wheat farm in 1885, Lane and his family bounced from Minneapolis to Canton, Ohio, and finally to the beaches of Cape Cod, where 7-year-old Ferdinand fell in love with nature. He also adored to travel, and eventually circled the globe seven times with stops at the North and South poles. His first job after graduating from Boston University was as assistant biologist at his alma mater, before he moved on to the Massachusetts Commission of Fisheries and Game. He loved to write about his experiences, too, and before long he decided to do the same with another of his passions, baseball. He became so drawn to it that he accepted a position at the new, Boston-based monthly devoted to the sport, *Baseball Magazine*, which printed much longer, in-depth stories than either daily newspapers or weeklies such as *The Sporting News*. Lane wound up spending the next 27 years using his own personal approach to the game—a scientific one—to analyze baseball through statistics in articles several generations ahead of their time.

Lane couldn't understand all the fuss over the 1910 Chalmers Award, that silly foofaraw over the batting averages of Ty Cobb and Nap Lajoie. Didn't people realize that-batting averages were a "worse than worthless" (his words) way to rank hitters? How could people so blindly ignore the differences between singles, doubles, triples, and home runs, and not try to figure out how many runs each hit led to? And what about walks and stolen bases? Not to mention accounting for how individual ballpark dimensions—like the Polo Grounds' short fences or cavernous fields in Boston and Cincinnati—affected statistics? Pitching and fielding numbers were a disaster as well, Lane claimed, and he went on a personal mission, several times a year, to impress this upon his readers in articles titled anywhere from "Where the Baseball Records Fail to Tell the Truth," "A Brand New System of Batting Averages," and "A Square Deal for the Base on Balls." Lane penned dozens of other inside features and interviews with baseball's stars—he was one of the few writers Ty Cobb invited to his offseason Georgia home—but no articles were so piqued as those involving statistics. "No pains should be spared to have the system," he wrote, "perfected to the extreme limit of human ingenuity."

Some allies joined Lane in the fight. In 1906, an unbylined writer in the Washington *Evening Star* examined scorebooks from 158 games to assess the value of the stolen base and sacrifice bunt—and while he was at it determined that of the 3,913 runners who reached first base, 2,106 reached second, 1,311 third, and 974 home again. Hugh Fullerton, a nationally known baseball scribe for the *Chicago Examiner,* wrote a long feature piece in the May 1910 issue of *The American Magazine* called "The Science of Baseball," where he analyzed 10,074 batted balls to learn that 3,602 were fly balls, 5,171 grounders, 957 line drives, and 344 bunts. He went on to measure not just how many balls certain fielders reached but the exact speed, thanks to his twentieth-of-a-second stopwatch, with which those grounders were hit. One exasperated reader replied that Fullerton "would have us believe that good ball can be played only by those men who . . . work with the assistance of a tape-measure, a tee-square, and an intimate knowledge of algebra and fractions."

Lane used those tools unabashedly, first to attack the widespread reverence for batting average. "Would a system that placed nickels, dimes, quarters, and 50-cent pieces on the same basis be much of a system whereby to compute a man's financial resources?" he wrote in 1916. "And yet it is precisely such a loose, inaccurate system which obtains in base-ball . . . Pretty poor system, isn't it, to govern the most popular department of the most popular of games?" Lane acknowledged that determining the relative value of singles, doubles, triples, and home runs was a difficult one. (Interestingly, he never once suggested adding up a player's total bases and presenting them either per game—a method popular in the 1860s and 1870s before Chadwick's distaste for power hitting snuffed it out—or per at-bat, which would be today's slugging percentage.) He wanted some-thing more grounded in logic, with what actually happened on the dia-mond, and spoke with Heydler about the dilemma.

"I admit that the system of giving as much credit to singles as to home runs is inaccurate to some extent," the National League president said. "But it has never seemed practicable to use any other system."

"Simply because a problem is hard to solve," Lane replied, "is no ex-cuse for failing to make the attempt."

So he made it himself. Lane kept strict account of 62 major league games in order to identify exactly one thousand hits. For each one he assigned the percentage of a run each represented on its own—.25 for a single, .75 for a triple, etc.—and then added the average advancements runners on base made as well. After a few manual adjustments for runners left on base and whatnot he wound up with these run values for each type of hit: singles (.30), doubles (.60), triples (.90) and home runs (1.15). Lane then took the figures and applied them to two well-known hitters: Brooklyn first baseman Jack Daubert, a singles artist who had recently won two National League batting titles, and the Phillies' Gavvy Cravath, who had just led the league with 24 home runs. Daubert's 1915 batting average was above the magic .300 mark (.301, actually) while Cravath's was just .285, but Lane demonstrated the hidden value of slugging with this chart:

	Daubert		Cravath	
Hits	#	Value	#	Value
Singles	133	40	87	26
Doubles	21	13	31	19
Triples	8	7	7	7
Home Runs	2	2	24	27
Total Run Value		62		79
at-bats		544		522
Total Run Value / At-bat		.114		.151

"The batting average of Jake Daubert, reckoned on any sane basis, is not equal to that of Cactus Cravath by a very wide margin. In fact, the two are not in the same class," Lane wrote. "And yet, according to the present system, Daubert is the better batter of the two. It is grotesqueries such as this that bring the whole foundation of baseball statistics into disrepute."

Some colleagues didn't appreciate Lane's shaking that foundation. William A. Phelon, the well-known baseball editor of the *Cincinnati Times-Star*, harrumphed at Lane's approach in a subsequent *Baseball Magazine* piece. "The present system is about as good as any, and it seems really impossible" to do any better, he wrote. Lane immediately snapped back: "There are many men who are fond of making an unsupported statement under the apprehension that they have posited an argument . . . Let's not make any effort to improve the present system which Mr. Phelon admits is grossly inaccurate. If there is any logic in this contention it escapes our feeble intellect."

Over several years, and through several more long and increasingly sanctimonious articles—loneliness can do that—Lane refined his approach to value singles as worth .457 runs, doubles .786, triples 1.15, and home runs 1.55.* Lane also cited the importance of walks, which, having been kept officially by Heydler just a few years before, was generally ignored. Lane called walks "the orphan child of the dope sheets" and determined they were worth .164 runs apiece. Lane's new approach of merging non-singles into a catch-all average certainly found a friend in Cravath, the Philadelphia slugger who complained that reliance on conventional batting average had cost him several thousands of dollars in salary each year. "If batting means anything at all, it means smashing offensive work for your club and ability to demolish the defense," he said. "[But] most of my seasons . . . I have hit under .300 and therefore have not been a particularly good batter according to the numbskull system."

Alas, baseball in the teens was not a slugger's game. Pitchers still were dominating the batters and had, almost constantly, since they adjusted to the 60-foot-6-inch distance two decades before. Offenses were centered around swift, slashing singles hitters like Detroit's Ty Cobb and Pittsburgh's Honus Wagner, who could steal bases to generate one run at a time; home runs were still frowned upon by the game's conservatives as

---

*These values are almost exactly the same as those that statistician Pete Palmer, working some 60 years later on a method he called Linear Weights, came up with through sophisticated computer regression analysis.

shameless displays of brute force. The game did receive a jolt in 1910, though, when a new, cork-center baseball with a zippy layer of rubber was quietly put into play. The livelier ball caused the average team's scoring to jump 18 percent, from 3.8 runs per game to 4.5, and produced some spectacular statistics. Cobb hit .420 in 1911 and .410 the next year, while Cleveland's sensational right fielder, "Shoeless" Joe Jackson, batted .408 and .395. But pitchers soon adjusted once again, thanks in large part to their widespread tendency to slather the ball with spit or otherwise scratch it with emery boards and belt buckles, making pitches dance and drop with ease. Hitting declined once more to almost unprecedented lows. By 1918 the sixteen major league teams averaged only 15 home runs per team for the entire season; Washington hit just four. How important could slugging be, conventional logic went, if so few bothered to do it?

Lane couldn't believe his ears. Now editor of *Baseball Magazine*, he evangelized the importance of the power game while scrutinizing almost every statistic there was—tearing down the use of pitchers' wins and losses, all but excoriating fielding percentage, and more. Charts listed the easiest batters to strike out and the best control pitchers. Long features examined the balance between pitching and hitting that the moundsmen were so dominating. Other studies looked at teams' average margins of victory, the value of multiple-run innings and more, to assess the effectiveness of certain strategies.

Just as important, Lane encouraged his readers to join the effort. "There are many fans, no doubt, who have thought deeply upon [statistics], and will be able to make valuable suggestions," Lane wrote, adding that *Baseball Magazine* "will be only too pleased to give publicity to any such helpful suggestions." Letters poured in that first winter of 1913, forming the first community of baseball stat mavens.

From J. H. Hamel of Kalispell, Montana: "What we need is a system by which the batter will get credit for the number of bases that are gained with his help. My plan is to give the batter credit for all bases gained [by baserunners] with his help plus the number of bases he himself hits for, and to divide [this] by the number of times he goes to bat. For instance . . . Banks goes to bat four times and gets two singles, one with a man on first [who goes to second] and one with a man on second who scores. Thus he gets credit for five bases, or a batting average of 1.250."

From F. M. Thayer of Orange, Texas: "The present method of rating the base stealers [total steals per game] is not very satisfactory . . . My scheme would be to . . . take the percentages of bases stolen out of the number of attempts, instead of the percentage of steals per game. It is a well-known fact that John McGraw's policy is to pilfer (or try to) as often as possible; consequently the Giants have a larger percentage of steals per game than other clubs, but whether or not they have a good percentage out of the number of attempts is unknown. My scheme would show them up, and it would be an easy matter to see if they are the Mercuries that their reputation claims them to be. [Note: Caught Stealing would not be kept by the two major leagues until 1920.]

From John O. Linden of Hannibal, Missouri: "I propose to credit the pitcher with 3 points for every inning he pitches. Charge his record 3 points for every run made by the opponents. But if the opposing team makes a run with the help of an error by the pitcher's team-mates, he should lose only two points. Let us see how this would work out in actual practice . . ."

While the study of statistics was getting more sophisticated in the second decade of the twentieth century, the keeping of them remained strikingly haphazard.

The National and American leagues had for years compiled end-of-season statistics for the annual guides, but those numbers didn't become available until weeks after the season ended. This left amateurs, occasionally newspapermen but often simply rabid fans, to keep them on their own throughout the season; when they disagreed with official tallies, as they often did, no one knew which to believe. Official statistics were not above suspicion by any means: in 1897, according to the historian Harold Seymour, one of the owners of the Washington Senators conspired with the club's official scorer to give shortstop Gene DeMontreville a few dozen extra hits to keep his average over .300 and boost his sale price to Baltimore. (The owner claimed such behavior was widespread.) The year before, when a *Boston Herald* statkeeper had Philadelphia Phillies catcher Jack Clements batting .402, the NL initially reported his average at .324, a whopping 78-point difference. His average was later adjusted to .362, no doubt through means anything but exact.

The situation wasn't a whole lot better in 1910, when the Chalmers Award fiasco evidenced the slipshod method in which batting averages

F. C. Lane and Al Munro Elias. (*National Baseball Hall of Fame Library, Cooperstown, N.Y.*)

were kept. All statistics, in fact. That September, Walter Johnson "broke" the American League strikeout record believed to be 301 by Rube Waddell six years before. But not only was the Waddell figure way off (Moreland, the *Balldom* stat fiend, later corrected it to 343, and that wasn't even right), people couldn't even decide how many strikeouts *Johnson* had in the current season! Moreland's tally read 308, others 307, while the league's official sheets weren't up-to-date enough to help much at all. When Johnson struck out 10 Chicago White Sox on September 28, the *Washington Evening Star* report read, "By striking out ten of the White Sox yesterday Walter Johnson established a new strike-out record—it will take the official count to decide whether he has fanned 307 or 308 to date . . ." This murkiness, not uncommon back then, would today be downright laughable.

Al Munro Elias didn't find it funny at all. So what if he was just a run-the-mill salesman, traipsing across the country hawking shoes and salad oil? To him, baseball was the most important thing in the world, the only home he truly had. Statistics were the foundation of that home; any imperfection within them weakened the entire structure. And if no one would keep the stats accurately, then by golly, he would.

He already had experience. Along with his brother Walter, another salesman, Elias always brought three items on his frequent trips to watch his beloved New York Giants from the bleachers of the Polo Grounds: lunch box, bottle of milk, and his scorebook, in which he would painstakingly record the goings-on. The work didn't end at the ballpark. After getting back home, he and Walter, scribbling on the backs of old envelopes, would figure statistics for their favorite Giants no one else had: the batting totals for the second baseman, Larry Doyle, each week as the season progressed; what catcher Chief Meyers hit against the Phillies; the teams that fared best against their pitching hero, Christy Mathewson. Before long, Al Munro Elias, suitably armed for combat, could win every baseball argument he got into, usually by asphyxiating the other side with his homegrown statistics. One friend claimed there were only two ways to deal with Elias when he got to talking baseball: "One was to listen to what he had to say. The other was to kill him."

When a persistent stomach ailment in 1914 left him too weak to lift his suitcase of salad-oil bottles, Elias, then in his 40s, decided to see if he could make a living keeping and selling his baseball statistics. He talked Walter into joining him. Within a few days Al was pestering newspaper editors who, one observer recalled, "gently but firmly" threw him out of their offices. But the Eliases did find some customers: mostly billiard parlors, which would buy cards printed with statistics and other facts for a dollar per 100, then offer them to their own clientele as grist for diamond discussions. Several restaurants and bowling alleys bought pocket folders of statistics called "Food for Fans," succumbing to Elias's indefatigable sales pitch. "His procedure was simple and effective," a friend recalled. "He buttonholed the proprietor, talked him into a comatose condition and when the poor man was utterly exhausted and helpless, put over the deal." Al Munro Elias considered his statistics vital to any serious fan. He would soon make them so.

Elias got his big break three years later when Jack Knox, sports editor of the *New York Evening Telegram*, bought some of his tidbits. From there the icy resistance began to crack. Bill Farnsworth of the *New York American* joined in. Then Walter Elias, usually the quiet one, had an epiphany. He saw how a Cleveland newspaper ran a daily box with updated statistics of the American League's three best hitters: Ty Cobb, Joe Jackson, and Tris Speaker. What a neat idea! Keeping up with out-of-town players was all but impossible; papers typically ran statistics only of the hometown team. There was no way to monitor the batting race as the season went on or follow the feats of other stars. The Eliases proposed to Farnsworth that they would furnish the *American* with the top three batters in both leagues every day.

"Make it the five leading hitters," Farnsworth said, "and I'll buy it."

The daily leader box was born. The feature became so popular so fast with fans that it sold to newspapers throughout the United States and Canada. The Eliases beefed it up to include the top five not just in batting average but also home runs, stolen bases, runs scored, earned run average, and won-lost percentage. They printed special editions of their statistics and box-score oddities in 1918 and sent them to fans overseas with the message, "To Our Fighting Boys in France." Before long the Eliases were offering up-to-date statistical totals of every player for Sunday papers, a feature that, like their League Leaders box, lives to this day.

The Elias brothers brought unprecedented zeal to the task of keeping timely statistics. Getting the information to newspapers still was rudimentary—lists were usually sent through the mail—but they strove to make the numbers as current as possible. To ensure Thursday and Friday games were included in the weekly lists, Walter would wait at the foot of the Brooklyn Bridge for the *Brooklyn Eagle*'s late box score edition to hit the streets at around 1:30 A.M. Saturday morning, rush up the subway to his office—actually the spare room of their sister, Hannah—in upper Manhattan, and work through the next afternoon getting the statistics ready. The brothers tolerated no mistakes. No transposed digits, no miscarried 1s. "There are only two kinds of statistics," Al often said. "Accurate and worthless."

The Eliases made their numbers worth more than they ever dreamed. The top five and Sunday lists that appeared in newspapers caught the attention of National League president John Heydler, a statistics buff for years, and in 1918 he hired the brothers to handle the NL's official numbers. (The American League had been serviced by Irwin Howe of Chicago since 1911.) The company, renamed the Al Munro Elias Baseball Bureau, saw revenues climb from $1,400 in 1917 to $3,400 the next year to $12,000 the year after that. When the Associated Press signed on to wire Elias statistics to more than 250 papers, the brothers gave up shoe sales for good. More than 80 years later the operation they built is still going strong: Now known as the Elias Sports Bureau, and located on the same corner of 42nd Street and Fifth Avenue to which Al and Walter first upgraded, it is the official statistician not just for both of baseball's major leagues, but for the other three major professional sports leagues as well.

Al Munro Elias foresaw the widespread appeal of baseball statistics more keenly than anyone in the first half of the twentieth century, sensing what newspaper readers wanted before the editors themselves. But he also got lucky. Getting into the baseball business in the late teens meant being on hand for an arrival of almost messianic proportions, a player who did things no one had ever done before—and whose numbers, as astonishing as they were colossal, made baseball statistics part of the national parlance. He pitched for the Boston Red Sox. His name was Babe Ruth.

Babe Ruth. (*National Baseball Hall of Fame Library, Cooperstown, N.Y.*)

3

The Sultans of Stats

This year will be unique in baseball history for there are three races on in the big league circuits. There is the usual pennant race in the National League and in the American League. In addition, there is the added feature of a race between Babe Ruth and the (home run) record. And that is, perhaps, the most exciting race of all.

—F. C. Lane
Baseball Magazine, June 1921

Babe Ruth's swing and swagger had already lassoed the imagination of the baseball public before he was sold from the Red Sox to the Yankees in January 1920. Only a few years removed from being the best left-handed pitcher in the game, Ruth had firmly established himself as a "champion home run hitter" and the "Home Run King," as two newspapers described him. The six-foot-two, 215-pound giant hit baseballs over grandstands no one had reached before; he swung with awesome, contorting vigor. Yet statistics were not yet part of the allure. Reporters did not dwell on the numbers. The day after he was sold to Gotham, for example, the *New York Herald's* story only parenthetically mentioned, and midway through, his record 29 home runs the year before, and that was the only statistic cited at all before the next-to-last paragraph. This would change, and change very quickly.

Just as Ruth sent pitches thrown at him hurtling in the opposite direction with one mighty wallop, the new Yankee soon put up statistics so marvelous, so downright preposterous, year after mind-boggling year, that journalistic coverage of him also shot off in a different direction. No longer mere stats, his 54, then 59, then 60 home runs became as legendary as the player himself, the digits as vibrant as the letters R, U, T, and H. His statistics kept climbing higher and higher, inspiring awe, wonder . . . and, most of all, conversation. Baseball was becoming the numbers game.

Ruth came along just in time. Baseball in the teens, after its brief bender with the lively ball, had basically degenerated into tedious, daily pitchers' duels. Runs scored one at a time, manufactured piecemeal by the steal-and-sacrifice style advanced by New York Giants manager John McGraw, and before long complaints percolated that the games were "monotonous" and "listless." It didn't help that pitchers had all but perfected the spitball, emery ball, and other offerings then perfectly legal. (Pirates hurler Marty O'Toole would stand on the mound and literally lick the ball; opponents sometimes counteracted by applying noxious liniment to it between innings.) These "freak deliveries" helped the New York Highlanders' Jack Chesbro win 41 games in one season, and the White Sox's Ed Walsh 40, statistics that surely will never be matched again. As run-scoring plummeted, fans lost interest in watching at all. Attendance began to deteriorate in 1913 and got worse through the rest of the decade.

Ironically, a pitcher would change that. George Herman "Babe" Ruth, a troubled kid from Baltimore who had spent much of his life in a boys' home, joined the Red Sox in 1914 and quickly established himself as one of the top lefthanders in the American League. He averaged 20 wins a season from 1915 to 1918, leading the Red Sox to three World Series titles during that span. (He twirled 29⅔ straight shutout innings in those World Series, a record that would stand for 43 years.) Yet it was in the batter's box—where even full-time hitters, let alone pitchers, could barely do any damage—that he was his most tantalizing. In 1915, his four home runs (in just 92 at-bats) led all of his Boston teammates. Two years later, although Ruth came to the plate just 142 times, his .325 batting average trailed only Ty Cobb, George Sisler, and Tris Speaker in the American League. By 1918 fans came to Fenway and other ballparks to see this Babe Ruth not pitch, but hit; the Red Sox soon let him play first base, and then outfield, less for competitive advantage than as a gate attraction.

He didn't disappoint. In his first two games as a position player in

1918, Ruth hit home runs; he soon was batting .484, hit home runs in four straight games, and was being called the "sensation of baseball." When he slammed his 11th home run of the season in the tenth inning to beat the great Walter Johnson on June 30—remember, no American Leaguer had hit more than a dozen for the previous 15 years—the intrigue spread quickly. According to Ruth biographer Robert Creamer, "A naval officer noted that the wireless report that went out from Arlington every night at eleven included a quick rundown of the day's baseball scores. Just the bare results were given, except for Boston's games. Here the operator would interrupt the report to advise whether Ruth had hit a home run or not." Newspapers began to capture Ruth's accomplishments not just in words, but numbers; charts and graphs displayed how his "extra bases," the ones beyond those of run-of-the-mill singles, dwarfed those of Cobb, Sisler, and other stars.

Home runs at that time were like triples today—freak hits that were too rare to be fully appreciated. Even Ruth didn't flaunt his circuit clouts early on. In a wonderful *Baseball Magazine* article from 1918, a first-person story titled "Why a Pitcher Should Hit," Ruth rarely mentions home runs. He sticks to the stats more valued at that time. "I believe I could qualify as a true .300 hitter," he writes. Later, "If there is any one thing that appeals to me more than winning a close game from a tough rival, it's knocking out a good clean three bagger with men on bases." Ruth did indeed hit 11 triples that season, but his 11 home runs led the American League. His towering flies made onlookers wonder just what Ruth could do in 1919. Alas, the slugger's celebrity did not impress the Giants' McGraw, the hard-nosed traditionalist who hated home runs and strikeouts, feats at which Ruth was equally adept. "If he plays every day," McGraw complained before the 1919 season began, "the bum will hit into a hundred double plays before the season is over." But the game McGraw had mastered was slipping from his hands.

The 1919 season began one month late because of lingering war issues, but Ruth started just as hot as expected. On July 29 he tied "Socks" Seybold's American League record for home runs with his 16th; journalists waited anxiously for two weeks before he would break it. Ruth hit seven home runs in one 12-game stretch, an unheard-of explosion, and spread his fame by going deep in every American League ballpark. Would he break the all-time season record for home runs? It was commonly believed that Gavvy Cravath owned the modern (post-1901) standard with 24, and "Buck" Freeman the pre-1901 one with 25, and Ruth's march past those marks met with appropriate fanfare. Then, after his twenty-sixth, someone discovered that Ned Williamson of the 1884 Chicago White Stockings had hit 27; though Williamson's mark had always been tainted by the fact that his ballpark had a fence just 215 feet from the plate that season (the guy never again hit more than nine), his 27 was indeed the record. But Ruth quickly passed Williamson, too, becoming perhaps the first and only player in sports history to shatter the same all-time record twice in one season. He finished with a staggering 29.

Ruth was sold to New York that offseason, and speculation ran rampant on what the Babe could do in a full season in the Polo Grounds with its short right-field fence. F. C. Lane, the numbers-savvy editor of *Baseball Magazine*, suggested that Ruth could pass 29, perhaps easily, because he was getting out of Fenway Park, in which he had hit just 9 home runs compared to 20 on the road. The *Spalding* guide, however, had its doubts: "Perhaps, and most likely, Ruth will not be so successful in 1920. The pitchers will eye him with more than ordinary caution and they will twist their fingers into knots to get more curve and still more curve on the ball. They will give one another private little tips." The editor, John Foster, penned this verse:

> *King of the Realm of Swat,*
> > *Omnipotent in the Land of Slug;*
> *You surely set a mark*
> > *At which others will plug—and plug;*
> *To beat that "29"*
> > *Will take some breadth of shoulder,*
> *And when they put a "30" up*
> > *Well—we'll most likely be some older*

It took only a few months. Ruth hit 12 home runs in May 1920, another dozen in June and slammed number 30 on July 19, barely halfway through the season. Fans flocked to the parks to see him swing. The Yankees doubled their attendance that season; spectators, even those outside New York, booed when Ruth was walked, just as Mark McGwire and Sammy Sosa followers would several generations later. Those fans were not coming to see the Yankees as a team, but Babe Ruth individually. This was downright blasphemous. After one-third of a Polo Grounds crowd left following a Ruth eighth-inning strikeout, Yankee pitcher Carl Mays complained, "Can you imagine it? One man out in the eighth and they are through for the day. They know Babe will not come up again and they have seen what they paid to see. When Babe is through, they are through." The fans Ruth attracted were not the die-hards who put up with the soporific game that baseball had become before and during the war. These were new fans who wanted to see runs score, and relished the thrill of watching Ruth swing mightily to make that happen. "I hit big," the Babe crowed, "or I miss big."

Ruth's style of hitting caught on. While many people thought (and still think) that a new "rabbit" ball was introduced for the 1920 season, accounting for Ruth's 54 home runs and offense jumping throughout both leagues, the inside of the ball was not responsible. It was the *outside*. The previous winter, after a decade of controversy, baseball banned all but two pitchers per team from throwing spitballs, removing one of their most potent weapons. This allowed hitters to zone in on pitches that were straighter and take harder whacks at them, just like Ruth. John Heydler, the former National League secretary-statistician and now president, said that baseball had "undergone a complete metamorphosis," and that "Ruth and his home-run hitting have done more to change the style of the modern game than all other agencies combined . . . The hitters are going to keep right on stepping into the ball and slamming it as far as they are able. They've seen Babe turn the trick, and all want to be Ruths." Though it paled in comparison to Ruth's 54, George Sisler of the St. Louis Browns hit 19 homers in 1920, seven more than any AL player not named Ruth since 1903. All hitters went deep more often; over two seasons home run frequencies more than doubled.

Baseball historically had responded to such jumps by trying to restore the balance between pitching and hitting, but after news broke late in 1920 that the Chicago White Sox had thrown the previous year's World Series to the Cincinnati Reds, the league powers simply gave the public what it wanted: more offense. All sorts of rule changes were considered, including lowering the walk threshold from four balls to three, taking away fielders' gloves, returning runners to their bases to begin the next inning, and even a permanent pinch hitter for the pitcher, to which many now refer bitterly as the designated hitter. But those more drastic measures proved unnecessary. Tragedy intervened.

On August 17, 1920, immensely popular Indians shortstop Ray Chapman was killed by a Carl Mays fastball that slammed into his head as if out of nowhere. The ball, like most used at that time, was dingy brown from overuse, and Chapman barely even saw it. That offseason rulemakers tightened restrictions on the spitball (though the pitch from Mays probably wasn't one) but more importantly instructed umpires to replace dirty balls with new white ones that hitters could pick up better. As a result slugging shot up over the next several seasons, right along with attendance.

Not everyone liked how home runs and doubles were trampling the game they knew. "It ain't the old game which I have lost interest in," Chicago baseball writer Ring Lardner complained, "but it is a game which the magnates have fixed up to please the public with their usual good judgment." The more fatalistic F. C. Lane commented, "It may be a triumph of brawn over brain. It may suggest the dominance of mere brute strength over intelligence. It may show a preference for the cave man over the finished artist. It may be what you will. But rest assured it's a fact."

Lane reveled in the Ruth phenomenon because he could capture it in numbers. His many articles on Ruth during his ascent from 1918 to 1921 featured examinations of his extra bases per hit, weekly batting average graphs, and more. While cooing mythmakers in the press such as Grantland Rice lavished Ruth with adjectives—"herculean," "majestic," and so on—Lane preferred citing the statistical records the slugger cut to snippets. "Babe is particularly good at shattering records," Lane wrote in 1920. "His favorite stunt is to break a record so old that it has grown mouldy [sic] and crumbly, setting up a brand new one of his own creation in its place and then, in a fit of dissatisfied petulance, thrusting that new record roughly to one side to make room for a still fresher creation." When Ruth wound up with 54 home runs in 1920, Lane wrote that his 29 from the year before "sinks to ridiculous obscurity," as if a sprinter had just run 100 yards in eight seconds. Lane went on: "Two years ago if you had made the statement that it would be easier for a batter to hit .500 throughout a season than to rap out fifty home runs, ninety-nine ball players out of a hundred would have agreed with you."

Fewer still thought that Ruth could come back in 1921 and break his record of 54, but Lane did. As the news of the Black Sox fix avalanched upon baseball during that the offseason of 1920–21, Lane contended that the biggest question facing the game was not whether Joe Jackson and his seven teammates had taken the bribes, but, rather, "Can Babe Ruth Repeat?" Lane examined Ruth's month-by-month production from the previous season—particularly his zero homers in April—and declared that the record would fall once again. "His chances to set up a new mark are excellent," Lane wrote. "He will race against Ruth, the Ruth of 1921 against the Ruth of 1920. It will be a unique race, a race of feverish excitement, of thrilling interest from start to finish. The spectators will number many millions." Lane also figured out that Ruth had batted .500 in games in which he homered, which surely blew the derbies off readers' heads.

Ruth did the same from the moment the 1921 season started. He careened toward 54, swatting five in April, 10 in May, and 13 more in June. The *Pittsburgh Gazette-Times* began running a "Truth about Ruth" feature almost every day, describing all the pitches thrown to the Babe and the damage he invariably inflicted upon them. Amazingly, even with all this attention, the fact that Ruth was in the process of breaking the *lifetime* home run record went unnoticed. Roger Connor, who annually hit between 11 and 17 home runs during the late 1880s and early 1890s, finished his career with what is now considered 138, but home runs were so uncelebrated back then that Connor's records were neither exact nor even accessible when Ruth came barreling along. It was such a fait accompli that Ruth was or would be the lifetime home run king, when he passed Connor in July 1921 New York's *Daily News, Times,* and *Tribune*— and even the Bible of Baseball, *The Sporting News*—wrote not a word.

On September 15 Ruth hit his 55th, breaking his own seasonal record again. He finished the year with statistics—59 home runs, a .378 batting average, 171 runs batted in, and 177 runs scored—that simply staggered the fans who followed them. And there were more of those than ever before. "While thousands cram the grandstands to be actual spectators," Lane reported, "literally millions scan the [box scores] for word of what Babe has done."

R uth had changed the game, all right—not just on the field but in the stands, and at breakfast tables across the United States. The millions who surveyed the box scores for Ruth's exploits began doing the same for other players who were posting statistical totals that never had been reached before. In 1922, Rogers Hornsby, the brilliant young second baseman for the St. Louis Cardinals, batted .401 and smacked 42 home runs, almost doubling the post-1900 National League record. Three American League batters went deep 35 times or more. Rampaging offense prompted the leagues to adopt two new official statistics. The Run Batted In, formerly the personal province of *New York Press* sports editor Ernie Lanigan, finally became official for both leagues in 1920 (though for its first eight years the statistic was called Runs Responsible For). In 1923, National League president John Heydler, former champion of the ERA, added slugging percentage to the NL stat sheets. (Ruth's own American League strangely did not follow suit with slugging percentage until 1946, but the statistic was widely used by writers in both leagues.) Spotlighting players' statistics in greater detail than ever began a tectonic shift in sports, as intrigue that once focused mostly on teams began to go to individual players and their statistics lines. "The player, even the greatest star, was [once] an inconspicuous fraction of the game itself," Lane wrote. Yet with the Elias and Howe bureaus disseminating up-to-date statistics to newspapers around the nation, more and more articles focused on the game's numerical side.

Stars were taking aim at records left and right, shooting the statistics down like ducks at a carnival booth. Walter Johnson passed Cy Young for the all-time strikeout lead in 1921. Tris Speaker's 59 doubles in 1923 beat Ed Delahanty's 1899 mark of 56 (a figure later corrected to 55). Ruth inched his own record upward by slamming 60 home runs in 1927, the same year his new slugging mate, Lou Gehrig, topped the Babe's RBI record with 175. Over in the National League, two of Hornsby's marks for that circuit fell in 1929: home runs (to Chuck Klein of the Philadelphia Phillies, who hit 43) and RBIs (to Hack Wilson of the Chicago Cubs, with 159). In August of that year, Grover Cleveland Alexander broke Christy Mathewson's National League record with his 373th career win.* As America throughout the 1920s expanded its economy, women's rights, and Fitzgeraldian love for liquor, baseball's statistics grew right in step.

More and more young hitters joined the slugging revolution. In 1930, offense went completely haywire, leaving a residue of numbers that cast that season forever as the Year of the Hitter: The National League batted .303 as a whole; Wilson drove in 190 runs** and set an NL mark with 56 home runs; and Bill Terry of the New York Giants hit .401, the last time any Senior Circuit player topped the .400 level. Fans came out to watch the orgy in record numbers, despite the stock market crash of the previous October. The 10.1 million patrons at major league parks was the highest attendance major league baseball ever had before 1945.

Even so, the leagues reportedly deadened the ball slightly to restore

---

*Mathewson had a 373rd win discovered in the 1940s and today shares the mark with Alexander.
**Now officially 191; see chapter 8.

some semblance of order. But offense continued throughout the 1930s to define what baseball had become and wanted to be. It was a game more and more described by numbers, and large ones. Any new statistical news got its share of ink, even fielding. On July 30, 1933, when Cardinals ace Dizzy Dean struck out 17 batters to break the modern standard, he shared top billing in the *New York Times* headline with his catcher, Jimmy Wilson: DEAN FANS 17 AND WILSON GETS 18 PUTOUTS FOR TWO NEW RECORDS AS CARDS WIN TWICE.

This is not to say that the people keeping the records always knew what the records were. Even after the Howe and Elias bureaus brought some semblance of order to things by the 1920s, screwups became a tradition all their own. Whether it was Walter Johnson's strikeouts or Christy Mathewson's wins, there tended to be a degree of uncertainty whenever a statistical mark was printed. Much of this came from how official scorers of the time resembled the batters they watched: They were a hit-and-miss sort of bunch. Their tallies of a game's goings-on occasionally bore scant resemblance to what actually had occurred. And then those sheets were often mistranscribed to official Howe and Elias ledgers that were added up at the end of the season, with workers transposing digits or miscarrying 1s left and right. In the days of pencil and paper, long before even mechanical calculators, official statistics sheets were strewn with these types of errors. Just ask Ty Cobb.

In 1922, still going strong at age 35, Cobb finished the season with the Philadelphia Athletics with a batting average of .401. Or so everyone thought, based on information furnished to newspapers by Irwin Howe, the American League's official statistician. Because official scorers' reports arrived slowly and only sporadically through the mail, Howe would use Associated Press box scores to compile statistics during the season. These wound up giving Cobb his .401 average that newspapers widely reported. Problem was, when Howe proofed his tabulations against the official scorer's sheets, a game at Yankee Stadium on May 15 found a maddening discrepancy. All because Fred Lieb wanted to stay out of the rain.

That afternoon, Lieb, the AP writer who also kept its box score, left the open press box when it started drizzling and sought shelter under the grandstand. In the second inning, Cobb hit a grounder to Yankees shortstop Everett Scott, who bobbled the ball and threw too late to get Cobb at first. Lieb took the conditions into account and decided against charging Scott an error; he marked a hit for Cobb. Yet back in the press box, the official scorer, a rookie writer named John Kieran (who later became a famous columnist for the *New York Times* and a regular on the *Information Please* radio quiz show) gave Scott an error, meaning no base hit for Cobb. Lieb's incorrect ruling went out over the wires, into newspapers nationwide and even into Howe's ledger sheets until weeks after the season ended, when the discrepancy was discovered. Applying Kieran's official ruling, Cobb's average declined from a magical .401 to a close-but-not-quite .399.

Howe asked AL president Ban Johnson to settle the matter. Citing how Kieran's official box score contained several blatant errors, which he oddly claimed was commonplace, Johnson decided he would go with Lieb's unofficial interpretation of the ground ball, giving Cobb his third .400 season. The press went nuts; even Lieb, whose ruling on the play had been upheld, claimed that the official scorer's ruling must always prevail. "I do not believe that a league president or a league statistician has any more right to overrule an official scorer on a question of judgment than he has a right to overrule an umpire on the question of what is a strike or a ball, or whether a base runner is safe or out on a close play at first," Lieb told *Baseball Magazine*. He later said, "The use of baseball records will be undermined when records are deliberately tampered with in order to favor any batsman, whether he be a star or a mediocre player." Yet Johnson's ruling stood, and Cobb's 1922 record finds a .401 average to this day.

Mistakes by official scorers continued. On July 28, 1930, in the second game of a Cubs-Reds doubleheader at Wrigley Field, the scorer incorrectly assigned a run batted in to Cubs first baseman Charlie Grimm when it truly belonged to Hack Wilson, who just happened to finish the season with 190 RBIs, an all-time record that still stands—sort of. The scoring goof went undetected by the National League office after the season, and didn't get picked up for half a century. A researcher in 1977 stumbled upon it, and a controversy just as impassioned as Cobb's, this time over whether Wilson had 190 or 191 RBIs, broke out all over again.

W ho cared about this stuff? Who would actually lose sleep over one hit or two strikeouts? More people than anyone imagined. Proof of that came in September 1944 when an earthquake shook Manhattan, and baseball statistics fell out.

Hy Turkin was a sports writer by trade, for the New York *Daily News*, and had covered baseball since 1938. (His first assignment just happened to be the first night game at Ebbets Field, when Cincinnati Reds left-hander Johnny Vander Meer threw his second straight no-hitter.) Five-foot-six, thin and shy, with a goofy affinity for bow ties, Turkin was not the most talented writer at the *News*, but his colleagues hailed him as a numbers whiz who could figure averages in his head and proof a box score—making sure all the totals added up properly—in seconds. These skills served him little, though, when the 1944 earthquake hit, and his apartment building began to rumble. He wrote a first-person account of the event for his paper, which happened to mention his address. One reader, a Broadway musician and baseball fan named S.C. Thompson, noticed that he lived right around the corner from Turkin. He decided to pay a visit.

"I'd like you to come to my house sometime, Hy, and look over my baseball collection," Thompson said. "I know you'll find it interesting."

Turkin didn't just find it interesting. He couldn't believe his eyes. With plenty of time on his hands between gigs, Thompson had spent 20 years amassing statistics for every man who had ever played major league baseball, all the way back to the National Association's first season of 1871. He'd been doing this since he was a kid. It all started when he wanted to settle an argument over the makeup of the 1919 Reds, who had beaten the infamous Black Sox in that year's tainted World Series. Thompson decided to make it his hobby to give each player an index card and comb through old guides and newspapers to fill in his yearly statistics. (It didn't hurt that Thompson also helped out part-time at the Al Munro Elias Baseball Bureau, the National League's statistics house.) As the project grew, and as he toured the country as a professional musician—he eventually played in John Philip Sousa's band—Thompson would carry a "Data Wanted" folder everywhere he went in case he came across a number he needed.

The day after the earthquake, Turkin trembled at the sight of all this information. He wanted to make a book out of it. Nothing resembling a comprehensive statistics encyclopedia existed or ever had. Ernie Lanigan, the champion of the RBI while at the *New York Press*, published a book called *Baseball Cyclopedia* in 1922 that listed every one of the 3,500 players to that point, along with their teams each year, but no statistics. *Daguerreotypes*, published by *The Sporting News*, featured statistics for a few hundred of the game's best all-time players. *Who's Who in Baseball* had every active player. But no book gave numbers for each major leaguer past and present, star or scrub. Over the next seven years Turkin and Thompson teamed up to provide just that.

In 1951, their *Official Encyclopedia of Baseball* was published by A. S. Barnes and Co., then the world's largest publisher of sports books. It included oodles of other features, like all-time standings, field dimensions, annual league leaders, and more, but the stats were the stars. The data today appears sparse: just games played, and then either batting average for hitters or won-lost records for pitchers. At the time, though, these were the principal statistics most fans and writers cared about. Finally, numbers on every player in major league history could be found between two covers. The book was a hit, selling more than fifty thousand copies. "It created more of a stir than you'd think," recalled Jack Lang, who covered the Dodgers for the *Brooklyn Daily Press*. "Nobody had put anything together like this. Nowhere else could you get this information. It was like a gold mine had been found in Manhattan."

Across the East River in Brooklyn, another seismic shift was just beginning, at the offices of the Brooklyn Dodgers. Some of the team's decisions had become downright bizarre. After the 1947 season, in which right fielder Dixie Walker had hit .306, he was shipped off to Pittsburgh. In 1949, Jackie Robinson, a .296 hitter with just 12 homers the year before, was moved into the cleanup spot. In May 1952, with catcher Roy Campanella batting .325, he rode the pine against Cincinnati in favor of Rube Walker, who was batting in the low .200s. Why would the Dodgers do this? the writers wondered. What could they possibly have up their sleeve? Only one man truly knew: Allan Roth.

Roth was the Dodgers' numbers man, as vital to Brooklyn boss Branch Rickey as Robin was to Batman. The first full-time statistician ever hired by a major league club, Roth spent his days churning out figures that no one had ever seen before: runners advanced and bunting success rates; batting averages in every ball-strike count; and performance against lefty and righty hitters or pitchers. He kept diagrams of where each batter's hits went, what we now call "spray charts." Every one of the 40,000 pitches in Brooklyn's season called for up to a dozen notations onto Roth's yellow legal pad, which he then collated for hours after every game, all so that he could discover any little edge the Dodgers could exploit.

Why was Dixie Walker traded? In part because the hit-location diagram indicated he wasn't the pulling the ball anymore, a sign of immutable aging. (Sure enough, Walker was out of the majors two years later.) Why was Robinson moved to cleanup? Because while he hadn't hit for much power the year before, he had batted .350 with men on base. (Robinson responded by batting .342 with 124 RBIs in 1949 and was named National League MVP.) Why did Campy sit against the Reds? Because he owned a lifetime .065 batting average against that day's pitcher, Ewell Blackwell, a tidbit that no one but Roth knew. Statistically based strategies like these, long before computers made them commonplace, were born in Brooklyn, at the end of Allan Roth's pencil. "Baseball is a game of percentages," he once explained. "I try to find the actual percentage."

Roth wasn't alone in his attempt—often pooh-poohed by the traditionalists—to develop ways to rate players beyond conventional batting and earned run averages. First there was F. C. Lane's *Baseball Magazine* community of letter writers in the teens. In 1944, a Los Angeles man named Ted Oliver self-published a pamphlet-sized book, *Kings of the Mound*, in which he unveiled his Weighted Rating System for pitchers. Oliver hated how good pitchers stuck on bad teams tended to have mediocre won–lost records. (One particularly snakebit hurler of that time, Hugh Mulcahy of the dreadful Philadelphia Phillies, earned the nickname "Losing Pitcher Mulcahy" because his name appeared that way so often in box scores.) Oliver instead looked at the difference between every pitcher's won-lost percentage and that of his club, which unveiled the Mulcahys of baseball as surprisingly competent, while pitchers like Red Ruffing and Lefty Gomez of great Yankees teams were exposed as rather run-of-the-mill. Oliver's was one of many such methods to rate pitchers more accurately. In 1951, a man named Alfred P. Berry designed a system to rate them by bases allowed per inning.

Roth, however, was the only zealot lucky enough to work for a major league team and to get to test his theories firsthand. He would spend hour upon hour holed up in his office, piles of notebooks and ledgers strewn about him, collating his figures and trying to devise others. He hated RBIs, because opportunities for them varied widely by position in the batting order, and instead kept track of the percentage of RBI chances converted, which we now call batting average with runners in scoring position. He measured which opposing hitters lunged at the first pitch or stayed patient. Whatever performance splits he was pinpointing— lefty-righty, home-away, different batters versus different pitchers—he sought out what he called "extremes," numbers that were so far away from normal that they had to mean something. They just *had* to. Amazingly enough, Roth didn't like math very much, and hated numbers outside baseball. He didn't even do his own taxes. But when it came to his favorite of sports he amazed people with the statistics he could keep and rattle off in seconds. Roth could never explain his dexterity with baseball statistics. Can a shortstop *explain* how he gobbles up a routine ground ball?

Roth was born in 1917 in Montreal, and within three years wowed his parents by counting backward from 100 by twos. Ten years later he was keeping his own statistics for the International League, which included his hometown Montreal Royals, the Dodgers' top farm team. He had to pass up a scholarship to prestigious McGill University to help support his family as a salesman for a neckwear and suspenders company, but in 1941 Roth was compiling numbers part-time for the National Hockey League. After serving in the Canadian army, he decided to approach Branch Rickey about keeping new statistics for the Dodgers.

Rickey, Brooklyn's general manager, was known to be the most progressive thinker in his stodgy industry. Beyond more high-profile moves like signing Jackie Robinson and developing the modern farm system, Rickey put players on handball courts to improve eye-hand coordination and introduced the first "Iron Mike" pitching machine. Michigan-educated with a law degree, Rickey took a similar approach to statistics. While old-timers would discount them (even batting average) by harrumphing, "My eyes tell me everything I need to know," Rickey wanted to know more. While running the St. Louis Cardinals in the 1920s and 1930s, he retained the services of a fellow named Travis Hoke, who rated players by counting the number of bases their hits accounted for, not just for themselves but the advancement of any base runners. (A home run with runners on second and third would count as four plus the two for the man on second and one for the man on third.) Later, in 1944, Rickey was intrigued by this pushy Canadian, Allan Roth, who showed up at spring training in Bear Mountain, New York, and cornered him at his restaurant table. Roth showed Rickey his data on RBI percentage. He flashed the Dodger batters' records against lefty and righty pitchers, numbers the Brooklyn boss had never seen. As soon as Roth got his visa, which took two years, Rickey hired him. Roth arrived in Brooklyn within hours of Jackie Robinson, just before Opening Day, 1947.

Many of Rickey's decisions later hailed as brilliant—trading the aging Dixie Walker for 1950s mainstays Preacher Roe and Billy Cox, for instance—were bolstered by Roth's information. Rickey liked to swap an old player one year early rather than one year late; his accuracy was helped by Roth's data. The stocky and thin-haired Roth would sit jacket-and-tied behind the plate every game, charting every pitch, making sure to avoid liquids so he would never have to get up to visit the rest room. He prepared a detailed study of the club every two weeks and was available for questions at the drop of Rickey's fedora. The boss rarely made any decision without surveying Roth's statistical landscape. "Baseball men like to call baseball a percentage game, but quite often they don't actually know what the percentage is," Rickey later said, eerily echoing his numbers man. The press soon picked up that something weird was going on inside the Dodgers front office. "Roth is a spy," one article in 1948 whispered. "He constitutes Branch Rickey's intelligence department."

Roth's statistics were forwarded to the manager's office, naturally, though there they met a far less receptive audience, particularly after Rickey left the Dodgers in 1950 to run the Pittsburgh Pirates. (Roth stayed behind.) Hired as Brooklyn manager was Charlie Dressen, then in his early 50s but a man getting an early start on stubbornness. A hunch gambler and master sign stealer, Dressen had little use for the sheets of statistics that Roth would deliver to his office at Ebbets Field. Dressen would say thank you, wait until the door closed behind Roth, and shove the papers in the trash.

With Rickey gone, Roth wound up moving from behind the plate up to the press box, where he generated statistics for the writers and club broadcasters. He found an instant fan in a bright, young radio voice named Vin Scully. Scully was only 22 when Rickey hired him after the 1949 season, and Rickey suggested the kid familiarize himself with the club's players by helping Roth compile his year-end statistics report. Roth would joke for years that he would guarantee the 100 percent accuracy of his statistics except for 1949, "the year Scully helped me."

The two took an instant liking to each other, and the friendship helped Roth brook his later demotion to the press box. Roth would update every hitter's batting average, home run, and RBI totals after each at-bat. He armed Scully with batter-versus-pitcher stats that made the broadcaster look downright wizardly. "Gil Hodges is 0-for-20 lifetime off of Johnny Antonelli," Scully would say, before Hodges rapped out a hit. "Now he's 1-for-21!" Scully has called Dodger games every season since but still remembers what the quiet Canadian did for him during those formative years. "Long before there was Mary Poppins, there was Allan Roth," Scully recalled fondly. "If you had some question that came to you in the middle of a game, he would reach down into this bag, and next thing you knew you'd have your answer. It was marvelous."

Roth's work became anything but secret. Newspapers marveled that someone could make his living churning out statistics; headlines called him a "Human Univac." WHO BUNTED ON A FRIDAY IN 1947? one asked, while another declared, SLIDE RULES AND LOGARITHMS HELP SOLVE DODGER WOES. He was profiled in *Newsweek*, making Roth the patron saint of closet baseball stat freaks; several sent their work to him asking how they could get similar jobs, while numbers-oriented kids grew up wanting to be the next Allan Roth. (We will meet some of them later in this book.)

Nothing made Roth more famous than when a formula he helped develop for Rickey became the subject of a ten-page spread in *Life* magazine, then the nation's most widely read periodical. The 1954 story was headlined GOODBY TO SOME OLD BASEBALL IDEAS and had Rickey, standing professorially at a blackboard, pointing to a long line of gobbledygook as majestic as it was befuddling:

$$\left(\frac{H + BB + HP}{AB + BB + HP} + \frac{3(TB - H)}{4AB} + \frac{R}{H + BB + HP} \right) -$$

$$\left(\frac{H}{AB} + \frac{BB + HB}{AB + BB + HB} + \frac{ER}{H + BB + HB} - \frac{SO}{8(AB + BB + HB)} - F \right) = G$$

The equation was heralded as the long-awaited Grand Unifying Theory of baseball, the end of a scientific quest that rivaled those of physicists over at Princeton. (Not surprisingly, the Princetonians were enlisted to perform a correlation analysis on the formula.) Each term was a gear in a magic meat grinder to which Rickey held the crank. It took every aspect of batting, pitching, and fielding and crunched them into one indisputable number. Just eight years after signing Jackie Robinson, Rickey clucked with his typical arrogance, "It is the most disconcerting and at the same time the most constructive thing to come into baseball in my memory."

Roth was relegated to deputy status in the article—Rickey always demanded center stage—but clearly was the driving force behind the equation's ideas. Silly as it looks, it held some concepts forty years ahead of their time. The first term was what we now call on-base percentage, a statistic Rickey emphasized in the story as drastically undervalued. The second term captured pure power, a sort of slugging percentage without the singles. The third tried to quantify base running ability by looking at how many times a runner scores per time on base. The other terms applied to pitchers and fielders. Needless to say, the equation was so complicated that the baseball community reflexively mocked it. No evidence suggests that anyone took it seriously.

Back in Brooklyn, the Dodger writers did appreciate Roth's work, particularly when it helped them. Roth would prepare statistical notes for the press before each game—each hitter's batting average against that day's starting pitcher, the pitcher's lifetime record against the Dodgers, and whatnot. Few baseball journalists at the time cared for such esoterica, but young Dodger writers such as Lang came to value the material. "Clubs didn't hand out stat sheets back then. We were lucky," Lang recalled. "We could keep track of a 15-game hitting streak or something we were following, but Allan came up with stuff we weren't aware of. Red Schoendienst had just a .227 average against Preacher Roe? Who knew that?"

Baseball journalism was beginning to change around this time. Writers such as Grantland Rice, who "godded up" athletes through the 1940s with flowing prose and praise, had been replaced by thoughtful scribes such as Red Smith, Leonard Koppett, and others who developed a style more grounded in realism. They were getting more interested in actual information. New York's *Daily News* ran a daily column called "Diamond Dust" with all sorts of baseball tidbits, many of them statistical. Meanwhile, Dodger beat writers tossed Roth's information into their own notes columns, often just to fill space, and couldn't believe the reaction they got. "Fans chewed it up," Lang recalls. "They loved it!"

Sure enough, readers only clamored for more and more numbers, chewing on them like billygoats. They couldn't get enough. Baseball statistics were beginning their rise to full-fledged cultural phenomenon.

Sy Berger didn't know what to do. It was late 1951, and the young accounting graduate had spent several years at the Topps Chewing Gum Company unsuccessfully trying to spruce up its trading-card line. Sets of "Hopalong Cassidy" pictures sold fine, but his boss, J. E. Shorin, wanted to try a set of athletes, particularly baseball players. This wasn't exactly a new idea. It had been done for more than half a century by cig- arette makers, and still was by the Bowman Gum company. Berger's first attempts at a baseball set in 1951 pictured players but was more of a base- ball card game than anything else—cards read "double," "walk," and the like—and it sold horribly. Berger needed to add something that would grab and interest kids. He needed a hook.

"We ought to do statistics," he told himself.

Berger knew that would attract children, because years before, he *was* the market. Growing up in the Bronx 10 blocks from Yankee Stadium, Berger was a statistics nut. As a young boy he would scan the newspaper's box scores for his favorite players and mark down what they did on a mas- ter sheet, add the totals, and do the long division so he could monitor their batting average through the season. He won the math medal at P.S. 64 elementary school. Twenty years later, those skills came in handy when he sat down to include statistics for the 1952 Topps baseball card set. When he looked at 1951 season statistics in various sources—news- papers, *The Sporting News*—they didn't agree. So he simply did them all himself, from the box scores.

Berger put each player's lifetime and 1951 statistics on the back of the 1952 cards, but hedged his bet by calling the 1951 stats "YEAR"—in case the cards took more than a season to sell, they wouldn't look too dated. But they flew off the shelves faster than Berger ever dreamed, in large part because of the statistics. Kids couldn't get enough of them.

Batting averages made math cool, or at least worthwhile. (If nothing else, they legitimized the existence of long division.) Future doctors, lawyers, and captains of industry cut their figurative teeth on baseball numbers. "That's how I learned to do math—and I'm sure I wasn't alone," remembered Peter Hoffman, a retired partner at the worldwide consult- ing firm of Deloitte & Touche. Hoffman was one of the thousands of young boys of the early 1950s who dove into the gleaming pool of base- ball statistics. While growing up a rabid Wiffle ball player in Norwalk, Connecticut, Hoffman and a friend staged hundreds of games in his backyard, pretending to be their two favorite teams, Eddie Mathews's Boston Braves and Willie Mays's New York Giants, and dutifully recorded every at-bat in a Spalding scorebook. At the end of each game, they would tally the records for each player and even type up stat sheets and league leaders. "It was weird—when we did up the numbers, the better real-life players always did better," Hoffman recalled. "When Willie

Mays or Joe Adcock was up, or a .300 hitter, I think psychologically we always tried harder."

Hoffman's passion for baseball statistics only grew after a trip to Stoll's Drug Store, where he bought his first pack of 1952 Topps cards. The numbers on the back transfixed him. As he flipped cards with his friends, arguments over who was better—Duke Snider or Mickey Mantle, Sal Maglie or Johnny Sain—invariably summoned their statistics. "We'd debate different trades, and yell at each other over who should bat cleanup," Hoffman recalled. Topps baseball cards joined box scores as the major pipelines that fed statistics into young boys' brains. In 1957, Berger put full year-by-year stats for every player on the back, only adding to the carnival. "Statistics lent an importance to the card," Berger recalled. "A credibility." Topps quickly bought out Bowman's business and dominated the baseball-card market for another thirty years.

Backyard Wiffle ball tournaments were but one means for boys to generate their own baseball statistics. Others did so through a game called All-Star Baseball, a tabletop pastime that used the real statistics of major league players to let kids simulate games indoors. It became a sensation soon after its birth in 1941 because it was so darned realistic. All baseball games to that point had been pinball-type affairs, with little bats hitting marbles into holes denoted "single," "double," and whatnot, or card decks that determined the fates of players paying no heed to their real-life performance. Sometimes kids made up their own games. One imaginative teenager in Lowell, Massachusetts, in 1935 invented an entire universe with more than 100 fictional ballplayers on six teams he named after cars, like the Pontiacs and the Chevvies, and kept detailed stats in addition to writing a league newsletter. His name was Jack Kerouac.

But All-Star Baseball gave each major league player a disk whose circumference was divided into segments that, when placed under a spinner that came to a stop like a roulette ball, would mimic the *real-life* skills of the player. If Joe DiMaggio hit doubles 10 percent of the time and walked 4 percent of the time, then the appropriate slice of circumference was laid out accordingly. Kids marveled at the large home run areas for sluggers like Ralph Kiner and Hank Greenberg. They watched in suspense as the spinner neared those longballs, which were, of course, tantalizingly sandwiched in between "flyout" and "strikeout." Each spring a new set of cards came out reflecting the statistics from the previous season. This was a grand slam for realism, and the game's inventor, Ethan Allen, knew it: Allen had been a .300 hitter in the major leagues for six teams from 1926 to 1938, and understood baseball enough to coach at Yale University, where his star first baseman was one George H. W. Bush.

Kids all over the nation played Allen's All-Star Baseball on weekends, after school, and as late into the night as their parents would allow. They dutifully kept statistics and practiced their long division with nary a complaint. There were only two problems. The game completely ignored pitchers—at-bats were determined solely by hitters' disks—and the spinner would wear down and lose its randomness.

One boy, an 11-year-old from Long Island named Harold Richman, would become quite perturbed as he watched Harry Heilmann bat 60 points too high, and Joe DiMaggio hit only 12 home runs a season. This was wholly unacceptable, particularly to a fifth-grade DiMaggio fan. So Richman sat down to roll the dice—literally—and began inventing a new game of his own. His version would generate real major leaguers' batting, pitching, fielding, and base running statistics with unprecedented precision. You know it as Strat-O-Matic.

Hal Richman feared his father. Irving Richman, an insurance man with an eighth-grade education, grew up in the first decade of the twentieth century in the hardscrabble Mulberry Street section of Manhattan's Lower East Side, a Jew among Irishmen. He had two choices to handle the abuse he took: either hide in synagogue and bury his nose in the Torah, or fight back. He fought back. Growing into a big man for the time, almost six feet tall, Irving lifted weights at the local firehouse, developing a tremendous chest and muscular arms that he swung at the slightest provocation. He once knocked a man out cold for 35 minutes with one punch. He beat up someone at the age of 81. His impetuous physicality found its way into his child-rearing, with his belt his weapon of choice. His son Hal sought shelter in the family basement, playing Ethan Allen's All-Star Baseball.

Hal spent hour upon hour spinning disks into statistics, and by age 11 decided that the game wasn't realistic enough. He wanted pitchers to be involved, and to make strategic managerial decisions like calling for steals and sacrifice bunts. And he wanted the results to mirror those of the actual major leaguers. But how would he do that? How could he use these events' true probabilities when he had never heard the word "probability" in his life? Luckily, Hal had enough mathematical instinct (he always finished his multiplication tables faster than anyone) and youthful pluck to keep thinking. He knew that dice could be used to make random numbers, but how often did each one come up? No one had yet taught him that snake eyes came up 1 in 36 throws, 7 came up six in 36, and so on. So he sat down and threw the dice over and over, a mind-numbing 5,000 times, to figure it all out himself.

Armed with those probabilities, Hal mapped them to the statistics he found in his *Sporting News 1948 Baseball Register*. Since Joe DiMaggio had 20 home runs in 601 total plate appearances that season, he deserved to get one every 30 times up in this new game. That meant one snake eyes (one in 36) and a small portion of threes (one in 18) would give DiMaggio his homers. (In addition, these would vary depending on the strength of pitcher he was facing.) Hal did similar calculations for singles, doubles, triples, outs, strikeouts, and walks, plus stolen base ratings. When he was done, he and his three best friends—the ones still afraid of girls, like him—could play baseball manager against each other realistically. They made up three teams of all-stars and one of scrubs. They called that last club, fittingly, the Misfits.

While the boys around him wanted to be lawyers and businessmen, Richman decided he wanted to refine his game and sell it as his career. He

Hal Richman's boyhood index cards, the forerunners of Strat-O-Matic. Note the use of playing cards in the left-hand column. (*Courtesy of Hal Richman*)

added a second layer of suspense to the game: a player could hit a long fly ball, and only a second roll of the dice would determine if it was caught at the wall or went over for a home run. In high school he changed over from dice to a custom deck of playing cards to determine the random events, and at 17 got his first patent. His old man, of course, thought it was all nonsense. Even Richman's mother, a more understanding sort, said he shouldn't mention his game on college applications. "They'll think you're odd," she told him.

Richman kept the baseball game under wraps while earning his accounting degree at Bucknell University, but emerged in 1958 determined as ever to make a go of it professionally. A family acquaintance with some knowledge of the toy industry said it was intriguing but not commercial enough. It had to be more realistic, and the deck of playing cards seemed too kitschy. Discouraged but not demoralized, Richman went back home, where his father was insisting he join the family insurance business, and sat down at the kitchen table. He tossed his dice dozens then hundreds of times, hoping they would tell him what to do. The plastic cubes bounced across the formica and came to rest in zillions of ways. Richman sat there for 45 minutes, tossing those dice and peering into their randomness, until they stopped and stared back at him with an answer.

It lay in the basic premise that baseball is 50 percent hitting and 50 percent pitching. Crudely translated, that meant the batter determined the outcome half the time and the pitcher the other half. Richman's epiphany was to have one die make that separation: A one, two, or three would send the at-bat to the hitter's card, where his skills took over, while a four, five, or six would summon the pitcher's card. That way the players' real-life statistics could be recreated fairly. Strikeout pitchers would get their slew of whiffs. Home run hitters could go deep regularly, but less often when facing Whitey Ford. Richman seized upon this solution, redid all his cards, and began searching for a name for the game. One day he was flipping through a book and saw the word "strategicalmatical," which, mercifully, never caught on but captured his fancy at the time. He fiddled around with it, remembered how gadgets that he saw on TV sounded even cooler with the suffix "matic" (think "Veg-O-Matic" and the like) and came up with Strat-O-Matic.

Richman borrowed $3,500 from friends in 1961 to launch a commercial version of Strat-O-Matic Baseball, which had only 80 all-stars, because mapping the players' statistics to the dice rolls—with no help from any calculator—took him all winter. He made 1,000 games and sold 350. He beefed up the player count to 120 the next year but again lost all his money, forcing the ultimate indignation: He told his father that if he could borrow $5,000, another bust in 1963 would mean he would join Pop in the insurance biz. Almost literally, Hal Richman was betting his life.

He never had to pay up. Ads in *The Sporting News* and *Baseball Digest* helped Strat-O-Matic catch on that summer, selling thousands of copies, and Richman never looked back. Kids marveled at how they could pretend to be the manager of a real major league team with players who behaved (at least statistically) just like actual big leaguers. Within a few years kids were playing entire 162-game seasons with the game, keeping box scores, standings, and, of course, detailed statistics. One group of kids from New York played by walkie-talkie, while another sang the National Anthem before every game.

Forty years later, Strat-O-Matic has sold close to a million sets, many of them to kids who grew up to be major leaguers. "You really know you've made it," outfielder Ken Singleton said when he reached the bigs, "when you get your own Strat-O-Matic card." Broadcasters Bob Costas and Dan Patrick played Strat-O-Matic as teenagers. Spike Lee and Tim Robbins, too. Keith Hernandez, now a television announcer for the Mets, is currently replaying the entire 1964 National League season to see if the Phillies choke to the Cardinals again. Richman even does personalized cards for Little Leaguers to cast their statistics into Strat-O-lingo. Strat-O-Matic and its main competition, another dice game called APBA, became so realistic through the 1960s and 1970s, with kids learning how to build lineups, call for steals, and remove pitchers to best improve the percentages, that they gave children who weren't athletic a way to connect to the game, to learn its intricacies, like never before. In a 2002 *Baseball America* survey of major league teams' front-office executives, half of them said they played Strat-O-Matic or a similar game as a kid.

But Strat-O-Matic, All-Star Baseball, APBA, and the like were not merely child's play. Based on a kid's game, perhaps. Yet the strategic theories and statistical arguments they spawned also intrigued grown men, many of whom had far better things to do. Military officers charged with designing flight formations would blow off their command to try figuring out how many runners scored from second base on a single. Veterans of the Manhattan Project, dissatisfied with merely unleashing the awesome power of the atom, zeroed in on the inner forces of baseball strategy. Baseball was attracting legitimate scientists, and statistics were their microscope.

Earnshaw Cook. (*Walter Iooss Jr./Sports Illustrated*)

4

Darwins of the Diamond

The Georgian Bay off Lake Huron lay peaceful and still, tall trees standing sentry over the scene's verdant tranquility. A solitary rowboat bobbed out in the distance. In it was a fisherman, out for bass, but one whose pursuit of a bite or two was surely impeded by the crackling dissonance coming from the heavy, dusty box that sat in the boat with him. He didn't mind. To this fellow, fish were but a pleasant distraction. The Toronto Maple Leafs were playing baseball on radio station CFRB, and Lt. Col. Charles Lindsey had statistics to catch.

This was the passion of Lindsey's retired life. Like many Toronto families in the 1950s, every summer weekend the Lindseys drove their old Model T two hours north and rented a lakefront cottage. Mothers would tend to the kids as fathers drank whiskey and told war stories into the night. Charles Lindsey owned more than a few. The strapping, decorated infantry officer had spent four years in the Canadian army during the Great War, then five years in World War II. His free time after retirement, though, begged for something to occupy him. So Lindsey, a lifelong baseball fan, decided to help his son George with that . . . well, that "project" of his, as the rest of the family dubiously referred to it.

George Lindsey, you see, had a day job: figuring out how to intercept Russian bombers before they reached Halifax. A pioneer in the new military field of Operations Research that grew out of the Cold War posturing of the 1950s, Lindsey modeled flight formations and tactical strikes for the Canadian Department of Defence, assessing risk and cost and strategy. Yet something nagged at him. Data was murky and incomplete. Combat was too fluid to pinpoint the value of decisions each side made. Where could he find a system whose patterns lent themselves to such analysis? Which had built-in stoppages of time, clear strategic decisions, with distinct, calculable states that could be expressed in manipulable numbers?

"Doggone it," Lindsey said to himself, "you can do that with baseball."

And so he did. Lindsey spent the next 15 years, whether stationed in Quebec, Colorado, Washington, or under a distinctly disapproving Norwegian commander in Italy, devoting his days to military modeling and his nights to the study of baseball games. Was the stolen base a good strategy? The sacrifice bunt? How many runs scored after each decision, and did they wind up worth the effort? For the first half of the twentieth century, baseball fans had been content to debate these matters with little to no statistical proof. George Lindsey would dig deeper than anyone had before.

"Baseball is the highest form of human activity—it *should* be analyzed," recalled Lindsey, now 84, grinning as mischievously as he surely had then. When he was through, the nuclear warheads his department had feared remained in their silos. But George R. Lindsey, along with his father and his rowboat, had become the first to use formal statistics to split the atom of baseball strategy.

F ive hundred miles south in Brooklyn, Allan Roth was keeping his own statistics for the Dodgers, figuring players' batting average versus lefthanded and righthanded pitchers, at home and away, during various months, and more. But Lindsey had different goals in mind. As a military strategist, he was more interested in how various maneuvers (singles, steals, walks, and so on) fit together as if advances on a battlefield. Lindsey's original passion as a boy growing up in Toronto was hockey—he received some professional offers as a goalie—but that sport was too fluid, with too few stops in the action and therefore measurable states of combat, to lend itself to such analysis. Baseball was perfect, though finding proper data was impossible. The annual *Spalding* guides Lindsey bought since childhood had only the players' final season statistics, which told nothing of how the hits and outs interacted within innings. Even daily box scores, detailed as they were, recorded the events of each game only by summing up the feats of individual players. Lindsey wanted the *inning's* feats—the players to him were not Mantle, Mays, and Musial, but home run, stolen base, and single. How did they combine to score runs? What mixtures were most successful? No one, at least publicly, had quantified such data. Lindsey would have to tabulate it himself by keeping score of live games off the radio. He did just that, night after night after night.

This was not necessarily conduct becoming a Lindsey. Besides being a military officer, George was a direct descendent of William Lyon Mackenzie, the first mayor of Toronto who later advocated open rebellion to break from the British throne; he also was a cousin of William Lyon Mackenzie King, Canada's prime minister during World War II. Nor did Lindsey's household provide much encouragement for his baseball endeavors. "I developed a great loathing for baseball," his wife, June, harrumphed to me during a visit to their Ottawa home. June Lindsey, a Yorkshire-raised woman of striking intellect, holds a Ph.D. from Cambridge University in X-ray crystallography. At Oxford she worked on the molecular structure of vitamin B12 with Dorothy Hodgkin (later winner of the Nobel Prize) and modeled the structures of adenine and guanine that two doctors across the hall, named Crick and Watson, incorporated into their celebrated model of DNA. So she can be forgiven her distaste for a sport that stole much of her husband's attention for most of their marriage's first 15 years. "If you turned the television to baseball," she said, "I would leave the room." She did that often.

George Lindsey, his wife aghast, watched and listened to roughly 400 games during the mid-1950s, scoring them with exacting precision so that he could investigate several questions that always had dogged him. Specifically, to what extent did platooning—sending up a righthanded hitter to face a lefthanded pitcher, and vice versa—improve batting averages? If a team loads the bases, how many runs typically score? And how much does a player's batting average fluctuate due to luck? During his breaks at the Air Defence Command center in St. Hubert, Quebec, Lindsey examined his scoresheets, tabulated the totals, and wrote up his findings in a paper called "Statistical Data Useful for the Operation of a Baseball Team." It was accepted and published in the March/April 1959 issue of the journal *Operations Research*.

"It may occur to the reader," Lindsey wrote, "that the amassing of statistical data on baseball has already exceeded all reasonable bounds . . . But in one application, the interpretation of data on past performance in order to influence decisions regarding future situations, there may be some thoughts still worth developing." Using tables, equations, and distribution graphs, Lindsey detailed his findings. When hitters faced pitchers of the opposite handedness, batting averages did go up, by 32 points. When a team loaded the bases, 2.3 runs usually scored with none out, 1.6 with one out, and 0.9 with two. As for the luck issue, Lindsey also showed how a manager who reacted to a hitter's slump—say, a .180 batting average over one week—by pinch-hitting for him was probably panicking; binomial probability theory showed that a true .300 hitter would often bat .180 over seven games through the vagaries of randomness.

Most in his military community considered Lindsey's findings amusing but didn't pay them much attention. One journalist from Washington, D.C., came across the article, probably because of *Operations Research*'s readership among military types, and phoned Lindsey not for a story but to recommend he contact the Washington Senators about consulting for the city's floundering ballclub. But the franchise moved to Minnesota the following year. "I got invited to give talks at mathematical associations and statistics groups," Lindsey recalled, "but they were mainly looking for something to keep people awake."

Lindsey pressed on. His next quest was to determine the relative value of different leads, i.e., how each type of advantage (one run after the third inning, four runs entering the bottom of the eighth, etc.) resulted in a win or loss. He analyzed 782 games from the 1958 season and discovered, for example, that the visiting team won about 15 percent of the time if down by three runs after the top of the third; the home team, if ahead by two runs after the seventh, would go on to win 88 percent of the time. *Operations Research* saw too little of a strategic nature in this paper, though, deeming it merely statistical, so Lindsey got it published in September 1961 in the *Journal of the American Statistical Association* under the title, "The Progress of a Score During a Baseball Game." That article was merely the beginning of a larger study, though, that Lindsey knew would be his most significant.

Since the days of John McGraw and Connie Mack, managing "by the book" had meant employing fairly routine strategies that over time had grown universally accepted. Managers would defend the use of the sacrifice bunt by puffing, "I don't mind giving up an out to move a runner into scoring position." They reflexively would attempt to steal second if down by one or intentionally walk a batter to set up the possibility of a double play. Okay, Lindsey thought, but by how much do such moves alter the chances of scoring? And, depending on the inning and score, how do they increase or decrease the probability of winning the game? Many fans might have harbored similar questions, but there were no Internet databases or computerized play-by-play data to consult. Only Lindsey, with his father's help, actually scored more than 1,200 games and spent hundreds of hours interpreting the sheets in order to finally find out. "G. H. Hardy once said, 'Here's a toast to mathematics—may it never be of any use to anyone,'" Lindsey said with a smile. "I wanted my mathematics to be of use to somebody, whether it's a baseball manager or a war general."

George Lindsey (right) with his father, Charles. Also, one of the sheets on which the Lindseys tallied their data. (*Courtesy of George Lindsey*)

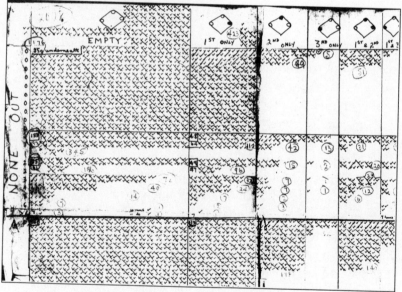

Lindsey's father gladly enlisted in this effort. Freshly retired from the service, Charles Lindsey had kept track of most of the 782 games for "Progress of a Score." He then kept in even greater detail the play-by-play of 373 more, comprising some 6,399 half-innings, on special green quadrille graph paper and in custom notation he and George had devised. In painstaking, loving penmanship, Charles scored every ballgame he could get his ears on—his wireless could pick up broadcasts from as far away as Wheeling, West Virginia—often two whole games a day, one in the afternoon and one at night. Charles delivered the scoresheets in bunches for George to sit down and decipher.

George wasn't even on the same continent when he pored over these sheets. By this time he, June, and their two young children had been transferred to the village of San Terenzo in Italy, living in a gorgeous hilltop villa. Not that George looked up from his baseball work much to notice. "I have to do everything around here!" June would complain. "When I need any help, you're doing baseball all night, working on these papers, these *statistics*!" George's military commanders at the antisubmarine research center run by NATO, many of them European, were even less impressed, especially his straightlaced Norwegian supervisor. "To study something called baseball, which he'd never even heard of, was unbelievable," Lindsey recalled. "He strongly disapproved of it. Then he thought, 'If this guy writes it and it's published, and it says that he was in the Saclant ASW Research Center, I'll be the ridicule of Norway.'"

Lindsey kept a low profile. He carried bundles of his father's scoresheets, some still redolent of Lake Huron, back and forth from Italy and for two years went though every batter on every sheet to track scoring patterns. Each time a batter came up with a man on second and one out, a tick was marked in the appropriate box on a master sheet; obviously, he had no computer to handle the computation, though back then, this heavy lifting was half the fun. The sheets filled up with so many hundreds of ticks, all in neat groups of five, that they resembled those of a prisoner recording days on his cell wall. But each one got George closer to the point where he could count everything up and report his results.

Much to the relief of his wife and young family, that time finally arrived in the summer of 1963 when *Operations Research* published Lindsey's seminal 24-page article, "An Investigation of Strategies in Baseball." Lindsey's study dove head-first into the following:

- Expected runs in any situation: exactly how many runs scored depending on the number of outs (none, one, or two) and any runners on the bases (empty, man on first, bases full, and so on). For example, with runners on second and third and one out, no runs were scored 27 percent of the time, one run 24 percent, two runs 28 percent, and more than two 21 percent. The average total runs scored after each of the 24 possible situations:

		Bases Occupied							
		0	1	2	3	1,2	1,3	2,3	Full
	0	.46	.81	1.19	1.39	1.47	1.94	1.96	2.22
Outs	1	.24	.50	.67	.98	.94	1.12	1.56	1.64
	2	.10	.22	.30	.36	.40	.53	.69	.82

- The sacrifice bunt: giving up an out to move a runner, typically, from first to second. The above chart clearly shows how this can help or, as often is the case, hurt a team. For example, with none out and a man on first, teams score an average of .81 runs. A successful bunt would leave the runner on second with one out, which typically results in just .67. A sacrifice becomes worthwhile only when a club needs one and only one run late in a game. (This assumes an average hitter both at the plate and on deck, however, and real-life managers would surely take this into account. But the concept as Lindsey asserted it was irrefutable.)

- The stolen base: At what success rate is it worthwhile to attempt to steal second, say, with one out? Using the chart, the benefit (1.19 expected runs versus .81, or in increase of .38) must be weighed against the risk of getting called out (and winding up with .24 expected runs, or a decrease of .57). Simple algebra puts the breakeven point at 59 percent. Once again, however, the state of the game is significant, and trailing by only one run can make stealing an advisable risk. (This no doubt could have provided some solace to Babe Ruth, who, with his New York Yankees down 3–2 to the St. Louis Cardinals in the bottom of the ninth inning, was caught stealing second to stunningly, and controversially, end the 1926 World Series.)

- The infield in: With the bases loaded and none out, the defensive team can choose to either play its infielders deep, in hopes of turning a double play (one run scores, man left on third with one out), or play them in and nail the lead runner at the plate (no runs score, but the bases are left loaded with one out). Teams almost always should go for the double play, Lindsey discovered. Only when a team is tied or ahead by one run late in the game, with none out, will playing the infield in pay off on average.

- The intentional walk: often used with runners on either second or second and third to set up a possible double play. This maneuver, Lindsey determined, more often than not *increased* the expected number of runs that would score in the inning. (Double plays, however tantalizing, don't happen often enough.) In real life, of course, a manager will walk a good hitter to get to a less dangerous one, but for simplicity's sake Lindsey's model could not account for different types of hitters. Lindsey foresaw a world when that could be possible, though: "The concept of an electronic computer in the dugout is a distasteful one," he wrote, "but, if progress demands it, this is the type of calculation for which it could be programmed."

"An Investigation of Strategies in Baseball" concerned mostly managerial maneuvers. But Lindsey ended his paper with a strikingly ahead-of-its-time application of the expected runs matrix, that being to evaluate individual hitters. The batting average, he asserted—as F. C. Lane had 50 years earlier in *Baseball Magazine*—drastically undervalued extra-base hits, while slugging percentage, which arbitrarily weighted long hits by their number of bases (doubles were worth two, triples three, and so on), overvalued them. By manipulating the chart algebraically in ways that will be skipped here, Lindsey determined that a single was worth on average .41 runs, a double .82, a triple 1.06, and a home run 1.42. (These values were, in fact, not terribly different from Lane's more rudimentary calculations from way back in 1917.) Lindsey applied his findings to a recent controversial trade between the Detroit Tigers and Cleveland Indians. The Tigers' Harvey Kuenn, a singles hitter who had just won the 1959 American League batting championship at .353, had been dealt straight-up for the Indians' Rocky Colavito, who had batted just .257 but tied for the league home run lead with 42. Who was the more valuable hitter, in terms of the runs generated by the weight values of each player's hits? Even though Kuenn had hit virtually 100 points higher in batting average—still by far the most popular measure of batting ability—it was Colavito, 114.5 runs to 112.6.

This new analysis did not shake baseball; it caused nary a tremor. No teams contacted Lindsey. No journalists wrote a word. His Norwegian superior got over it, too, because soon after "Investigation of Strategies" was published, Lindsey and his family moved back to Ottawa, where George, his curiosity in baseball strategy fulfilled, returned his focus to more military matters. He remained with the Canadian Department of Defence, and later became head of the Operational Research and Analysis Establishment, before retiring in 1987. He continues to handle selected projects on strategic nuclear weapons and ballistic missile defense.

Lindsey's baseball work is all but forgotten (if it was ever known to begin with). His name is barely recognized, if at all, by even the most knowledgeable fans of baseball statistics. His papers appeared only in obscure journals, a full 20 years before Bill James's *Baseball Abstract* series popularized the field. Still, as we examine Lindsey's work today, it goes down as the first time anyone compiled reams of play-by-play data, applied sophisticated statistical analysis to weigh various strategies, and published the results.

Lindsey, for one, didn't realize how groundbreaking his work truly was. "It was really just out of curiosity," he admitted, sitting on the couch of his Ottawa home. He got up and went to his attic to fetch the old scoresheets, which he kept all these years. Flipping through them for the first time in decades, his enthusiasm bubbled anew. He looked through his reading glasses, settled far down his then-82-year-old nose, and remembered all those nights scoring games with his father and vexing his wife—all to use baseball statistics in a new and exciting way. He wore the blue blazer of his old Operations Research division, whose crest on the left breast pocket featured a Latin phrase, *A Posse Ad Esse*—"From the Possible to the Real."

His skittish commander notwithstanding, Lindsey was not the first to publish an article about baseball in an academic or technical journal. In 1952, Frederick Mosteller of Harvard University analyzed the World Series in the *Journal of the American Statistical Association*. Mosteller questioned whether a best-of-seven series was an adequate way to decide which team was better—and in fact, through 25 pages of binomial probability theory, he proved it to be quite unreliable. Four years later, John H. Smith discussed in *American Statistician* a method to adjust standings for the strength of each team's schedule. And in 1960, Donato A. D'Esopo and Benjamin Lefkowitz, of the Industrial Operations Research department at the Stanford Research Institute in Menlo Park, California, presented a paper to the American Statistical Association called "The Distribution of Runs in the Game of Baseball," which appears to be the first advanced attempt to combine the probabilities of hits, walks, outs, and more into a model of how runs score. All these studies, however, were read only by tiny audiences, many of whom blanched at the idea of allowing so frivolous a subject as baseball into their otherwise important affairs. It would take a commercially published book to introduce statistical analysis of baseball beyond academia and to the more average fan. That book arrived in the summer of 1964: *Percentage Baseball*, written by a bowtied Baltimore gentleman named Earnshaw Cook.

Cook was a most unlikely sort to devote four years to the study of baseball statistics. Grey-haired in his sixties, the stern and iron-faced Cook was an aristocrat at heart—conservative to the core, constantly complaining about the "Japs" and inflation, and always, always wearing a smoking jacket, sport shirt, and tie (often a clip-on). He spoke with a faux English accent to lend an elitist aura, and his gruff bearing was so authoritative that his Chesapeake retriever would, on command, fetch the newspaper and then go to the closet and bring down his bedroom slippers. He signed all correspondence with his blueblood pedigree: Princeton '21.

Cook had played varsity baseball at Old Nassau, and even was a distant cousin of George Earnshaw, the former big league pitcher, but went on to a distinguished career as a metallurgist, studying metals and their alloys down to the protons and electrons at their core, primarily for the American Brake Shoe Co. of Mahwah, New Jersey. He wrote *Engineering Properties of Heat Resistant Alloys* and other light classics. He served as a consultant on the Manhattan Project and for the Atomic Energy Commission before retiring in 1945 and ultimately nesting in a small estate in Baltimore. With little to occupy his time thereafter, other than training his dogs and playing golf at the nearby Elkridge Club, he decided to prove, once and for all, damn it, that Ty Cobb was better than Babe Ruth.

This Cobb-versus-Ruth, slapper-versus-slugger debate had raged for generations and became almost religious for each sect's most ardent followers. Cobb was the master of the single-and-speed game prevalent during his prime of 1907 to 1922, ringing up a .366 lifetime batting average (still the all-time major league record) and 892 stolen bases (a mark that lasted almost 50 years). Ruth's awesome power diverted focus from batting average to home runs, much to the chagrin of fans clinging to the game's original style. Cobb himself complained in a letter in 1952, "Now they have gone to the hit per distance game. They look as if they will be lucky to hit .340 or maybe less . . . The hit and run, stolen base, bunt, and sacrifice are deteriorating from unuse and they only hit for their amusement and pleasure for the home run." Everyone agreed that a home run was more valuable than a single, but by how much? To what extent did stolen bases and the venerable sacrifice aid in the scoring of runs? Come to think of it, what was the optimal lineup order? How should relief pitchers be used? Unaware of George Lindsey's work, Cook didn't want to go "by the book," blindly accepting the time-honored answers to these questions. So he wrote a book of his own.

In fits and starts over several years, Cook holed up in his study, overlooking the golf course, and pounded on baseball statistics. (Actually, much of the pounding was done by his Friden STW mechanical calculator, a contraption the size of a briefcase that clicked and clacked its way through the heaviest arithmetic. You can see it in the photograph on page 66.) His slide rule and colored pencils stood at attention above his angled drafting table, piles of The Sporting News and the Baseball Register at the ready.

Cook used his research to teach math to his teenaged nephew, Bryson. Bryson returned the favor with one heck of a public relations coup. Bryson Cook's best friend was Gil Deford, whose big brother Frank had just begun writing for Sports Illustrated. Frank Deford learned of this quirky baseball scientist and mentioned him to his editor, who dispatched the young writer to interview Cook during the winter of 1964. The editor liked the piece so much he made it the lead feature story of the March 23 issue, with the headline BASEBALL IS PLAYED ALL WRONG.

Deford breathlessly previewed Cook's discoveries: The sacrifice was generally worthless. Platooning was a waste of time. Sluggers should bat first. Games should be started by a "relief" pitcher who would leave for a pinch hitter at the first opportunity, followed by a "starting"-caliber pitcher who would then pitch four or five innings. All this, Cook claimed, would add a total of 250 runs and perhaps 25 wins to a team each season, numbers clearly absurd today but in 1964 as arresting as a Bob Gibson fastball at the noggin. "Right now," Deford gushed, "Earnshaw Cook knows more about baseball than anyone else in the world."

Cook asserted that by employing his theories, a .500 club could instantly become a pennant winner. Deford naturally presented baseball personnel as being alarmed, even humbled, by these findings. "If these figures are correct," Los Angeles Dodgers manager Walter Alston told SI, "Cook must have something . . . Maybe we've just been playing what we assumed was the proper way." Bill Veeck, the renegade owner of the Chicago White Sox, loved the idea of minimizing at-bats by weak-hitting pitchers. "By all means," Veeck raved, "get the pitcher out of there!" But privately most team personnel brushed Cook's theories aside. Pulitzer Prize–winning New York Times columnist Arthur Daley wrote, "It is highly unlikely that Cook, the iconoclast, will influence one manager to alter his

pattern to the slightest degree . . . What was good enough for John Mc-
Graw is good enough for them."

The recalcitrance of baseball executives only hardened when Cook's
full-length book, *Percentage Baseball*, came out a few months later. It was
barely intelligible to even educated readers; beyond sprinkling the text
with haughty Latin phrases and quotations from the likes of Francis Bacon, Cook might as well have put a statistics textbook in a blender. Pages
of graphs, equations, and probabilistic gibberish, such as:

$$\text{Eqv. p.SHS.y} = \frac{1.1564 \text{ DX.y} + 1.4370 \text{ DX.z} + .1507}{2.3225 \text{ DX.z} + .2477}$$

made much of his methodology hopelessly inaccessible. (This surely
added to Cook's aura as a sort of baseball Merlin. His hometown *Baltimore
Sun* would consult him for pennant-race predictions—*"projections,"* he insisted—and use headlines such as BIRDS TO FINISH 3D, STATISTICIAN DE-
CLARES, and COOK, BASEBALL'S SEER, IS PITCHING ORIOLES.) Cook loved
the attention. While beguiling readers with a blizzard of figures and charts,
Percentage Baseball represented the first comprehensive effort to model all
aspects of baseball through applied probability theory, and was met with
apprehensive awe.

Cook rooted his approach in a statistic he developed called the Scoring Index. He examined the relative chances of all offensive events—single, double, sacrifice, steal, and so on—and all the ways they can be
strung together to score runs before three outs end an inning. (For example, a single can be followed by two straight outs, a steal, and a single. A
batter can reach on an error and jog home on a later batter's home run.)
Cook concluded that the probability of scoring a run was proportional to
the chances of reaching first base multiplied by the chances of advancing
that runner. His final formula looked like this:

$$\text{p.R} = (K) \times (\text{p.H} + \text{p.BB} + \text{p.E.o} + \text{p.HB} - 2\text{p.SH} - \text{p.XBH}) \times (\text{p.TB})$$

This equation, however disguised in ugly and cumbersome notation,
was actually rooted in concepts some 20 to 30 years ahead of general acceptance. Each "p." merely denoted the probability of the event that followed it (for example, p.BB meant the probability of a base on balls, i.e.,
walks per plate appearance) so the entire equation can be seen as having
plate appearances (PA) as its denominator. Ignoring errors and the sub-

traction of sacrifices and extra-base hits for the moment, the right-hand side's two terms reduce to:

$$\frac{(H + BB + HB)}{PA} \times \frac{(TB)}{PA}$$

This is far more recognizable to modern fans of statistics: It's essentially the product of on-base percentage and slugging percentage, and greatly resembles the approach Bill James took to developing his renowned Runs Created formula in the late 1970s.

Armed with his scoring index and other statistical tools, Cook examined dozens of baseball strategies and trends. Summarizing them here would require another entire book. But these were the most significant matters Cook analyzed, with his conclusions:

- The best hitter ever: Lo and behold, Ty Cobb, with a scoring index of .2161, beat out Babe Ruth (.2109), Ted Williams (.1962), Lou Gehrig (.1828), and Mickey Mantle (.1743). Cobb's score was actually .1574, but Cook, citing how Cobb had performed mostly in the "dead ball" era when home runs were very rare, adjusted his figure upward by comparing his performance to that of his contemporaries. Cobb and Ruth, at the time widely considered the best two hitters ever, had never before stood numbers one and two in any statistic. Scoring index let them rise to the top.

- The base-out matrix: While George Lindsey charted actual games to determine how many runs scored in each situation (bases empty and one out, man on first and two out, and so on), Cook generated his chart through his probability equations. His estimates were generally somewhat lower than Lindsey's (see page 73):

		Bases Occupied							
		0	1	2	3	1,2	1,3	2,3	Full
	0	.34	.77	.94	1.04	1.36	1.46	1.63	2.06
OUTS	1	.18	.47	.63	.72	.92	1.01	1.17	1.46
	2	.07	.21	.32	.38	.46	.52	.64	.78

- The stolen base: Cook determined that an average runner trying to swipe second base typically was a bad risk with none or one out, but a good risk with two. He went considerably further than Lindsey in assessing how the breakeven points fluctuated depending on the abilities of the runner on first and the hitter at the plate. For example, Minnie Minoso, the speedy outfielder for the Chicago White Sox, was successful in just 57 percent of his stolen-base attempts from 1960 to 1961; Cook claimed he should never run while any hitter with a .258 batting average or higher was up.

- The sacrifice bunt: Like Lindsey, Cook maintained that this was a bad play, except under certain conditions: when a hitter was as poor as the typical pitcher, or when just one run was needed in the late innings of a close game. Outs were that precious. "There are two primary objects in baseball," Cook explained. "The first is to score runs. And the second is *not* to make outs." The latter concept didn't become understood by a majority of baseball executives for 35 years, and continues to baffle more than a few franchises.

- The batting order: Most lineups put a speedster at the top, a bat-control artist second, and then the three best hitters third, fourth, and fifth. But because roughly 22 percent of games end when the first or second batter makes the final out, the best hitters often miss a chance at another at-bat. Cook claimed that the lineup should always just put the best hitter first, followed by the second-best, and so on; even though sluggers such as Hank Aaron or Willie Mays might get fewer RBIs because they would bat with fewer runners on base, that cost would be overcome by their getting roughly 40 more at-bats over the course of a season.

- Platooning hitters: Cook asserted that managers trying to match up righthanded batters against lefthanded pitchers, or vice versa, instead of simply playing their best eight hitters every day, cost teams up to 125 runs a year. He based this conclusion upon the belief—without statistical inquiry—that such matchups made no difference. He was mistaken, of course: Lindsey, unbeknownst to Cook, had already shown that the strategy boosted batting averages in general by 32 points. It is here that Cook appears to begin veering away from pure analysis to rampant iconoclasm.

- Platooning pitchers: Cook estimated that pitchers' horrible skills at the plate cost the average team 113 runs per season, and suggested that those players virtually never be allowed to come to the plate at all. Given that complete games were already becoming rare in the early 1960s (they since have all but disappeared) Cook advocated starting a relief-caliber pitcher for two or three innings and pinch hitting for him at the first opportunity, and then using a starting-caliber pitcher to throw the next five innings or so, batting no more than once. Cook designed a ten-pitcher rotation to accomplish this.

- Other assertions: Baseball's enlargement of the strike zone prior to the 1963 season had decreased offense up to 15 percent; a team's winning percentage should equal .484 times its ratio of runs scored to runs allowed (he offered no derivation of this); and the intentional walk is often a poor strategy. One should be ordered, Cook wrote, "only if the actual 'DX.z' of the third batsman is less than his own equivalent 'DX.z' . . ."

Cook's rigorous mathematics ultimately failed him on both ends of the reader spectrum. Baseball fans were spooked by the intercept coefficients, distribution curves, and bizarre graphical techniques that recalled too many failed algebra quizzes. Professional statisticians, meanwhile, accused *Percentage Baseball* of sloppy and amateurish use of probability theory. "The book is easier reading for a baseball fan than for a mathematician," *Scientific American* sniffed. George Lindsey all but excoriated the book in his review for *Operations Research*, citing "very inadequate numerical evidence," "no tests of significance, fit or correlation," and other crimes. "Some of the mathematical presentations which form the heart of the book are atrocious," Lindsey wrote. "Aside from a number of outright mistakes in manipulating probabilities . . . in a desperate attempt to relate [scoring index] to scoring the author is obliged to introduce a 'specific luck factor' that makes one's probability nerves twitch."

Cook did appeal, however, to a narrow band of audience: young, mathematically inclined fans who relished his application of probability to baseball, however flawed that application may have been. Several of them—Carl Morris, Pete Palmer, Art Peterson, and more—became noted academic and applied statisticians, and were heard from years later in the field of baseball analysis. We will meet them all in later chapters.

Some of Cook's readers actually worked for major league baseball teams, but were too young to have much influence at the time. Tal Smith of the Houston Astros was a thirtysomething statistics buff who, between semesters at Duke University, had worked at *The Sporting News* helping to compile the reams of numbers for its annual *Baseball Register* and *Baseball Guide*. He relished Cook's rigorous examination of accepted baseball opinion, but knew that altering that opinion was another matter altogether. "It was difficult to get anybody interested in any statistical information in the '60s—they only wanted batting average and ERA and not to be bothered with it," recalled Smith, now president of the Astros. "Our general manager, Spec Richardson, was so statistically challenged that I'm not sure he knew what a batting average was. Managers in those days, most of them were old school. [Cook's approach] was nothing they were raised with. When I came across it there wasn't any way to put it into any practical effort."

Lou Gorman worked in the minor league department of the Baltimore Orioles in the late 1960s, knew of Cook's work from articles in the *Sun*, and after moving on to the expansion Kansas City Royals in 1969 kept a copy of *Percentage Baseball* on the shelf behind his desk. One day, the Royals' owner, Ewing Kauffman, noticed it.

"What is that?" he asked.

"It's a book a scientist wrote about baseball," Gorman said. "He analyzes lineups, strategies, and other things with hard-core math and statistics."

Kauffman, who made billions in the pharmaceutical industry, took the book in his hands and flipped through the pages. "I want you to have this guy call me collect," he told Gorman. "I want to meet him."

One month later, Kauffman sat down with Cook in the owner's suite at Kansas City's old Municipal Stadium. "Ewing loved the book and what Cook said in it," Gorman recalled, "but it never got to the point where he would use it to run the club. He stayed out of baseball decisions." Gorman, however, went on to a distinguished career with the Royals, Seattle Mariners, New York Mets, and Boston Red Sox, always keeping *Percentage Baseball* in mind, and on his shelf.

At least one major league player took notice of *Percentage Baseball* and became an avid devotee. Davey Johnson, a young second baseman for the Orioles, just happened to also have a mathematics degree from Trinity University in Texas. Johnson read the book and noted that Cook lived in Baltimore, so he looked him up and visited his home. The two became friends, playing golf on occasion and always talking baseball. Johnson integrated some of Cook's ideas when he became a manager himself, leading the Mets to the 1986 World Series championship and later managing the Reds, Orioles, and Dodgers. Johnson credits Cook with underscoring the importance of on-base percentage (rather than speed) at the top of batting orders and the inadvisability of intentional walks. "I'd played for a lot of managers who would just make out their lineup the old-fashioned way—they didn't know what they were doing," Johnson remembered. "Cook showed how statistics could be used to run a ballclub better." In the end, the *Times*'s Arthur Daley was proven wrong: Cook did influence a manager, a future one. Like most groundbreaking ideas, Cook's were appreciated most by people young enough not to feel threatened.

Cook himself did not witness the moderate influence he ultimately had. Eight years after the original publication of *Percentage Baseball* he followed up with a second volume, *Percentage Baseball and the Computer*, in which he employed computer-simulation techniques to fine-tune, and usually validate, his theories. This book received considerably less attention than his first. In a 1975 letter Cook wrote, "At the age of seventy-five, I do not expect to survive to witness any changes of attitude . . . It is my opinion that the application of basic statistical analysis will eventually receive the attention of professional baseball—as it has in so many other fields of endeavor with increasing use of the ubiquitous digital computer." He spent a few years applying his mathematics to golf—he tried to prove that the great Bobby Jones was better than newcomer Jack Nicklaus—but ultimately discarded the idea. He died in late 1987 of a heart attack.

Before that, however, Cook was asked by the Hall of Fame in Cooperstown to donate the slide rule on which he did some of his calculations for *Percentage Baseball*. "I am more than content," he typed in a note of appreciation, "to present my last testament herewith to the Greatest Game of them all."

Not long after Cook finished *Percentage Baseball* in 1964, the digital computer began to grow into a tool for fields beyond the military. Most major corporations had some sort of mainframe, either from IBM or Sperry Univac, and while these monsters often filled several rooms and had none of the mouse-and-modem features we take for granted today—not even video displays—their power offered great possibilities to the few people who knew how to use them. The most cavalier were often teenagers (including two from Seattle named Paul Allen and Bill Gates, who accessed a mainframe through their school's teletype machine), but aficionados of all ages were devising new applications for computers every day. As the tape drives whirred and punch cards flew, it was only a matter of time before someone thought to employ computers not just to keep baseball statistics but to analyze them, too. That time arrived in 1969 when two brothers in their late 40s, Harlan and Eldon Mills, rented time on an IBM 1620 mainframe to pick at a knot that had confounded baseball fans for generations, and still does: just what a "clutch" player is, and how that can be measured. Three years later, the Mills brothers completed what some today consider the most innovative work ever done in the field of baseball statistics.

They're keeping the wrong data! Harlan would yelp, either while reading the sports section over breakfast or listening to some baseball announcer yammer on about batting average and RBIs. Sportscasters and writers kept talking about *what* a player did: seven hits in 25 at-bats, two doubles and a sacrifice, and so on. Precious little described *when* he did it, whether or not it influenced the outcome of the game. Did one of those doubles break a tie in the bottom of the eighth? Or did all the hits come during blowouts, when they didn't much matter? Mills was interested in the context of a player's performance—hits didn't matter unless they helped the team win the game. And few people on earth knew more about games than Harlan Mills.

Fifteen years before, Mills had been colleagues with some of the most brilliant minds in game theory, the new field that used sophisticated mathematics to analyze and design strategic approaches to games, economics, military science, and more. He worked at Princeton University's famed Institute for Advanced Study in the early 1950s with the likes of Albert Einstein, Kurt Gödel, and John von Neumann, a staggering intellectual bouillabaisse. "He loved talking about his smart friends," remarked one of Mills's future colleagues. "Of course, all of his smart friends were struggling to keep up." Mills had little patience for procedures that weren't optimal; for example, as a command pilot for the U.S. Army Air Corps during World War II, he was so dissatisfied with the training program for B-24 pilots that he simply rewrote it. A personable, six-foot-two Iowan, Mills later worked for General Electric, RCA, and IBM, where he became one of the most influential minds in applied mathematics and the nascent field of software engineering.

Eldon Mills. (*Courtesy of Eldon Mills*)

One of Mills's many passions was baseball. As a boy growing up in Fort Dodge, Iowa (his parents owned a dental laboratory that made false teeth), he and his younger brother Eldon would sit beside the radio and listen to Dutch (later known as Ronald) Reagan announce Chicago Cubs games on Des Moines station WHO. The pair would hitchhike 400 miles to see a game or two each season at Wrigley Field. Eldon was the more athletic and outgoing of the two. He was an all-state tackle for Fort Dodge High—back when a tackle could stand five-foot-eleven and 150 pounds—loved beer and girls, usually in that order, and flew 25 missions over Europe in the Air Force, earning the Distinguished Flying Cross. (His B-17, called the "Bomb'n Belle," was embossed with a painting of a naked woman splayed across a bomb with the slogan, "Layin' For You.") Eldon reenlisted during the height of the 1950s cold war (he often sat on the runway with an atom bomb in a B-47, waiting for a signal to bomb Moscow that never came) and later worked at the Pentagon, writing computer programs for data processing. In 1968, Eldon retired from the service to join his older brother, Harlan, and form a new company, Computer Research in Sports. They vowed to do what no one had done before: *Keep the right data.*

Conventional statistics and box scores couldn't tell the Mills brothers what they wanted to know. As George Lindsey understood, season statistics in the annual *Sporting News Baseball Register* didn't say *when* players got their singles and walks, and how those influenced individual games. Box scores were somewhat more decipherable, in that one could occasionally guess that Orlando Cepeda's double scored Lou Brock in the seventh to put the Cardinals ahead, but such discoveries were rare, tedious, and often wrong. Smaller player contributions were all but hidden forever: A reliever coming in with the bases loaded and getting a clutch flyout to preserve a tie earned him one-third of an inning pitched and nothing else; a batter's groundout that moved a runner from second to third before a game-winning sacrifice fly left him a positively unheroic 0-for-1. No way existed to meaningfully measure these accomplishments. So the Millses invented one. They called it Player Win Average. "We were excited all the time we were doing it," recalled Eldon Mills, now 82 and living in a DeLand, Florida, retirement community. "We were really onto something."

The logic behind player win average was beautifully simple. Each player has a goal: to do something, large or small, to increase the probability of his team winning the game. It might be a home run. It might be a walk to start a rally. But it must be something that leaves his team in a more advantageous state than before. Pitchers, of course, have the same charge, to get outs in such a manner that their team has a better chance to win. Every hitter–pitcher confrontation, no matter what the result, nudges the balance ever so slightly in one team's direction. The question was, by how much? And how might that be calculated?

The Millses tackled this in two stages. First, not unlike Lindsey up in Canada ten years before, Harlan designed a new scorecard that could record not just what a player did, but under what conditions he did it: the number of men on base, the number of outs, the inning, and the score. The brothers of course had no way to watch each of the thousands of major league games each season, so they called the only people who had access to play-by-play scoresheets: the Elias Sports Bureau, one of Major League Baseball's official statisticians. Eldon recalls paying $5,000 or $10,000 for this information, which he laboriously coded onto IBM punch cards. From there, Eldon wrote a FORTRAN program to run simulations of baseball games. For each of more than 8,000 starting situations, the computer would play thousands of games to see who wound up winning.

Here's one illustration of the Mills brothers' method: The home team is down two runs in the bottom of the sixth, with men on first and third, and one out. The simulator determines that teams in that situation win the game 39 percent of the time. Now, several things can happen with the next batter. Say he singles to leave his team down by just one, leaving men on first and second and still one out. The computer says that from that stage the team will win the game 46 percent of the time. The batter has increased his team's chances of winning by seven percentage points. If he'd flied out, he would have decreased it to 37 percent. Hit into an inning-ending double play, 29 percent. This was the essence of player win average—measuring exactly how much every contribution, large or small, makes in winning or losing a game.

The percentages were translated into point totals, the positives being termed Win Points and the negatives Loss Points, with most plays carrying around 25 to 75 points but some in the hundreds. Succeeding or failing in a tight, late-inning situation—right when the game is being decided—carried more weight than doing so in a blowout. (Bobby Thomson's three-run home run in the 1951 National League playoff game to snatch victory from the clutches of defeat for his New York Giants would have been worth a whopping 1,472 points; had it come while his team was down by 10 runs, it would have been one-hundredth of that, because under those conditions it would have been of little consequence.) This was a unique method of measuring "clutch" ability, the tendency to come through when it mattered most, something that had been debated for generations (and continues to be today).

A player's win average was his win points divided into his total points so that it resembled winning percentage for teams: .500 was average by definition, .600 very good, .400 poor. And of course clutch performances took place on the mound, too. The beauty of player win average was that it was a double-entry system: Every positive for a hitter was a negative for a pitcher (or a fielder, in the case of an error), and vice versa. Credit and blame were assigned to those responsible. Whereas slugging averages and ERAs are all but incomparable, a .520 PWA for a pitcher meant much the same as it did for a hitter.

Having determined the value of every event, the Mills brothers next had to input what actual major leaguers would do during the 1969 season. This came from Elias as well. For every game each player received an IBM punch card—a 7⅜-by-3½-inch slice of card stock much like current All-Star Game ballots—that coded all the events he participated in and fed them into the computer, where a program Harlan wrote assigned the appropriate win points and loss points and stored the data for later retrieval.

The full 1969 season involved about 310,000 events for both hitters and pitchers. Harlan and Eldon kept having to fix bugs in their programs, running them on a small scale until they worked properly. When they finally went through without a hitch, the answers they had sought for three years began clicking out of their printer:

NATIONAL LEAGUE BATTERS

Name	Team	AB	BA	HR	PWA
W. McCovey	San Francisco	491	.320	45	.677
J. Jeter	Pittsburgh	29	.310	1	.637
P. Rose	Cincinnati	627	.348	16	.611
D. Allen	Philadelphia	438	.288	32	.611
R. Carty	Atlanta	304	.342	16	.606

NATIONAL LEAGUE PITCHERS

Name	Team	IP	ERA	W	L	PWA
T. McGraw	New York	100	2.25	9	3	.651
H. Wilhelm	Atlanta	12	0.73	2	0	.644
L. Dierker	Houston	305	2.33	20	13	.612
T. Seaver	New York	273	2.21	25	7	.609
J. Koosman	New York	241	2.28	17	9	.601

AMERICAN LEAGUE BATTERS

Name	Team	AB	BA	HR	PWA
C. Motton	Baltimore	89	.303	6	.698
M. Epstein	Washington	403	.278	30	.641
C. May	Chicago	367	.281	18	.616
F. Robinson	Baltimore	539	.308	32	.615
H. Killebrew	Minnesota	555	.276	49	.608

AMERICAN LEAGUE PITCHERS

Name	Team	IP	ERA	W	L	PWA
K. Tatum	California	86	1.36	7	2	.643
E. Watt	Baltimore	71	1.65	5	2	.623
M. Lachemann	Oakland	43	3.95	4	1	.619
P. Richert	Baltimore	57	2.20	7	4	.607
J. Roland	Oakland	86	2.19	5	1	.595

The lists showed things the Mills brothers did and did not expect. It was no surprise that Willie McCovey came out as the best hitter in the National League; the San Francisco Giants slugger had led the loop with both 45 home runs and 126 RBIs, in addition to hitting .320. It was the best season in the future Hall of Famer's career, and he was bound to have done enough good things at the right times to emerge on top. As for the National League pitchers, it raised some eyebrows when Mets sensation Tom Seaver placed behind Houston's Larry Dierker—Seaver had run away with the Cy Young Award voting, mostly because he won five more games for a division-winning club—but their ERAs were almost identical. Bit players such as Johnny Jeter of Pittsburgh made it onto the leader board despite little playing time, but that happens with any "average"-type statistic.

Top relievers such as Tug McGraw and Ken Tatum shined, which was interesting considering how relief pitching at the time was only then starting to be appreciated; the clunky "save" statistic had became official that season. Player win averages could lend a whole new dimension to the conversation. Relievers scored highly because they were the ones who got key outs when games were on the line. Also, the PWA leaders were dominated by players on winning teams—13 of 20 played for clubs that finished first or second in their division—but that wasn't surprising, because the Millses designed the system to reward events that specifically aided victory. The method worked exactly as its developers had hoped.

The Mills brothers published their approach and results in a thin, *Reader's Digest*–sized book titled simply, *Player Win Averages: A Computer Guide to Winning Baseball Players*. The $1.95 volume read "1970 Edition" because they planned to publish each season's results every year. The back cover featured this odd claim written by a public-relations person: "Not since the appearance of the Earned Run Average has a really new system of evaluating the abilities of various baseball players come on the scene." Seeing that line again recently, Eldon cringed. "That still bugs me," he moaned. "It wasn't a strong enough declaration for what we had."

With not one word of the mathematics or computer mumbo-jumbo that had gummed up Earnshaw Cook's *Percentage Baseball*, the Millses explained the logic of their method in clear terms understandable to even baseball executives. Several were actually enthusiastic. Yankee officials read the book and invited the brothers to the suites of Yankee Stadium—the first time they'd ever been to the renowned ballpark—to discuss the possibilities of consulting for the team. The Mets made some inquiries, too, while Bill Veeck, then in temporary retirement, met with them as well. But the Mills brothers caused no revolution. Not even a mild uprising. Most club executives still trusted their eyes more than some computer. The book sold around 2,000 copies, Eldon recalled, not enough to publish again the next spring. The two later used their program to stage a faux tournament between all-time great teams such as the 1927 Yankees and 1954 Indians for an NBC special called "World Series of the Century," hosted by Curt Gowdy. But they did little work in sports ever again.

They do still have one big fan left, though: Mike Epstein, whose .641 win average in 1969 for the Washington Senators led all American League regulars, including Most Valuable Player Harmon Killebrew. Beyond his 30 home runs in just 403 at-bats (one of which was a two-out, bottom-of-the-eighth grand slam against Detroit to turn a 2–0 deficit into a 4–2 lead), Epstein also had gotten a large number of RBIs to put his team ahead as well as smaller clutch hits. So he came out on top. Epstein didn't even know this at the time—an indication of how little publicity *Player Win Averages* generated—but learned about it after retiring in 1974. "It came as a big surprise to me," recalled Epstein, who now teaches hitting to youth-league players in San Diego. "I knew I'd had a great year, but I didn't know it was *that* good. That, to me, is a real highlight of my career—to be recognized with these great hitters like Willie McCovey." To this day, "Led American League in Player Win Average, 1969" is on Mike Epstein's résumé.

Though it received little acclaim in its day, looking back, *Player Win Averages* rates as perhaps the largest leap toward quantifying something baseball fans have debated since the game's birth: Who has performed best with the game on the line, and how can that be measured? Allan Roth, the Brooklyn Dodgers statistician of the 1940s and 1950s, was the first to tabulate batting average with runners in scoring position. In 1980, a statistic called the Game-Winning RBI saluted the player who drove in the game's most pivotal run, but that became caught in a web of controversy over which was, in fact, the game-winning RBI. The Elias Sports Bureau and other modern statistics companies such as STATS Inc. measure a player's performance with runners in scoring position, in tight situations and the like, but to this day no one employs a system as tailor-made for the "clutch" question as player win average.

Well, that isn't quite true. After the 2003 World Series, *Business Week* ran a long piece on how a Yale Business School game-theory expert, along with one of his students, had come up with a new way of evaluating players by measuring their impact on the probabilities of winning the game. It was the exact same method that the Mills brothers had invented 35 years before. Their names appeared nowhere in the story.

I n their own ways, George Lindsey, Earnshaw Cook, Harlan Mills, and Eldon Mills were all ahead of their time. They were also products of it.

Men who grew up baseball fans and became scientists were bound to look at baseball through scientific eyes.

The 1960s found people beginning to care about baseball statistics like never before, and not just the analysis of them. For a sport nearly 100 years old, and in its modern two-league form for almost 70, the keeping of baseball's statistical history was in shocking disarray. Few reference works gathered comprehensive statistics. *The Sporting News Baseball Register* annually printed the career records of only active players, and *Daguerreotypes*, a *TSN* spin-off published every several years, featured lifetime statistics of old-time players, but only about 200 of them. The sole book that listed every player ever was Hy Turkin and S. C. Thompson's *The Official Encyclopedia of Baseball*, first published in 1951, but that merely collected the most basic three categories: games played, batting average for hitters, and won-lost records for pitchers. What about home runs? Stolen bases? Innings pitched? The growing gaggle of statistics fans hungered for more.

Luckily for them, the largest project in the history of baseball statistics was already under way. It was the national pastime's equivalent of the *Oxford English Dictionary*. Dozens of researchers all over the country scoured old newspapers, scrapbooks, and box scores to piece together the first all-encompassing statistical history of the game. It was a mammoth undertaking, and when it was unveiled on August 28, 1969, during a press conference at Mamma Leone's restaurant in New York, the six-and-a-half-pound behemoth served notice that the culture of baseball statistics would never be the same. It was called *The Baseball Encyclopedia*.

5

Big Mac

It was September 1965. The San Francisco Giants and Los Angeles Dodgers were fighting for the National League pennant, while the Minnesota Twins had just about wrapped up the AL crown and were awaiting their first World Series. Subscribers to *The Sporting News* picked up their September 25 issue, with Sandy Koufax on the cover, and found on page 20 stories on the floundering Red Sox and a Houston pitcher's $50 fine for plunking Ron Fairly. At the bottom, left-hand corner of the page, a tiny ad beckoned:

WANTED—A BASEBALL NUT

Group involved in sports history wishes to add to its permanent New York research staff a person who is thoroughly familiar with baseball history and statistics, particularly the 1871–1919 period. A knowledge and enthusiasm for history and statistics in other sports plus a record of success with administrative/managerial skills will also be considered in our selection. Salary will be commensurate with capabilities and experience. Please send resume and salary requirements to Box 10, 150 West 31st Street, New York, New York, 10001.

David Neft had been dreaming of this since he was a kid. A New York–based statistician, Neft grew up in the Bronx, within walking distance of both Yankee Stadium and the Polo Grounds, with two loves: baseball and numbers. At age 10, dissatisfied with the imprecision of All-Star Baseball's spinning disks (he actually used his protractor to confirm that Ted Williams's 1948 hit sector should have encompassed 132 degrees, not 129), he invented his own, more realistic baseball game with 100 playing cards. He rejoiced at the 1951 publication of Turkin and Thompson's *Official Encyclopedia of Baseball* and would bring it up to camp in central New York every summer. But in 1954, as a teenager, he read that volume with increasing discontent. Why did it print only batting averages for hitters and won-lost records for pitchers? How could you compare Lou Gehrig to Hack Wilson without annual listings of their doubles and RBIs? No book had everything for everyone. This was simply preposterous.

Neft went on to earn a B.A. in statistics at Columbia University, serve two years in the Army, work at the Pentagon, and become chief statistician for Lou Harris, the polling company. In 1965 his growing expertise was courted by Information Concepts, Inc., a New York firm that specialized in new types of computer data processing and was seeking new applications for it. During his ICI interview Neft broached the idea that had bounced around in his mind since his camp days. "What we really should do," Neft said, "is a computerized baseball encyclopedia."

The business of building a credible baseball encyclopedia was amazingly complicated, and Neft knew it. To compile the first definitive volume of statistics would require the dispassionate exactitude in which computers specialized—only their memory and power could handle full stat lines on every player, from every team in every season—but it went far beyond that. It was no secret that baseball's records, particularly before 1920, were an utter disaster: Turkin-Thompson listed "Iron Man" Joe McGinnity with 27 wins each in 1899 and 1900, while *The Sporting News's Daguerreotypes* had 28 and 29; *Daguerreotypes* gave Cap Anson the 1889 NL batting championship with a .342 average, and 15 pages later awarded it to Detroit's Dan Brouthers (.373); and what was Walter Johnson's lifetime win total, the 414 on his Hall of Fame plaque in Cooperstown or the 416 listed in the Elias Sports Bureau's *Little Red Book of Baseball*, which baseball considered official? Hundreds of less notable discrepancies abounded. League and team totals rarely agreed with the sum of their players—not by a longshot. Players were identified incorrectly or missing altogether. Was this any way for the history of the national pastime to be preserved?

Charged by ICI to head the project, Neft first had to assess whether this mess could ever be untangled. He visited the Library of Congress to research nineteenth-century newspapers and see how reliably they printed box scores. He hit the Hall of Fame library in Cooperstown to learn about its statistical archives, which were sketchy after 1900 and virtually nonexistent before that. As the scope of the work grew ever larger Neft placed the above ad in *The Sporting News* to hire four assistants, who were dispatched to libraries all over the country to scout out microfilmed newspapers and other resources. It quickly dawned on them that ICI would have to completely rebuild the game's statistical history, brick by painstaking brick, by recording new, day-by-day statistics for every player from 1871 through the early twentieth century. The numbers would have to be confirmed and checked and reconciled so that players didn't overlap and totals added up properly. That was the only way to get it all straight, to compile the book that baseball deserved. It would take thousands upon thousands of man hours to do it. But it could, in fact, be done.

Bob Markel immediately saw the potential. The executive editor of the Macmillan Publishing Company, Markel was an avid baseball fan himself, one who had just championed the publication of Lawrence Ritter's *The Glory of their Times*, memoirs of old-time players, which became a runaway hit. He was aware of Turkin-Thompson's deficiencies and, in a meeting with Neft in 1967, relished the idea of a proper, complete baseball reference work and expressed serious interest. The same could not be said for Macmillan president Jeremiah Kaplan, who knew nothing about baseball and almost coughed up a lung when Markel told him the book's cover price would be $25, a stunning amount in the late 1960s.

"How are you going to sell champagne to people with a beer pocketbook?" Kaplan asked.

"We're not selling it to them," Markel explained. "Forget bleacherites ponying up the 25 bucks. I'm telling you that there are 100,000 folks out there who can afford this book and will have to have it—or think they have to have it, which is the same thing."

Markel got the go-ahead to purchase rights to the project. ICI's advance helped it hire another 15 researchers, many of them college kids.

The staff of 21 thus began its two-year, Kerouackian odyssey all over the United States, from library microfilm rooms to long-lost graveyards, mortar and spades always in tow, to build the greatest book of statistics sports had ever seen.

The first order of business actually had nothing to do with numbers. Assigning statistics to players initially required figuring out who the players were. That meant a trip to Cooperstown to consult with one and only one person: Lee Allen.

No one in the world knew more about baseball players, so delighted in their demographic esoterica, than Allen, who in 1959 had succeeded Ernie Lanigan as the Hall of Fame's resident historian. For thirty years, somewhere between joyfully and obsessively, Allen had kept track of every major league ballplayer ever—height, weight, birth and death dates, postplaying occupations, and so on—in neat, loose-leaf notebooks. And not just the stars. The more obscure the player, the better. "I care very little for statistics. My concern is the players," Allen boasted. He contacted their kin with hundreds of letters and long-distance phone calls. He trolled around state record bureaus and, if necessary, cemeteries to add to his data. For years Allen hosted a Cincinnati radio program where he claimed no caller could name a big leaguer for whom he could not, off the top of his head, furnish the player's position, clubs, and debut year from memory; Allen nailed 57 of the first 74. Allen would discuss his quests for "missing" players, and listeners, often distant acquaintances or relatives, would write back with information. Allen told *Sports Illustrated* in 1959:

> There was a shortstop named Lewis Say with the Reds in 1880. I happened to read a note in an old issue of *The Sporting Life* reporting that Say was living in Baltimore. So I wrote to H. L. Mencken, who was a Baltimore authority, and he said that the name rang a bell, but he didn't remember. He suggested that I write to the widow of an old Baltimore catcher who might know. I did. She wrote me a 16-page letter that was an attack on Franklin D. Roosevelt and didn't answer the question at all. So then I began all over. I wrote a letter to the editor of the Baltimore *Sun*, and I got a letter from a reader of the *Sun* in Fallston, Maryland, informing me that Mr. Say had died there in 1930 at the age of 76. I got his death certificate, and we were in business.

Allen's was a lifelong obsession. Born Leland Gaither Allen in Cincinnati in 1915, the son of a notable Cincinnati lawyer and a sitting U.S. congressman, Allen fell in love with baseball at age 9, not long after he first leafed through Ernie Lanigan's *Baseball Cyclopedia*. The pudgy kid in knee pants soon made scampering three miles over to Redland Field for 3 P.M. Reds games an afternoon ritual. In high school, he kept track of pitch counts and gave them to Jack Ryder of the Cincinnati *Enquirer*, whose "Notes of the Game" column would amaze readers with the writer's keen attention to such detail. (No one noticed that he never printed pitch counts for away games.) Allen's first paid job came in 1931, when he read out-of-town scores off the Western Union ticker and phoned them to the stadium's scoreboard operator for 75 cents a game; alas, he often spent twice that amount on ice cream, pop, and peanuts.

Allen graduated from Kenyon College and assumed several baseball posts—public relations man, radio announcer, newspaperman, book author—while chain-smoking three packs of Kools a day, developing high blood pressure, and becoming what we now call an alcoholic. (Friends recall his rather morbid interest in ballplayers who drank themselves to death.) Yet he considered his work, tracking down the whereabouts and fates of ex-big leaguers, his purest passion, for as long as it could last. When Allen assumed his Hall of Fame post in 1959, the movers hauled 55 cartons of books and records, weighing over 5,000 pounds, to Cooperstown.

Allen's ledgers became the skeleton for *The Baseball Encyclopedia*. They told ICI the ballplayers' full names, nicknames, birth and death dates and places, heights, weights, years played, and teams. But Allen had unearthed only

Lee Allen. (*National Baseball Hall of Fame Library, Cooperstown, N.Y.*)

about half of the 10,000 big leaguers by himself. Then ICI landed on his doorstep, in the form of a 29-year-old Manhattanite named Jordan Deutsch.

Deutsch was one of the four assistants Neft had hired through the original help-wanted ad in *The Sporting News*. He arrived merely as a secretarial temp. Rather than type or file, though, he wound up assisting in a considerably more enjoyable pursuit: traveling to stadiums throughout the country to scout out their scoreboards. (Another ICI project was developing systems to deliver statistics directly to new, mammoth scoreboards that the just-opened Astrodome had made the rage.) Deutsch later did some early encyclopedia reconnaissance work at microfilm rooms in libraries, searching box scores in as many as three cities in one day, but wasn't as statistically oriented as other staffers, so he joined Allen in the demographic trenches. "I remember calling up a pitcher from the Phillies named Cal McLish," recalled Deutsch, now an artist living in Phoenix. "We had to confirm his name: Calvin Coolidge Julius Caesar Tuskahoma McLish. He was very sweet. He laughed, and that was it."

One of Deutsch's responsibilities in 1966 and 1967 was to ferret out "phantom" players: men who appeared in existing record books but had not, in fact, existed. He also had to distinguish between two names for the *same* player; it was not uncommon in the late nineteenth century for a young man who wanted to stay eligible for his college team to play professionally under a pseudonym, then afterward appear under his given name. ("We found a case where a rabbit once ran around the bases and was credited with a run," Deutsch later told the *New York Post*.) Allen didn't find these matters quite as humorous. To him, distilling fiction from fact was serious business. At one point a Catholic priest told Allen that he had played catcher for the 1920 St. Louis Cardinals. Allen checked it out and fired off this salty reply:

> The St. Louis Cardinals of 1920 had the following catchers: Vern James Clemons (112 games), William Martin Dillhoefer (74), Carlos Timothy Greisenbeck (5), George Lewis McCarty (5), George Louis Gilham (1), and William Gibbons Schindler (1). Clemons died in St. Petersburg, Florida, May 5, 1959, and I am in touch with his descendants; Dillhoefer died of typhoid fever at St. Louis, Feb. 22, 1922; Greisenbeck passed away on March 25, 1953 at San

Antonio, Texas, and his family is known to us; McCarty died at
Reading, Pa., and his identity is established beyond dispute;
Gilham, poor fellow, fell victim to Hodgkins disease and left this
sphere on April 25, 1937 at Lansdowne, Pa. That leaves Schindler
and he tells me he is very much alive at 303 North Walnut St., Per-
ryville, Mo. If you wonder why I have dropped my other duties to
devote so much time to your case, it is because historians, like
priests, are dedicated to the truth, which I would go to any length
to establish.

With Allen and Deutsch on the demographic front, the rest of
Neft's research staff, which swelled to 20, set their sights on making sense of the rat's nest in which they found baseball's statistical history.
They had to deal with four separate eras: 1871 until league offices began
keeping original day-by-day statistical sheets for every player, 1903 for the
National League and 1905 for the American; from that point into the
1930s, when sheets were kept but had more errors than the Browns infield; a brief period of about 15 years when sheets were checked, but not
by Seymour Siwoff of the Elias Sports Bureau; and the Siwoff era from
roughly 1948 on. Siwoff kept his statistics with the strictness of a fastidi-
ous bookkeeper. Prior to that, ICI found everything but.

As we have seen, professional baseball was only awkwardly finding a
footing in the second half of the nineteenth century. Its statistics were
kept more as a means to reflect the present—that day's game of the current season—rather than the past, of which at that time there was very
little. Arithmetic errors went unchecked. Unbalanced totals, such as
when players on the 1889 Cleveland Spiders combined for more at-bats
than their team line claimed, were neither reconciled nor, in all likelihood, even noticed. Not even Henry Chadwick complained about this.
The errors were fired into history in the next winter's *Reach* and *Spalding*
guides, and that was that.

Neft soon learned how striking, and transparently intentional, some
mistakes had been. "When a team owner was friendly with the league secretary and wanted to unload a player, somehow that player's average got
inflated in the stats," Neft recalled. The American Association, a major
league from 1882 to 1891, blatantly cooked the books to promote its
stars, such as Philadelphia's Harry Stovey, by crediting them with batting
averages 50 or even 100 points higher than they deserved. The National
League routinely rewarded the popular Cap Anson—whom Allen suspected

had provided his own reward of bribes—with boosted totals of up to 100 points. Neft quickly realized that the only way to sort out the nineteenth century, and the first few decades of the twentieth when early official sheets remained a disaster, was to start from scratch, play league secretary from day one, and have ICI build a new day-by-day statistical log for every one of thousands of players.

Amazingly, this process had been started years before, simply for the fun of it, by John Tattersall, a Philadelphia steamship executive who every night pored over baseball statistics like a monk copying parchment. Tattersall was the opposite of Lee Allen—quiet and studious, the kind of person who would camp out in his basement for days to examine 1884 Union Association box scores to see if Fred Dunlap of the St. Louis Maroons really did score 158 runs. (It was 160, by golly.) "I started in 1924, when my father gave me a *Spalding Guide*," he once told the *New York Post*. In 1941, Tattersall learned that the Boston *Transcript* was going out of business and, for $3,500, bought the newspaper's entire library of sports sections and scrapbooks, which enabled him to build books of his own that included box scores of every major league game from 1876 on, neatly presented by league and team. He compiled a list of every home run ever hit in the major leagues. But more importantly for Neft and Company, Tattersall also had constructed day-by-day stat logs for most players from 1876 to 1890. This already had come in handy for baseball's growing group of historians: In the early 1950s, Tattersall's research pinpointed that a typographical error in the hits column of the 1902 *Reach Guide* led to Napoleon Lajoie's batting average for 1901 being listed not at the official .422, but at .409, the figure that *Daguerreotypes*, Turkin-Thompson, and other books wound up printing for posterity. Tattersall's efforts helped restore Lajoie's .422.

ICI paid $25,000 for Tattersall's scrapbooks, an invaluable head start. But these day-by-days were by no means all that Neft sought. The charge of his *Baseball Encyclopedia* was not just to gather information between two covers, but to arm fans with the means of bringing old-time stars to life through more modern statistics. This was more difficult than one might expect. Two of the most evocative and meaningful statistics—runs batted in for hitters and earned run average for pitchers—did not exist until the early twentieth century. How could fans argue the relative merits of 1930s slugger Hack Wilson and Sam Thompson, a National League star from the 1880s and 1890s, without comparing their RBIs? Cy Young's career wins (511) were well known, but his

ERA? A total mystery. Tattersall's box scores couldn't tell the research staff who had driven in every run or when pitchers were let down by their defense. It was all uncrackable code. Or was it?

Early baseball newspapermen, before the rise of radio and later television, took a considerably different approach to game reporting than their descendants. Few readers had attended the game. Their listening to it or watching it through airwaves remained unfathomable. For reporters, telling people what had happened meant exactly that: running down *exactly* how every run scored. (This was often presented in mind-numbingly chronological paragraphs, in part because editors demanded "running" play-by-play during a game so they could give typesetters a head start.) The practice was so widespread, so comprehensively followed, that the blueprints of almost every major league game before 1920 could in fact be located in not just one but two or more newspapers from the following day. The RBI and ERA codes could, in fact, be deciphered. One game at a time.

For example, ICI would consult passages like these, from the June 15, 1893, edition of the *Philadelphia Inquirer* and the June 3, 1894, edition of the *New York Herald:*

> The Phillies were first at-bat and opened up briskly. Hamilton was hit by a pitched ball. Sam Thompson sent a grounder down to Bierbauer and [Hamilton] was forced out at second. Delahanty got his base on balls. Hallman rapped out a pretty single and Thompson crossed the rubber. Jack Boyle then faced Terry; Hallman was at first and Delahanty at third. Boyle met one of Terry's inshoots nicely and the ball sailed away over the right field fence. Three runs were tallied . . .

> The most exasperating failure came in the sixth. The score stood 2 to 1 in favor of St. Louis when the Giants went to bat for their half. Miller muffed Doyle's grounder as a starter and a wild throw sent him to second. Ward's out advanced him to third. Then Van Haltren sent him home by a safe grounder to left. Tiernan followed with a hit to centre, on which he went to second as Van Haltren beat the ball to third. Again there were men on second and third with one out . . .

In the first account, RBIs would go to Bill Hallman (for scoring Sam Thompson) and to Jack Boyle (for his three-run homer). In the second, Doggie Miller's error clearly led to the run, so that tally, belonging to the pitcher, Emerson "Pink" Hawley, went down as unearned.

Neft's research staff, which included about a dozen college students from New York enjoying perhaps the best side job in the history of higher education, traveled to libraries and historical societies all over the United States to sift through newspapers and recreate run-scoring innings from each one of the 87,000 major league games played from 1876 to 1919. At least two sources, one from each team's city, were used to maintain unprecedented accuracy; many times one run batted in or earned run would be researched in separate sources hundreds of miles apart. More than one hundred newspapers, reams of *The Sporting News*, and other periodicals were consulted in search of the most accurate information. Staffers looked for more than RBIs and earned runs, too. They sought explanations for any career interruptions of more than 30 days (injury, military service, suspensions and the like). They determined managers' won-lost records and even pitchers' saves, which wouldn't become an official relief statistic until 1969.

Each researcher's mission would end with a trip back to ICI's headquarters, catercorner from Penn Station in Manhattan, on the mezzanine level of the Penn Garden Hotel building. The information would be laid out on long tables, checked, and entered onto master sheets before being filed away for easy reference. Neft's lust for efficient organization kept the project as smooth as a repeating decimal. "He knew exactly where he wanted to be next," Jordan Deutsch recalled. "He had his game plan—the map was there, and he followed it to a T."

And yet the most ambitious aspect of *The Baseball Encyclopedia* still had to be tested. The book was born in part to test how computers could aid in this type of massive data storage and manipulation. There was no Microsoft database software; Bill Gates was only 12 years old. Information could not be sorted or even eyeballed on what we now consider computer monitors. For ICI's grand plan to work, a completely customized method of electronically recording, cross-referencing, and maintaining numerical and biographical data would have to be built from scratch. That job fell square in the lap of a 29-year-old Californian named Neil Armann.

Armann didn't follow even modern baseball, let alone passed balls from the 1800s; he didn't know Dan Brouthers from the Smothers Brothers. And he had learned computer programming only after earning a master's in history from the University of Connecticut, returning from the Peace Corps, and taking the hint from all the "Computer Programmers Wanted" ads he saw in the papers. He wound up at ICI, inherited the baseball project and had to learn, from scratch, the COBOL formatting and file reference structures required to build an efficient statistical archive that could sort data by team, player, and so on, and alert the user to balancing errors. He worked on an IBM 360 mainframe—the one with whirring, 12-inch magnetic disks straight out of James Bond films—but not in ICI's office, because the computer was too expensive at that time for a relatively small company to own. Armann had to schlep all over Manhattan to rent time from larger outfits. In the end his program had to be play nice with a new printing system at R. R. Donnelly in Chicago. While phone directories had taken advantage of such technology before, *The Baseball Encyclopedia* would become the first conventional book in the United States to be typeset entirely by computer.

Each player received a 17-inch wide sheet of printout paper on which researchers would fill in his yearly statistical totals. Coding all that data onto thousands of IBM punch cards, which would be fed into the computer, was so cumbersome that ICI sent the sheets to Israel, where a company specialized in quick, high-quality key-punching. Three or four weeks later, thousands of IBM punch cards would return from Israel and be loaded onto magnetic tape. Sorting the information inside the computer took hours, not the instants with which we are spoiled today. Armann couldn't even see the data unless he pulled a small portion off a tape and line-printed it; most of the time he had to feel around in the dark. "You couldn't pose a question and answer it immediately like you can now," Armann recalled recently. "You had to anticipate the questions and print it out in some form that somebody was going to be able to look at it." Working virtually alone until he inherited a few assistants, Armann spent months putting in 15 hours a day, seven days a week, to keep everything straight.

The most powerful feature of Armann's program was how it exploited baseball's double-entry personality. The sport's symmetry leaves every hitting event part of a pitcher's record and every pitching event part of a hitter's record; a strikeout, single, walk, or homer goes down on both sides, one never existing without the other. Other sports can't match this: a 10-yard run by a halfback or a point guard's breakaway layup cannot be assigned against any particular defensive player, leaving football and basketball immune from such crisp-and-clean scorekeeping. Baseball, however, is the most individual of team sports: In perfectly discernible packets the game reduces to one batter versus one pitcher, with each assuming responsibility for the other, every matchup a still photograph that flipped together form the moving picture we call nine innings.

Armed with this concept, Armann designed his system to scrutinize whether every league's combined hitting and pitching ledgers of at-bats, strikeouts, and the like represented the sums of its individual teams. At one level below this, team totals of batters' doubles, and so on, had to match the sum of their individual hitters. If anything were out of balance, an error message would appear. But where was the mistake? Which one of the 25 or 30 hitters was missing a strikeout someplace? The researchers would have to double- and triple-check every figure, hoping to pinpoint the discrepancy sooner than later; one bulb in a string of dozens or hundreds or sometimes thousands of Christmas lights would be out, and they had to find it.

Neft kept a log of these corrections on page after page of painstaking notation. The hundreds of lines detailed just how sloppy baseball's record-keeping had been, even after official day-by-day sheets had been used. An excerpt from Neft's master sheets:

Year	Team	Player	Categories	Officials	Actual	Explanation
08	Bos	Cicotte	G, IP, H, BB, SO	38, 204, 193, 57, 93	39, 207, 198, 59, 95	6/9—OS has Pruiett instead of Cicotte
16	Chi	Perry	BB Allowed	4	3	Adding error
12	Bkn	Northern	HR	2	3	6/25—HR not posted
08	Cin	Doscher	IP, BB, SO	43, 21, 6	44, 22, 7	7/16—OS has Dubuc instead of Doscher
08	Cin	Dubuc	IP, BB, SO	86, 42, 33	85, 41, 32	7/16—OS has Dubuc instead of Doscher
15	Phi	Wyckoff	W, L	11–21	10–22	4/15 L, not W
15	Phi	Harry Davis	G, AB	6, 6	5, 3	9/29 Bud Davis, not Harry Davis, change B.A.
15	Phi	Bud Davis	G, AB	20, 23	21, 26	9/29 Bud Davis, not Harry Davis, change B.A.

These pages are easy to decipher: The 1908 AL official sheets had Tex Pruiett mistakenly starting a June 9 game rather than Eddie Cicotte;

addition errors and other goofs abounded. There were more than 700 of
these mistakes. (Very few came from National League data after the late
1940s, when Seymour Siwoff patrolled those numbers.) Other errors were
rampant. One box score from 1901 had a Woodruff playing right field for
the Cleveland Blues (later the Indians). No one could find any record of
a Woodruff in any other game, on any other team in any other year, and
Allen had no demographic data whatsoever on this Woodruff fellow. Finally, a researcher realized that the Blues' regular catcher that year, Bob
Wood, played a few games in the outfield; the telegraph operator, clearly,
had mistaken the Morse code for "Wood rf" as "Woodruff." The correction was made, and the staff moved on.

Because ICI had secured Major League Baseball's blessing to produce
the game's first complete historical record, some decisions on what to
correct and what to leave alone were left to a relatively independent
Special Baseball Records Committee. The group consisted of David
Grote, the NL's public relations director; Robert Holbrook, assistant to
AL president Joe Cronin; Jack Lang of the *Long Island Press* and national
secretary of the Base Ball Writers Association of America; Joseph Reichler, public-relations director for Major League Baseball; and Lee Allen.
They met in March and November 1968 to review ambiguities, corrections, and other interpretations. The committee determined which
nineteenth-century leagues would be called "major." Batters' walks,
which in 1876 were scored as outs and in 1887 were scored as hits,
would always be treated in their modern manner, as neither out nor hit
nor official at-bat. The committee settled upon definitions of pitchers'
wins and earned runs in past eras, in addition to other smaller decisions.
The group had to balance correctness against the impression of monkeying willy-nilly with baseball's hallowed statistics. "On the one hand,
they wanted the records to be straightened out," Neft recalled. "On the
other hand, they didn't want people to say, 'The records can't be taken
seriously anymore.'"

With newspaper and other media-connected men populating the
committee, it didn't take long for news of corrections, many of them to
some of baseball's most storied numbers, to leak. Christy Mathewson was
losing six wins, going from 373 to 367. Ty Cobb's lifetime hit total, the
well-known 4,191, became 4,192. (Honus Wagner wasn't so lucky—he
lost 15 hits, more than one for each year he'd been dead.) The Nap Lajoie 1901 controversy was opened again; more than a decade after John

Tattersall's research restored Lajoie's .409 average to its proper .422, ICI researchers found three more missing hits for him, raising his average to .426. Neft informed the *New York Times* on March 31, 1968: "We have discovered an inconsistency in the official records of (Babe) Ruth's runs batted in. There is one game in which he hit a home run and never was given a run batted in. It's being checked out with various sources to find out how many men were on base when he hit it. Initial investigation, too, shows that Walter Johnson may actually have two more victories than he had officially been credited with." This was serious stuff.

Yet no controversy compared to the hullabaloo over Babe Ruth's lifetime home run total of 714, the most revered record in the sport. Leonard Koppett of the *New York Times* broke the news of how the Special Records Committee was adjusting Ruth upward to 715 not because of arithmetic error but based on an old, outdated rule change. On July 8, 1918, at Fenway Park, Ruth came to the plate for the Red Sox in the bottom of the 10th inning with the score tied 0–0, with one out and Amos Strunk on first. Ruth belted Stan Coveleski's pitch deep into the right-field bleachers. But this was not a home run, according to a rule in effect before 1920; it was only a triple, because Strunk's run effectively ended the game with Ruth at third. (Had Strunk originally been at second, Ruth would have gotten credit for a double.) Only after 1920 did "walk-off" home runs, as they are now called ad absurdum, go down as actual home runs. ICI discovered 37 of these phantom shots from before 1920, belonging to such legends as Sam Thompson, Jimmy Collins, and one George Herman Ruth. COMPUTER FINDS RUTH'S 715TH HOMER, the *Times*'s headline declared, sharing the era's wonder and distrust for the intimidating machines.

Newspapers all over the country followed up on how the legendary record was being changed. Fans couldn't believe their eyes. Neither, apparently, could Joe Reichler—he missed the November 14 meeting when the committee unanimously decided to change those 37 walk-off hits to home runs. Reichler went berserk. "It wasn't in the original concept of the committee to change rules," he carped to *The Sporting News*. "The idea was to correct obvious errors and establish ground rules. When you carry this a little further, what do you want to do about hits that bounced into the stands, and were declared homers?" (What we now call ground-rule doubles were, indeed, scored as four-baggers for a time.) Reichler ultimately was able to convince other committee members to change their

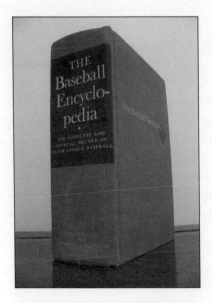

Macmillan's *The Baseball Encyclopedia*,
affectionately known as "Big Mac."

decision in May 1969, just before the book went to press. Ruth's homer total stayed at 714, and has remained there to this day.

By this time, ICI was putting the finishing touches on the other millions of digits in *The Baseball Encyclopedia*. Hitters would get seventeen categories per season, arranged more logically than ever: games, at-bats, hits, doubles, triples, home runs, home run percentage,* runs, RBIs, walks, strikeouts, steals, batting average, slugging average, pinch hit at-bats, pinch hits, and games broken down by position played.

Pitchers, meanwhile, got 19 numbers per year: wins, losses, winning percentage, ERA, games, starts, complete games, innings, hits, walks, strikeouts, shutouts, and seven categories devoted solely to any relief appearances. But the book went far beyond a simple player register. All-time statistical leaders were presented with unmatched authority. All-Star Games and every World Series game had a line score and summary. Managers' records were compiled for the first time. One other goal, pulled off beautifully, was a section called "The Teams and Their Players," which presented rosters, individual statistics, standings, and leaders for every team and league from 1876 on, all cross-referenced and checked by Armann's masterful COBOL programming.

In the end the book ran 2,338 pages and weighed six and a half pounds. "It took just seven hours to print," Neft later exhaled, "but a year and a half to tell the computer what to do." Holding the book in one's hands for the first time was like cradling more than 10,000 ballgames at once; opening it was like diving tongue-first into a giant vat of chocolate.

---

*Why was the strange and rarely used home run percentage (homers per 100 at-bats) included? It was Neft's nod to the game he had invented as a boy with 100 playing cards, for which he figured all statistics per 100 at-bats.

Sadly, Lee Allen, whose historical files and dogged research gave the book its vital demographic skeleton, never had a chance to experience the awesome feeling. Driving back to Cooperstown from a speaking engagement in Cincinnati that May, he suffered a fatal heart attack at age 54. By that point he had secured birth dates and places for 95 percent of baseball's 10,400 players. "My saddest memory of the whole project," Neft later recalled, "is that Lee died just before publication."

Preparing for the launch, back at Macmillan's New York offices, Bob Markel knew he had a hit on his hands. He arranged to send a copy of *The Baseball Encyclopedia* to every influential baseball writer and columnist in the country. Fancying the book as "the ultimate argument settler," he considered selling a model specifically for saloons with a hook and chain bolting it to the bartop, for sure and easy reference. The only advertising Markel took out was a small ad in *The Sporting News* that overwhelmed Macmillan with response.

Markel's most brilliant marketing stroke never saw the light of day. He wrote and designed a full-page ad for the *New York Times*'s Sunday Book Review section that presented a simple photograph of two books sitting on a table. One was the King James Bible, the other *The Baseball Encyclopedia*. "VOLUME TWO," the ad declared. Alas, with the hoo-ha over John Lennon's "We're more popular than Jesus" remark still in their minds, skittish Macmillan executives feared the image was too sacrilegious. "Everyone would be talking about it, which is what we want!" Markel told his boss, Jeremiah Kaplan. "Run the damn ad, and then run for cover!" The ad never appeared.

But nothing could dampen the excitement of the book's unveiling on August 28, 1969. New commissioner Bowie Kuhn joined Hall of Famer Hank Greenberg, future Hall of Famers Whitey Ford and Monte Irvin, and other luminaries to celebrate the occasion at a press luncheon at Mamma Leone's restaurant in Manhattan. Markel stood at the podium and introduced everyone, including his publishing superior who originally thought the book would fail. "This is Jeremiah Kaplan, the president of the Macmillan Company," he said, "who has had the courage of my convictions." The crowd roared.

And reviewers raved. The *New York Times* devoted three full-sized appraisals of *The Baseball Encyclopedia* in different sections by three of its most notable writers: Koppett, Christopher Lehmann-Haupt, and Jimmy Breslin. "Big for a book, small for an amusement park," Lehmann-Haupt called it. "I got lost in it for nearly two days. My wife had to ask me to stop reading it at red lights and during meals . . . It's still the book I'd take with me to prison." Breslin, while he didn't know what slugging average even was, delighted in how the book gave almost-forgotten players a permanent place among the big boys. "Look at this book—it proves baseball is the toughest business in the world," Breslin giggled. "Bill DeKoning strikes out once 25 years ago and they still publish books about it."

The Baseball Encyclopedia flew through its first printing of 50,000 books and ultimately sold more than 100,000 copies. But not everyone was thrilled. Traditionalists—of which baseball never has suffered from any shortage—railed against the altering of numbers that they preferred the old way, chafing the way linguists rue the brutish acceptance of "donut." Robert Creamer of *Sports Illustrated* groused at how Christy Mathewson's win total had been whittled from 373 to 367. "This is illogical, historically invalid, and personally upsetting to Christy Mathewson fans," he wrote. Almost every major star from before 1940—Cap Anson, Cy Young, Ty Cobb, all of 'em—had his numbers altered, and the debates ensued. But for the first time, these arguments had a true starting point: a reaching up to the shelf, or below the bar, to haul out *The Baseball Encyclopedia.*

The book began a new era of fanaticism for baseball statistics. Stars who had remained in obscurity came alive. No one had known what a fantastic RBI man Sam Thompson had been for the 1890s Philadelphia Phillies before ICI pieced his record back together. Addie Joss, star pitcher of the Cleveland Naps (later the Indians) from 1902 to 1910, before John Heydler had invented the earned run average, emerged with a 1.88 ERA, the second lowest of all time. Both Thompson and Joss, as well as nineteenth-century standouts such as slugger Roger Connor and pitcher Amos Rusie, were soon elected to the Hall of Fame, in large part because of the awareness of their records that ICI had created.

*T*he Baseball Encyclopedia* showed how much of baseball's past still remained hidden, even to baseball historians who had devoted much of their free time to digging it up. Men such as Tattersall, Allen, Tom Shea, Frank Marcellus, and others had enjoyed a loose affiliation with each other, tracking down factoids when sufficiently moved, but they were just friends, with no official organization to provide a teamlike sense of direction and focus. Then one of them, Bob Davids, had an idea.

A 45-year-old former officer at the Atomic Energy Commission and later a speechwriter for Sen. Robert Taft, Davids also contributed freelance articles on baseball history and statistics to *The Sporting News* in his spare hours. Davids decided it was time for baseball history buffs like him to band together. In early 1971, he wrote to 40 men he knew who might be interested, and 16 of them met in—where else?—Cooperstown that August. They quickly drew up a constitution for their new organization, The Society for American Baseball Research. The group caught on so quickly that within 15 years it had swelled to more than 6,000 members, a flock of fans striving to preserve and understand baseball history like never before.

Strangely enough, the man who would soon do more than anyone in the twentieth century to advance the public's understanding of baseball was not at that first SABR meeting. Heck, he was too poor to spend $25 on *The Baseball Encyclopedia*. Bill James had just graduated the University of Kansas and was getting ready to enter the Army.

Bill James. (*Lane Stewart/Sports Illustrated*)

6

Bill James

The old widow was in her seventies, maybe even her eighties. She lived on Illinois Avenue. Many afternoons, while she tended to her tulips outside, passersby would see her poking in her garden, listening to the Kansas City Royals on the radio. Every minute or so she would pause, grab a pencil, and scratch something on a piece of paper. One day a neighbor, a tall, scraggly fellow lumbering to work as a night watchman at a Lawrence, Kansas, bean-canning plant, couldn't help but notice this, and struck up a conversation with the woman. She was keeping score, she said. Keeping stats. *Didn't everyone?* It was the summer of 1976, and while fireworks burst all over the United States, Bill James felt an atom bomb go off, right there in the old lady's tulip patch.

How much more corroboration could one man need? James had always suspected that he wasn't the only person fascinated by baseball statistics, and could even make a living writing about them. But hard encouragement was painfully scarce. People only considered him odd when, as friendly talk turned to baseball, he would rattle off home-road splits for Fred Lynn's batting average, or statistics proving how Lou Brock's base stealing actually didn't mean much. The listeners would invariably ask, "How in the world do you know that?"

"I figured it out," he replied.

"What do you mean?"

"I sat down and figured it out."

After a bit of a double-take to size up this nut with the oddly serious look, they all said the same thing: "I like this stuff, sure, does anyone else?"

As always, James did the math. Lawrence was a town of 50,000 people. At least 50 had admitted to him they were into baseball statistics, either from *The Baseball Encyclopedia,* Topps baseball cards, Strat-O-Matic, or just being a red-blooded fan. Those 50 extrapolated to what, 200,000 people across the United States? James knew there was a market. He just *knew* it.

After one final, symbolic push from that widow in her garden, Bill James gave it a try. He did indeed write about baseball statistics, and before long he was making not just a living, but an earthquake that rocked all of baseball, one from which it has yet to stabilize. From 1977 to 1988 James's annual *Baseball Abstract* books combined statistics, analysis, and wit into one potion that statistically minded fans guzzled like beer in the bleachers. Bill James didn't invent statistical baseball analysis—F. C. Lane, George Lindsey, Earnshaw Cook, and others had done similar work without the fanfare—but he, more than anyone, *popularized* it, introducing the subject to a public that only clamored for more. The dozen *Abstracts* wound up as baseball's version of Euclid's *Elements,* textbooks for generations to come.

His influence went far beyond that, though. James rounded up fans to keep leaguewide statistics themselves—shunning the Elias Sports Bureau—through his populist venture called Project Scoresheet. He helped relaunch STATS Inc., the now-behemoth supplier of sports statistics to fans, teams, and media worldwide. And of course there was a downside to all this. The tools that James introduced did not always find their way into the hands of nimble craftsmen; broadcasters and writers began to regurgitate meaningless numbers so indiscriminately that James himself called the new landscape a "Chernobyl of statistics."

No one would become more identified with baseball's 1980s statistical infatuation than Bill James, whose widespread influence left him revered by one side, reviled by the other, but either way the standard bearer for the phenomenon. When San Francisco Giants outfielder Willie McGee was asked by a reporter in the early 1990s about his low batting average in home games, he snapped, "Hey man, I ain't no Bob James." Close enough.

Mayetta, Kansas, in the 1950s had no movie theater and barely little else. The tiny town sat 15 miles north of Topeka on the edge of the Potawatomi Indian Reservation, an outpost nondescript enough that Jesse James was rumored to have hidden out there. Most of Mayetta's 209 inhabitants made do without television. The James family, George and

Mildred and their six children, was no different. Baseball was their summer entertainment. George, a carpentry contractor who made his home
across the street from the Methodist church, took his kids to watch the
Kansas amateur farm leagues. When Bill, his youngest, grew old enough to
play ball himself, the distressingly unathletic boy was placed, he later
recalled, "wherever they were least likely to hit it."

Bill preferred to listen to the Kansas City A's on the radio, a
masochistic rite if ever there was one. The dreadful local club had arrived
in 1955, when Bill was five years old, and proceeded to lose considerably
more games than it won in each of its thirteen seasons in Kansas City
through 1967, often trading its best players to the big-city bullies from
New York, the Yankees. However torturous rooting for the A's could be,
though, young Bill counted the minutes before every broadcast. He would
pace the floor on the rare occasions when the A's threatened to score.
And he loved all the numbers. He always loved the numbers. Without being asked, Bill decided to keep statistics for his elementary school softball
team, and discovered that the big, burly kid who hit cleanup was actually
hitting just .143. "As I recall," James later said, "he did not appreciate receiving this information."

In 1961, when he was 11, Bill bought dozens of boxes of Post brand
cereals (of such weird varieties the family refused to eat them) so that he
could cut out and collect the baseball cards printed on the backs. The
cards had pictures of the players, sure, but underneath the photo were
their statistics both for 1960 and their career. Young Bill carried the cards
everywhere and used them to learn the game. He learned quickly, so
much so that he began to teach himself. When he heard a Cardinals announcer claim that so-and-so bench warmer was so good on defense that
he could save his team a hit per game, Bill took that one hit per game,
added it to the player's offensive totals, and discovered that if this hit-per-
game business were true, the guy's value likened that of a .430 hitter. Bill's
planned one-page protest to The Sporting News evolved into a screed so
long he never bothered sending it in.

High school study halls became dreamlands of baseball statistics. Bill
would take the daily newspaper and diddle around with the numbers as a
chemist would salts and solutions, wondering what potion might evolve
of them. One pastime found him taking the daily statistics of, for example, every shortstop that had played the previous day, adding them together, and pretending the total was a brand-new shortstop himself, who
could be pitted against other players from that day. For Bill James, baseball

statistics were distinctly animate objects, with the power to whisk him away to alternate worlds. This wasn't unique to James. Baseball statistics had this escapist effect on many people, such as Jack Kerouac, and in 1968 inspired the delightful novel by Robert Coover, *The Universal Baseball Association*. The book's hero, 56-year-old J. Henry Waugh, was so fanatical about playing his Strat-O-Matic type dice game that he created an entire universe with fictional players (Willie O'Leary, Frosty Young, Damon Rutherford . . .) for eight teams that played entire 84-game seasons, all the while keeping copious records, standings, and leaders to make this world come alive. Waugh didn't need real baseball, he said. "I found out the scorecards were enough."

Reality beckoned Bill James, however, so after graduating high school fifth in his class of 18, he went off to the University of Kansas. As a dual Economics and English major, he found two primary influences: textbook author Paul Samuelson, whose crisp, mathematical modeling showed how different financial forces were quantitatively related, and William Faulkner, whose writing eschewed convention knowingly, confidently. James also wowed his classmates with Rain Man–like numbers tricks. He could multiply or divide three-digit numbers in his head in seconds. James graduated in 1971 and spent two years in the Army before returning to Kansas and putting in another year in graduate school to become a teacher. But in 1975 an adviser informed him that even a Ph.D. in English would not guarantee him a decent job. He virtually quit on the spot and decided to take a whirl at writing about his first love, baseball statistics. Even if his friends in Lawrence thought he was nuts.

James quickly wrote three articles for *Baseball Digest*, a small, hardcore monthly that provided an outlet for the numbers nuts. The first story, "Winning Margins: A New Way to Rate BB Excellence," appeared in November 1975, and was a relatively uninspired examination of the greatest spans by which home run, RBI, and other statistical leaders had led their leagues. (For example, Dazzy Vance's 2.61 ERA in 1930 was 1.15 better than his closest competitor.) The third was even more mundane, a list of pitchers who won 20 games and hit .300 in the same season. It was James' second piece, in between, that portended his future work. "Big League Fielding Stats *Do* Make Sense!" was an all-out assault on fielding statistics that had remained stagnant, and just as misleading, since the days of Henry Chadwick.

Only three principal defensive statistics had existed—putouts, assists, and errors—for more than 100 years, with errors by far the most scrutinized. Fans and media assessed a player's miscues or, in the case of fielding percentage, the portion of plays made without them. This struck James as patently absurd, and to illustrate he examined two American League second basemen. The Yankees' Sandy Alomar had a .985 fielding percentage the previous season, with just 11 errors. The Orioles' Bobby Grich fielded eight points lower, at .977, and in the same number of games (150) made a whopping 21 errors. Yet everyone knew Grich was by far the better defender. How could that be?

Looking more closely at the numbers, Grich had made far more successful plays (putouts and assists) than Alomar, enough to make a vast difference in their ultimate value. Alomar made 4.7 per game, compared to 6.0 for Grich. That might not sound like much, but over the course of a season that could equal the difference between a .220 hitter and a .360 hitter—in other words, far more than anyone realized. James proposed measuring fielders not by fielding percentage but by plays made per game, which he called Range Factor. "If one fielder gets to plays another would miss, shouldn't the record books reflect that?" James asked. His passion for reform harkened back to Chadwick, who in fact had proposed the exact same fielding measure around 1870 when he wrote, "The best player in a nine is he who makes the most good plays in a match." The statistic was actually printed in Chadwick's 1872 *Beadle* guide, was reexamined forty years later by F. C. Lane in *Baseball Magazine,* and even was included in Macmillan's *Baseball Encyclopedia.* But James's rhetoric struck a chord.

James was bursting with ideas like these, fresh ways of examining baseball and its mantras through its statistical footprints. So much of the sport, after all, is invisible. The naked eye cannot tell the difference between an average (.275) and good (.300) hitter—just a hit every two weeks over the course of a season—without looking at the numbers. What else might they evidence? Did pitchers receive different amounts of run support? Did base stealers take advantage of catchers or pitchers? Were some batters more likely to hit well in colder or warmer months? The topics ricocheted inside James's head until it hurt. There was no way *Baseball Digest* or *The Sporting News* could publish all his ideas, even if they were interested. So in January 1977, he decided to write a book. He would venture into his dark corridors of curiosity, with statistics as his flashlight.

The project immediately consumed James's every waking hour, particularly his 6 P.M. to midnight minimum-wage shift as night watchman at the Stokely–Van Camp factory in Lawrence. The sprawling plant canned baked beans (the company's specialty) and other midwestern staples like corn and ketchup. James had earned a few extra bucks in college working for Pinkerton Security, and with his plans for teaching dashed, treaded water at Stokely as he figured out his next move. Two factors made this bearable: One, William Faulkner himself had watched a boiler while beginning his own literary career, and two, it gave James oodles of hours to study box scores. "I'd spend five minutes an hour making sure the furnaces didn't blow up," he later recalled, "and 55 minutes working on my numbers." Seventy years after a clerk at the Swiss patent office named Albert Einstein blew off his regular job to develop relativity theories that set physics on its ear, it was at the Stokely–Van Camp plant in Lawrence that Bill James set about reordering the world of baseball.

He sat in a room that had 14 desks—all empty because he worked the night shift—and took the one that was tucked behind the door so any passersby couldn't see what he was doing. Every now and then he would unfold his six-foot-four frame from his chair and, wearing his blue Pinkerton shirt, gray pants, blue hat, badge, and nightstick, would check to make sure all the doors were locked. Sufficiently reassured he would sit back down with his stack of *The Sporting News* and continue banging away on his statistics. (Occasionally he would entertain himself by writing sarcastic reports to his supervisor, including one on Christmas Eve that described how he had been disrupted at midnight by a crazy, white-haired fat man in a red suit.) For a while James would sit in the boiler room, a dark and drafty outpost that forced him to wrap a blanket around himself to keep warm. But he barely noticed the conditions. He was too engrossed in what he called, to those who demanded he explain what he was up to, his "secret project." One of his fellow security men who occasionally stopped by recalled recently: "Bill had immense powers of concentration. He didn't like to be disturbed. He could be quite irritable. A lot of guys would be glad to see you because they were lonely or bored. He'd say, *'What the hell do you want?'* It was like disturbing a big bear."

James worked on his statistics so that he could write essays about his findings, but the sheer numerical computation took the entire three months of offseason that remained. For each of the almost 2,000 games from the 1976 season he would enter all the data on paper—from stolen bases allowed by each pitcher and catcher, to hitters' performance by month to time of game by umpiring crews—often so furiously that he couldn't read his writing afterward. James had no access to a computer.

He didn't even have a calculator. He did all the computation in his head. The resulting book, which had about 90 percent numbers with precious little analysis (and a throw-in simulation game like Strat-O-Matic, using a deck of playing cards rather than dice) was called *1977 Baseball Abstract—Featuring 18 Categories of Statistical Information That You Just Can't Find Anywhere Else*. Pecked out on a manual Olympia typewriter by his girlfriend and soon-to-be-wife, Susie, the 68-page compendium sold for $3.50 through a one-inch classified ad James took out in *The Sporting News*:

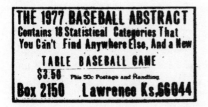

THE 1977 BASEBALL ABSTRACT
Contains 18 Statistical Categories That
You Can't Find Anywhere Else, And a New
TABLE BASEBALL GAME
$3.50   Plus 50c Postage and Handling
Box 2150   Lawrence Ks. 66044

The classified ad that began it all. (*The Sporting News*)

The book cost James $112.73 in materials to produce. He sold seventy, so with the $38.50 ad his profit for four months' work stood at $93.77.

A discouraging start, perhaps, but what perturbed James most was that some of the data wasn't precisely accurate, and could never be. To figure out how many bases were stolen off each pitcher and catcher, or how many double plays were turned behind Tommy John, he needed not just box scores, but the full play-by-plays from each game. His efforts to get them were stonewalled at every turn. When James wrote to the leagues and individual clubs asking for the scoresheets, they either ignored him as some Kansas crackpot or shooed him toward the league statistics houses, the Sports Information Center outside Boston (American League) and the Elias Sports Bureau in New York (National League). That didn't help, either. Teams didn't send SIC and Elias play-by-plays, just box scores. James's only hope came when he learned that Elias independently gathered comprehensive play-by-play information on its own. At last, the data he was looking for.

Elias told him he couldn't have it. For several years, James wrote or called the corporate office in New York asking for the game logs but was repeatedly turned down by Elias president Seymour Siwoff, who claimed the information was proprietary. James grew so frustrated that he eventually wrote about Elias' denials, excoriating the company in general and Siwoff personally. The feud eventually grew so nasty, so publicly vitriolic between James's readership and the Elias camp, that to this day Siwoff can barely utter the name of his nemesis. He refused to be interviewed for this book and threatened termination to any Elias employee who was, because the name "Bill James" was in its pages.

S eymour Siwoff had rescued the Elias Baseball Bureau. The company that Al Munro Elias and his younger brother Walter had started in 1914 by supplying restaurants, bowling alleys, and finally newspapers with their "Food for Fans" statistics had gradually deteriorated since two strokes left Al an invalid in 1937. When he and Walter died soon after, the Bureau was still the official National League statistician and had arrangements with about 1,000 newspapers across the United States. But without its leaders, the shop lost its verve and could hear the locomotive of bankruptcy bearing down on it. Siwoff whisked it off the tracks, saved the business from certain oblivion, and protected it like his child ever since.

It has been a lifelong attachment. After growing up in the Brighton Beach section of Brooklyn, Siwoff worked for Walter Elias at the Bureau as a $12 a week part-timer while a freshman at St. John's University in 1939. He spent three years in the Army, got his stomach shot up in northern Italy as an artilleryman in the Eighty-eighth Division, and returned home with a Purple Heart. He finished his accounting degree but decided to take his skills back to the Bureau. By 1952 he had bought the place from the Elias brothers' heirs, kept the name out of respect for his mentors, and went about rebuilding the operation. With black-and-white accountant sensibilities, he demanded the utmost accuracy from his loggers. He worked seven-day weeks for months at a time. (He still does.) He reassured the National League that the place was in good hands, and would only get stronger. When he convinced the young National Football League commissioner, Pete Rozelle, in 1961 to let him keep the NFL's official statistics, the revamped Elias Sports Bureau was back in business.

And Siwoff ran it like a business. With his gravelly, Brooklyn cackle atop a bony, five-foot-nine frame, Siwoff had only one item to sell—timely, accurate statistics—and jauntily packaged them for whomever he could. Newspapers and wire services bought their statistics from Siwoff. The National Basketball Association made Elias its official statistician in 1970. Television networks signed on, too. Wanting statistics from Elias generally meant that you paid for them: While Siwoff occasionally gave away data to people he wanted to help jump-start (Hal Richman got stats for Strat-O-Matic gratis during his early years), Siwoff's business was *selling* them. Sy Berger of Topps recalled the dawning of a new era in the late 1950s, when he learned that putting statistics on the back of his bubble-gum cards would now be more expensive: "I was paying Seymour $2 a card, and one year he sends me a bill for $8 a card. I told him that $8 was ridiculous. Seymour said, 'I'm doing the first series for eight. After that it's 10.'"

As mercantile as he could be, though, Siwoff was a baseball fan, and could become downright mushy when it came to the statistics themselves. "Statistics can be cold and trivial. But they also can be alive and full of drama," he said in 1973. "What I enjoy most about statistics is the chance they give you to relive the past. When Nate Colbert drives in 13 runs in a doubleheader it gives you a chance to recall when Jim Bottomley drove in 12 in a game. In looking up things like that, I can see these guys in my mind as clearly as if they were playing again." He cultivated an office with workers as passionate as he was. Nothing made his ledger loggers happier than when a player came along and broke a record, the new number justifying the keeping of thousands of anonymous others. The moment that the New York Mets' Tom Seaver struck out 19 San Diego Padres in 1970 to set a new standard, the Elias crew, huddled around the television together, exploded in glee.

Siwoff loved being a baseball insider, close to the club executives and media people who covered his favorite sport. He answered dozens of questions a day when they phoned for some esoteric factoid. But neither he, nor anyone working for Elias, would answer questions from fans. They were probably using the information to settle bar bets, Elias decided, or for more insidious gambling purposes. Scores of such phone calls were dispatched with abruptly. As the business grew more famous for being able to answer any press question—anything!—about sports statistics, over time there developed a certain "We're the Elias Sports Bureau and you're not" mentality to the place, an imperiousness that distanced the company from the masses they ultimately served. One afternoon, as Siwoff looked out from his 58th-floor window on 42nd Street and Fifth Avenue, he gazed down at the majestic New York Public Library below. Elias, he sighed, was "one font of knowledge overlooking another."

Siwoff's statistics were always more accurate than those of the Howe News Bureau, the American League's chosen outfit, but when the AL

Seymour Siwoff (sitting). (*National Baseball Hall of Fame Library, Cooperstown, N.Y.*)

switched to the computer-savvy Sports Information Center after the 1972 season, Siwoff knew he had to computerize for his paper-and-pencil operation to compete. (And, he dreamed, get the AL account for himself.) "I have to do this," he once recalled telling his wife. "I'll be swept by the wayside." Siwoff added manpower in the form of recent Fordham graduate Steve Hirdt, who had worked on David Neft's *Baseball Encyclopedia* stat-collection crew while in college, and soon thereafter grabbed Steve's brother Peter as well. He hired a crack programmer named Chris Thorn. Elias' plan was to set up a private network by which it would secure play-by-play scoresheets from every game across the major leagues, then computerize everything for examination afterward. This process would generate statistics that overloaded mere humans: batting average with runners in scoring position, how pitchers tired as games went on, flyball and groundball data, and more. Months upon months of writing and debugging code finally paid off in 1975, when Elias produced the most comprehensive and staggering statistical look at baseball that anyone had ever seen.

That is, those who saw it. *The Player Analysis*, a mammoth set of landscape printouts that weighed around 40 pounds, was sold only to the half-dozen major league clubs who cared to sift through the stuff. Still, nothing like it had ever been available before. Every player's performance was fractured into a dozen situations, called "splits": in home or away games, facing lefties or righties, and in all sorts of inning, out, and on-base configurations. Teams could use the data either to evaluate players or to negotiate against them at contract time. (Faced with a slugger's reputation for coming through in the clutch, a general manager could point to the printout and respond, "Actually, with runners in scoring position after the sixth inning, *he hit only .218.*") Elias did give some data to ABC's *Monday Night Baseball* crew as part of its contract, but Elias made no effort to market it to the public. There were various explanations. Siwoff later told the *Dallas Times-Herald*, "We just didn't think any fan would be interested." But Siwoff also did all he could to keep the information away from everyone but the teams who paid for it. When a reporter from the *Los Angeles Times* learned of *The Player Analysis* in 1980 and phoned Elias for a story (later headlined SECRET STATISTICS OF BASEBALL'S BOSSES), Siwoff grew gruff and clandestine. "How'd you hear about it?" he demanded. "I've got to be careful. I have a fiduciary interest with these clubs."

It was during this period that an unknown guy from Kansas, Bill James, wrote Elias to ask for those play-by-play scoresheets. The answer was *no*.

Having to comb through the box scores himself, to add up things that others already had but kept secret, only focused James's rhetorical aim on baseball's haughtiness. He started work on his next *Abstract* far earlier than the first one and it showed: With time for more exploratory essays, the 1978 edition became more of what he wanted the series to be. Its 115 pages included commentary on all 26 teams and their key players. Every pitcher was listed by his average run support, double plays behind him, stolen bases against him, average time of game, and attendance for games he started. (Amazingly, Tom Seaver was only the third-most-watched Reds pitcher, behind noted gate-packers Paul Moskau and Fred Norman.) James introduced his new Defensive Efficiency Rating, which quantified team glovework through the true charge of position players, the rate at which they turned batted balls into outs. (The Yankees at 70.8 percent scored best, and not coincidentally won the World Series.) He discussed the imprudence of signing players in their early 30s with impressive résumés: "When you acquire a player with a good record you are looking backward, building a great past." After a year of rote computation, he was *writing* about baseball, and like no one had before.

The 1978 *Abstract* sold only 300 copies. James was encouraged by the growth, but was so burned out that he questioned whether he would return with a 1979 edition. Then he peeked at his mail one fall morning, and found a letter from a reader named Dan Okrent.

Okrent was young freelance writer and such a statistics buff that he played Strat-O-Matic into the night as an adult. He bought the 1978 *Abstract* after seeing the ad in *The Sporting News* and, he recalled recently, "Couldn't believe my eyes. I was stunned. A whole new world opened up for me. I began a correspondence with Bill: 'Who the hell are you? Where did you come from?'" Okrent sold *Sports Illustrated* on a full-length profile of this renegade outsider. He flew to Kansas, filed the story, and promptly ran into a brick wall.

A fact-checker named Kathy Andria wasn't nearly as enamored with James's findings. Everyone knew Gene Tenace couldn't hit, so who cared what his walk rate was? And how could this clown write that Nolan Ryan didn't draw large crowds, when common sense suggested he did? (As Okrent later described James, "He was Galileo, and they were Ptolemaists.") Andria also proofed some of James's statistics with *SI*'s data provider, the Elias Sports Bureau, and found many inaccuracies. For example, the number of double plays turned by the Dodgers with Tommy John on the mound was not 38, but 36. Bases stolen off Johnny Bench were off by one or two. Andria suggested that James's whole book was surely filled with such mistakes. With increasing frustration, Okrent tried to explain that the numbers disagreed because Major League Baseball, via Elias, barred James from receiving scoresheets from the games and forced him to estimate the data himself through box scores.

"We have fact-checkers for a reason," one editor said. "It doesn't check out."

"But this is *why* it doesn't check out!" Okrent yelped.

The story became mired in *SI* politics for two full years, alternatingly resurrected and killed, until it finally saw the light of day in the magazine's May 25, 1981, issue. By then *Abstract* sales had grown by mere word-of-mouth to about 2,600 books, but Okrent's feature instantly brought Bill James out of the woodwork (or, in his case, out of the bean factory). Okrent's almost giddy support was paying off in other ways, too. That spring, he had shown the 1981 *Abstract*, still mimeographed and stapled, to another friend, Dick Krinsley of Ballantine Books. Krinsley loved it.

"This is fantastic!" the publisher said. "This is great for you and me and other people who are nuts about baseball. But there isn't enough real audience for this."

"Dick, you can have this book for an advance of $3,000," Okrent replied. "This guy should be brought to public attention."

"Well, I just can't justify it," Krinsley said. End of discussion.

Soon thereafter the *SI* story appeared, and five top publishers were bidding on the rights to the 1982 *Abstract,* one of them Krinsley. He eventually won out at $40,000, 13 times the price he could have paid months before.

Ballantine launched James to stardom. It published the *Abstracts* nationally from 1982 through 1988, a seven-year period in which James took his new readers—150,000 at one point, putting him at number four on the *New York Times* bestseller list—on an amusement-park ride that shook them up and thrilled them in equal amounts. He didn't use statistics to win trivia contests, but to understand the game better. He would hear some announcer prattle on about how the game is 75 percent pitching, and dig into whether that made any sense. (It didn't.) When managers claimed that players reach their primes at ages 31 and 32, he checked the records to see if they were right. (They weren't.) With his readers transfixed and his detractors aghast, James looked into baseball strategy and conventional wisdom with a consistent, visceral skepticism: "Is this true? Or have we been duped into thinking it is?"

James's lines of discussion numbered in the hundreds. He developed statistics not for the sake of the numbers themselves but to unearth concepts of the game that previously had been hidden. These were perhaps the 10 most influential discoveries and statistical tools that, as if 3-D glasses, transformed the way his readers viewed baseball:

- Runs created: Rather than look at runs scored and runs batted in—conventional statistics that were heavily influenced by the lineup in which a batter performed—James sought to discover the relationship between individual contributions (doubles, walks, and so on) and team results (runs scored). He tinkered with various mathematical equations before finding a surprisingly simple one that did the trick:

$$\text{Runs Created} = \frac{(\text{Hits} + \text{Walks}) \times (\text{Total Bases})}{(\text{Plate Appearances})}$$

  James was theorizing that offense was essentially the product of the abilities to reach base and to advance runners through slugging. He wasn't the first to suggest this. Earnshaw Cook's cumbersome Dx method claimed the same 15 years before, and in the early 1970s, Society for American Baseball Research members Pete Palmer and Dick Cramer multiplied on-base and slugging percentages to determine what they called Batter's Run Average. James came up with his method independently. He also was the first to explain its importance so convincingly that it caught on.

- Stolen bases: While young base stealers like Oakland's Rickey Henderson and Montreal's Tim Raines were swiping 100 bags a year to great fanfare, James questioned their true impact by quantifying how costly taking risks on the bases could be. In the 1983 *Abstract*, using a statistic he called Leadoff Efficiency, James demonstrated that while Henderson had just shattered the single-season record with 130 stolen bases, his 42 times caught stealing made his rampant running all but inconsequential. "That's 42 outs he took away from some Oakland batter . . . The actual increase in runs scored resulting from Henderson's base running: 4½ runs. Four and a half goddamn runs, and they want to give him an MVP award for it."

- Stadium effects: Generations of fans knew that Fenway Park boosted offense while the Astrodome hampered it, but by examining home-road breakdowns James determined the various degrees and predicted real-life consequences with astonishing accuracy. A pair of swaps between the Red Sox and Angels before the 1981 season allowed his methods to shine. Because Boston's Fred Lynn, one year removed from an MVP season in which he hit .333 with 39 homers, was leaving cozy Fenway Park for cavernous Anaheim Stadium, James predicted that Lynn would decline to a .285 average with 18 to 24 longballs per year as an Angel. He was right: Lynn averaged .281 with 22 home runs. James said slugger Butch Hobson would be exposed as a Fenway fraud in Anaheim; he indeed floundered there, and was out of the majors two years later. Meanwhile, by getting out of Anaheim and to Boston's friendly confines, Carney Lansford would probably become much of the hitter Lynn had been; sure enough, Lansford won the 1981 American League batting title with a .336 average. Even Okrent, James's greatest supporter, suspected that James was simply trying to grab attention with these predictions. But they were dead-on, grounded in records no one had examined or applied so deftly.

- The Pythagorean formula: A team can have a good offense or a good pitching staff, but how do those combine to create a final won-lost record? James discovered the following relationship:

$$\frac{\text{Team Wins}}{\text{Team Losses}} = \frac{(\text{Runs Scored})^2}{(\text{Runs Allowed})^2}$$

For example, a team that scored 800 runs in a season and allowed 700 could expect to win about 92 games. This assisted in measuring the ultimate impact of adding or subtracting a hitter or pitcher from a particular team.*

- The Plexiglas principle: James discovered that if a team improves one season, it will probably decline the next. Also, teams with winning records generally slip back to the pack and those with losing records often improve. This was baseball's version of regression to the mean, a formal statistical concept that also helped explain the Sophomore Jinx: Standout rookies usually declined in their second season not because of any unexplainable voodoo, but because outlying performances generally fall back to the pack over time.

---

*James later adjusted this formula to one that analysts still use today.

- Theories of aging: While conventional wisdom held that hitters reached their primes between the ages of 28 and 32 before falling off toward retirement, James demonstrated that their best years came considerably sooner, from 25 to 29. More important, he proved that among groups of pitchers with similar won-lost records and ERAs, those who are power pitchers (with high strikeout totals) rather than finesse pitchers retain their value far longer. This discovery led to new understanding of the reliability of forecasting pitchers' careers.

- Brock2 career projections: Using many of the aging patterns he discovered in examining hitters' primes, this method helped predict the ebb and flow of a player's career years into the future. This was more fanciful than truly meaningful, yet when James applied Brock2 to budding stars like Barry Bonds and Will Clark, and foresaw career stat lines placing them among the game's greats, it proved as popular as catnip.

- Favorite toy: In the same spirit as the Brock2 system, this delightful little device estimated a player's chances of reaching certain magical statistical levels such as 3,000 hits or 500 home runs.

- Similarity scores: Baseball fans love to compare players, and this method examined all their statistics to determine just how alike they were. For example, Eddie Murray's career numbers at age 30 were most similar to those of Orlando Cepeda, with a 949 Similarity Score. Players from across different eras could finally be compared to one another not through the misty eyes of nostalgia, but by nonpartisan examination of their statistics. (This metric is now one of the most popular features of the seminal statistical Web site, baseball-reference.com.)

- Major League equivalencies: When James was in high school, he tried to figure out why Jose Vidal—an outfielder who had just won the California League's triple crown with a staggering .340 average, 40 homers, and 162 RBIs—couldn't hit a lick in the majors. He finally tackled the subject head-on in his 1985 *Abstract*, and discovered that major league numbers are, indeed, quite predictable through minor league statistics, as long as you take into account the characteristics of the player's home park and his league's level of competition. This encouraged a new understanding of how high-priced, mediocre major leaguers could be inexpensively replaced by players trapped in Triple-A.

Some major league executives began calling James's office over the winter, asking, "Do you have MLEs done yet?"

James became one-stop shopping for sportswriters, radio hosts, and even TV's *Today Show* to put a face on baseball's statistical fervor, and receive comment from its anointed guru. He would explain the term he coined for his science—"sabermetrics," which married the acronym for the Society for American Baseball Research and the Latin suffix for measurement—to hosts who nodded airily. (Ted Koppel once asked him on *Nightline*, "What surprises do you expect to see in the World Series?", which baffled its literal-minded guest.) James often was batted about like a piñata, invited specifically to absorb complaints from those who believed statistics were sucking the romance from the national pastime. The bearded, inelegant Kansan was occasionally portrayed as a numbers-obsessed hermit; one day a *Nightline* producer took his wife, Susie, aside.

"Do you cut his hair?" the man asked.

"Yes," she said. "I always cut his hair."

"Well, stop."

She didn't. Her husband didn't want to, either; iconoclasts don't primp for the cameras. Part of James's appeal to his audience was that he had come out of nowhere, springing forth from the heartland to lead a movement they only wanted to join. The game during this period, 1982 to 1985, was still coming to grips with the new dynamic of free agency, which allowed teams to acquire players and revamp their rosters easily. If a general manager wanted a new second baseman, he could *buy* one. A star lefthander could be his with a rip of his owner's checkbook. At the perfect time, James provided tools to evaluate which players would make the most difference in new settings, which were on their career upswings and downswings, and how all the pieces fit together. In a sport that had spent a century second-guessing managers, James allowed fans to play *general* manager like never before.

Only a few baseball people read him. Mets manager Davey Johnson, whose interest in statistical analysis had been stoked by his old friend Earnshaw Cook, bought the *Abstracts* and shared them with his bright young coach, Bobby Valentine. As for general managers, A's boss Sandy Alderson, a newcomer to baseball hired originally as team counsel, read the *Abstracts* with such devotion that he would later proudly call himself

a "Bill James disciple." But with baseball's resistance to new ideas baked
in over 100 years, James made little impact on front offices during the
early 1980s. It was with the *next* generation of general managers, then
teenagers or younger, that he found his most willing converts. A good
portion of front-office executives under 45 today, including general managers Jim Duquette (Mets), Paul DePodesta (Dodgers), and Theo Epstein
(Red Sox), read James early and bought into his theories from the start.
"It changed how you looked at the game, entirely," Duquette recalled.
"I've taken that stuff with me ever since." Indeed, on Billy Beane's book-
shelf in Oakland stand all 12 of James's *Abstracts*—not just the Ballantine
books, but the self-published and stapled mimeographs from 1977 to 1981
he got from a collector. In the end, James became the most influential
baseball writer of the twentieth century, the successor to Henry Chadwick, with whom he shares not just a facial resemblance but also the same
birthday, October 5.

Readers loved that James was an outsider and wrote like one, with no
regard for what his subjects thought of him. He lambasted Enos Cabell, a
favorite of Tigers manager Sparky Anderson, as a player who "can't play
first, can't play third, can't hit, can't run, and can't throw. So who cares
what his attitude is?" When Reggie Jackson claimed fellow slugger Eddie
Murray had the "character" and "fortitude" to get himself out of a slump,
James wrote: "Many athletes truly believe that they are successful at what
they do not because God made them strong and fast and agile, but because *they're better people than the rest of us* . . . That's where all the bull-
shit about clutch ability comes from." His barbs occasionally ventured
into alarmingly bad taste and had to be cut, as when he commented on
the Yankees installing Rick Cerone behind the plate after the fatal plane
crash of star catcher Thurman Munson: "Cerone is to catching more or
less what Thurman was to aviation."

James became particularly nasty when discussing the Elias Sports Bureau, the outfit that kept its play-by-play data proprietary while James,
and increasingly more readers, wanted access to its statistics. He called
them "bastards" and described their "naked display of greed" to an audience that came to view Seymour Siwoff & Co. as an evil empire bent on
stunting the growth of sabermetrics. "The problem with the Elias Bureau," he carped, "is that the Elias Bureau never turns loose of a statistic
unless they get a dollar for it." This was actually not true, as Hal Richman
of Strat-O-Matic and other people whom Siwoff had helped over the
years would attest, but James was on a roll. "I know it's important that

Seymour Siwoff die a wealthy man," he sneered, "but I don't really think that is supposed to be your primary objective."

In his 1984 *Abstract*, James had written about his inability to get play-by-play accounts of games from Elias, and suggested a response, a plan he called Project Scoresheet. All sorts of on-field questions James and his readers wanted to answer—how often a pitcher plunked the next batter after a home run; how many times different runners scored from second on a single; to what extent some pitchers gave up more ground balls or fly balls than others; the list was quite literally endless—were unanswerable without those play-by-play scoresheets. He screamed from the pulpit: "[We] are blocked off from the basic source of information which we need to undertake an incalculable variety of investigative studies. We need accounts; we are given [box scores]. We need access to an exact record of what happens. We are told that that is for the big boys, not for us measley [sic] fans. I feel this is very wrong." So wrong, in fact, that he proposed that the fans join together and record everything themselves.

More than 100 volunteers for Project Scoresheet flooded James's P.O. box with pencils drawn like muskets. Within months he had organized a nationwide scoring network of fans, by fans, and for fans, and they set to work not just scoring each of more than 2,000 games of the 1984 season, but thumbing their collective noses at the Elias Sports Bureau. "They *were* the evil empire," recalled Jim Baker, James's assistant during this period. "I loved the idea of circumventing the evil empire." Volunteers included teachers, bankers, and one postman who listened to games while sorting mail. Computer whizzes in the group wrote software to collate the data and distribute it to fans everywhere. The movement that James had dreamed of was beginning, the Elias Sports Bureau be damned.

In 1985, Siwoff and Elias decided to fire back. They took their *Player Analyst* printouts, the annual anvils of information available only to major league clubs, and released them to the public. If James thought Elias was making money, he hadn't seen nothin' yet.

Dan Okrent, even before he had discovered Bill James and introduced him to the masses through *Sports Illustrated*, saw a market for publishing the kind of statistics Elias was keeping for teams (performance in clutch situations, versus lefties and righties, and so on). Around 1977 he arranged a meeting with Siwoff at the Elias offices on Fifth Avenue, and soon questioned why Siwoff had taken the meeting at all. "I can still see Seymour sitting there in his office in his white broadcloth shirt with a neck six sizes too large," Okrent recalled. "He said, 'Boys, boys, boys! Nobody gives a shit about this stuff! Nobody's gonna ever read this shit!' He literally said that. He was so dismissive and patronizing." This wasn't Siwoff's only smoke screen. In 1980, he claimed to the *Wall Street Journal* that baseball statistics were in danger of being "overdone" by computers. "You press a few buttons and out come the numbers in new ways," he groused. "Trouble is, most of them don't add much to what we already know."

But by 1985, with the Bill James revolution in full swing, Elias went on the attack. It released its specialized numbers to the public in the form of *The 1985 Elias Baseball Analyst,* a 407-page tome of statistics that broke down the 1984 season into the subatomic quarks few fans had ever seen before. The heart of the book came in individual tables that gave each player's performance against lefty and righty pitchers, at home and on the road, on grass and turf, by month, and in 17 different combinations of outs and runners on base. Who had led the American League in batting average with runners on base? (Toronto's Rance Mulliniks, .375.) What did Yankees speedster Omar Moreno hit in June? (.205.) Montreal's Tim Wallach loved to face Padres pitcher Andy Hawkins, against whom he was 9-for-14 lifetime, while he hated to face Dwight Gooden (0-for-12). The introduction admitted, disingenuously avoiding Bill James's name, that the market for baseball statistics had changed. "Little did we realize, back in 1975," the section read, "that the interest of baseball fans in this statistical material would eventually dwarf the interest of the 26 teams."

Elias then answered its nemesis's barbs with some vitriol of its own. The book made the preposterous claim that Elias's *Analyst* printouts from 1975 to 1984—despite being top-secret—were the true spawning of sabermetrics. Those "served as the state of the art for a variety of imitators: various individuals and computer companies outside baseball were fascinated by reports of its contents and attempted to copy it, with a notable lack of success." (James, who says he never saw those printouts, was so unsuccessful he was writing bestselling books.) Elias then veered from silly to bitter: "You will find in this book no arcane formulas with strange-sounding acronymic names. You will not find what somebody thinks George Brett would have hit in 1914. And if you want to know the product of Brett's hits plus walks minus caught stealing, multiplied by his total bases times fifty-five-hundreths of his stolen bases, all of that divided by the total of at-bats plus walks, you must look elsewhere."

The Elias books did more than ratchet the Siwoff-James feud up a notch. The *Analysts* became the primary cause of the statistics epidemic of the 1980s and beyond, where fans were deluged with incessant statistical gobbledygook. They put millions of statistics in the hands of people who didn't know how to use them, like handing a chainsaw to a hyperactive teenager, with similarly grisly results. Announcers would cite Benny Distefano's slugging percentage with the bases empty in late innings as if it were meaningful. Writers would herald how Mickey Hatcher had gotten hits in 17 of his last 25 games, a statistic roughly as significant as the number of hairs on his chinny-chin-chin.

Elias did not educate its readers nearly as well as James did. It failed to reinforce the fact that the *Analyst* was at its heart a *reference* book; only one in 100 numbers held any real significance. Whereas people *knew* things through Elias' charts, they *understood* them through James's writing and wit. The old saying "Give a man a fish, he'll eat for a day; teach him to fish and he'll eat for a lifetime" is applicable here. Elias delivered fish. James taught fans how to catch them.

Still, when the public objected to the altogether fishy smell of statistics wafting through announcers' every sentence—many of them surely from the Elias *Analyst*—it was James who bore much of the public backlash. He was the face of a movement not everyone wanted to follow, particularly baseball insiders who felt threatened by rogues gaining respect and influence. When Joe Klein of *Sport* magazine brought up James's name in an interview, the executive he was speaking with replied, "Aren't you in the wrong place to ask questions about Bill James? This is a ballpark." Tigers manager Sparky Anderson replied to James's criticism, "This guy has never played baseball. I don't think he knows very much about it." James got hate mail from fans who said he was ruining the game.

Of course, complaints about the overuse of statistics had been common even in Henry Chadwick's time. In 1958, *Sports Illustrated* ran a long feature headlined "The Great Numbers Nonsense," in which veteran sportswriter Stanley Frank, a self-proclaimed "old sourpuss," groused, "The greatest menace to big-time sports today is neither the shrinking gate nor TV . . . It is a nonsense of numbers [and] the stupefying emphasis on meaningless statistics which is draining the color from competition." Even Bill James's journalistic hero, the syndicated sports columnist Jim Murray, wrote in 1961, "The game of statistics has begun to run away with the game of baseball. I mean, it's not a sport any more, it's a multiplication table with base lines." But as he became famous in the 1980s, and the computer (though he never used one) made statistics even more plentiful, James faced new and far more voluble complaints focused squarely on him. He responded with characteristic directness. "Information," he explained, "is not to be held accountable for every misleading claim that somebody can derive from it."

James grew tired of the arguments by the end of 1987. He was writing his twelfth *Abstract* and wasn't so sure he liked the world he had helped create. He would listen to ballgames and hear announcers babble in statistical mumbo-jumbo and wonder, "God, I hope I'm not responsible for that." Whereas formerly he would respond to critical mail by writing one "Dear Jackass" letter a year, he came to write 30. So at the end of yet another grueling *Abstract* crunch, in February 1988, he decided to write one big "Dear Jackass" letter. He wanted out. Sounding a bit like Einstein warning Roosevelt about the dangers of his atomic theories, James nastily warned his public, some of whom he called "nitwits," of what he feared he had wrought, turning his pen upon himself.

If there has been a growth in the access to and understanding of meaningful baseball statistics, there has been an unchecked explosion in access to meaningless ones. The idea has taken hold that the public is just endlessly fascinated by any statistic you can find, without regard to whether it means anything. The success of the *Baseball Abstract* proves that, doesn't it? . . . I would like to pretend that the invasion of statistical gremlins crawling at random all over the telecast of damn near every baseball game is irrelevant to me, that I really have nothing to do with it. It just happened. [But] I know better. I didn't create this mess, but I helped.

And with that, Bill James was gone.

7

From Field to Front Office

The cameras needed something to look at. Ever since television entered baseball in the 1940s, typically just one or two cameras shot the action, mostly panoramic views from inside home plate. Then, in 1975, after an NBC cameraman behind Fenway Park's Green Monster caught Carlton Fisk madly gesticulating for his Game Six home run to stay fair—it did, of course—television directors decided to show more of the game's emotions, the crises and strategies of the participants. They would focus on the eyes of the runner dancing off first base. The sweat dripping off a faltering reliever. And when they turned to the dugout during Orioles games, they zoomed in on Earl Weaver and his—what is he holding?—*index cards*.

Weaver didn't just look at statistics; he feasted on them. Most of his fellow managers in the 1970s would use a set lineup, and decide their pinch-hitters on hunches. Gut feelings. "My eyes tell me all I need to know," they invariably said. But Weaver wanted to consult hard information. He consulted all the data he could get his hands on, even during the game. In a tight spot, when an opponent brought in its top relief pitcher, Weaver didn't just go with his gut. He whipped out his index cards, on which he kept updated statistics for each of his hitters against every pitcher in the league. "Just because a guy is hitting .330 doesn't mean everything—he might be a .110 hitter against the guy who's pitching out there," he once said. "You'd be surprised how bad a .330 hitter can look if he's up against somebody he can't hit . . . The stats tell you which ones." They told Earl Weaver enough from 1968 to 1982 to win four pennants for the Orioles—and to usher in a new era for baseball managers, one where they relied on statistics more than ever before.

Since baseball's earliest days, its considerable zeal for statistics came almost solely from journalists (Henry Chadwick, Ernie Lanigan, F.C. Lane) or fans (George Lindsey, Earnshaw Cook, Bill James). Men managing major league teams, those who could actually put the information to some practical use, generally pooh-poohed it as a toy for outsiders. Skippers knew who their .300 hitters were, of course, maybe the number of errors their third baseman had, but consulted little else. Strategy was decided on feel: When New York Giants manager John McGraw saw the game moving toward power in the 1920s, he eased off his speed-oriented style and emphasized home runs. Suit-and-tied Connie Mack believed he could remember where every hitter had hit every ball, and would stand on the top dugout step, scorecard in hand, to signal to his fielders where to shift for each batter. Casey Stengel, who often had been benched himself against lefthanded pitchers during his own playing career from 1912 to 1925, popularized platooning while managing the great Yankees teams of the 1950s, while also using tons of pinch hitters and no set pitching rotation. But these decisions derived almost solely from instinct, which after long enough formed "The Book," the rules of game strategy from which one deviated at his own risk.* Baseball managers tend to cling to the oak of conservatism; it's much easier to defend a decision everyone else would make than one you brainstormed yourself.

The first modern skipper to publicly challenge some of baseball's tried-and-true strategies appears to be the Pirates' Bobby Bragan, who in 1957 explained his iconoclasm in a *True* magazine piece headlined WHAT PERCENTAGE PERCENTAGE? Formerly a brash utilityman for Branch Rickey's late 1940s Brooklyn Dodgers (where he befriended club statistician Allan Roth), Bragan claimed that lineups were being ordered foolishly. Like Earnshaw Cook would seven years later, Bragan endorsed batting his best hitter first, second-best second, and so on. But unlike Cook, he could actually *put it into practice.* Bragan used this lineup for the last quarter of the 1956 season, often batting his top sluggers, slow-footed Dale Long and Frank Thomas, leadoff—followed by hitters such as Bill Virdon and Roberto Clemente in descending order of batting average. Critics called it "Bragan's Brainstorm," particularly after the manager

---

*A science this was not. Heck, in 1951, St. Louis Browns owner Bill Veeck let fans in the stands manage the club for a day, holding up placards that said BUNT, STEAL, and whatnot. They won 3–2.

asked injured pitcher Dick Hall, a Phi Betta Kappa from Swarthmore, to prove mathematically how many runs it could add to the offense. The Pirates went 16-24 during the experiment, slightly better than their 14-26 in the forty games before, but dropped it because of the controversy. Bragan later tried his lineup while managing the 1966 Braves but never placated the doubters. "My biggest fault," he once said, "is that I didn't experiment enough."

From the day he took over the Orioles in 1968, Earl Weaver didn't experiment. Quite the opposite, he consulted hard-and-fast facts before making his decisions. He didn't simply trust his memory, like Mack and Stengel. Weaver personally kept track of how each of his hitters had fared against every pitcher in the league, and recorded the data on index cards. His first task upon arriving at the park was to consult his team's batting averages against that day's opposing pitcher; he decided his lineup in large part on this information. Weaver knew when slugger Boog Powell was batting in the mid .100s against Mickey Lolich, and finally benched him. He knew when his .220-hitting shortstop, Mark Belanger, somehow fared better off Angels fireballer Nolan Ryan, and always started him. (Weaver generally considered 20 at-bats enough to know whether one hitter had a pitcher's number, or vice versa, but even a four-for-nine could sway him.) Beyond his own calculations, he used Elias's secret *Player Analysis* printouts to learn opposing hitters' stats against lefties and righties, and with runners in scoring position. "I wanted all the statistical information I could get," Weaver wrote in his 1984 memoir, *Weaver on Strategy*. "Maybe I wouldn't use everything, but I wanted to see it."

Weaver saw and used more than any manager before him. He platooned at several positions at the same time, turning marginal players John Lowenstein, Gary Roenicke, and others into valuable gears in the Oriole machine. He brought his index cards into the dugout to choose his pinch hitters. Did the players ever get to see them? Of course not. "If you don't know what your stats are," Belanger told a reporter, "you won't get mad if you should be starting and you're not." Baltimore's top slugger, Frank Robinson, recalled recently: "We laughed at it. But in the end he showed it works."

Weaver used only pencil and paper to keep his statistics. He stored them neatly in a plastic index-card file. But by 1980, it was only a matter of time before a new device, one revolutionizing other industries, would dawn over baseball's horizon. They called it the personal computer.

For all of its stodginess toward change, baseball's history with computers actually goes back almost 50 years. In 1957, an RCA mainframe in Detroit, code-named "Bizmac," solved problems for the U.S. Army's Ordnance Tank-Automotive Command during workdays, but on weekends was commandeered by curious officers to track major league players' batting averages. The Cubs appear to be the first team to toy with a computer to process players' full statistics, around 1963, and two years later a GE-235 in Phoenix had every play from the 1965 American League season plugged into it so operators could figure out the best clutch hitters. (It revealed that Tony Oliva, the 1964 AL batting champ at .321, slipped to .192 in pressure situations.) Indians general manager Gabe Paul consulted those GE printouts on some roster decisions, but his manager, Birdie Tibbetts, bristled at the notion of ceding power to a machine. "A computer can't tell what's in a man's heart," Tibbetts said. Countered Paul: "Computers are coming. They are ready for us, but we are not quite ready for them."

One executive who *was* ready was Tal Smith. The GM of the New York Yankees from 1973 to 1975 before five years with the Houston Astros, Smith encouraged his colleagues to pay closer attention to the numbers, particularly when arbitration and then free agency sent player salaries skyward. In February 1975, Smith prepared a computer statistics report that detailed every player's batting average, on-base percentage, walk percentage, and more, all of it mapped to salary and service time. Smith loved this part of the game. He had been a stat freak since his childhood. Growing up outside Philadelphia, he was one of the few boys who bought Ted Oliver's obscure little book, *Kings of the Mound*, and was transfixed by Oliver's invention of a whole new way to rate pitchers. Between his junior and senior years at Duke University, Smith worked for *The Sporting News*, where he figured the magazine's fielding statistics and minor league averages. After two years as a lieutenant in U.S. Air Force he approached Reds general manager Gabe Paul for a job, was hired as a secretary, and worked his way up the executive ranks from there, always carrying a respect for statistics with him.

In 1977, a letter arrived in Smith's Astrodome mailbox that particularly intrigued him. A young Philadelphian named Steve Mann wanted to provide statistical analysis for the club through his own personal invention, the Run Productivity Average. Mann was a failed ballplayer trying to get back in the game: He had played on the same thirteen-year-old youth all-star team as Reggie Jackson, and later pitched at the University of Pennsylvania before his arm blew out. He turned to studying educational philosophy at Temple University, but after years of squinting through that discipline's fog of indeterminate theory, he decided to analyze something a little more tangible: baseball. Having played Ethan Allen's All-Star Baseball as a kid, Mann loved the probabilistic nature of the game. As luck would have it, a second-grade friend and Penn fraternity brother happened to be Dave Montgomery, who had become director of sales for the nearby Phillies. Mann got the club's 1975 play-by-play scoresheets through Montgomery and from them developed his run productivity average, a method by which every offensive act was worth some amount of runs: walks, .25; stolen bases, .15; and so on. (Much as F. C. Lane had done in *Baseball Magazine* sixty years earlier.) Mann wrote to every GM detailing how his method could improve personnel decisions, and received a serious response from just one: Tal Smith.

Smith took the plunge and hired Mann in 1979, making him the first full-time statistical analyst for a team since the Dodgers' Allan Roth a generation before. Mann's main project was to determine the effects of the Astrodome on the team's performance. In the late 1970s, the cavernous stadium was one of the worst hitter's parks in baseball, muting offense by up to 25 percent. Good hitters looked bad while mediocre pitchers thrived; with half their games divided among all the other parks, it was hard to look at the stats and unravel which Astros had talent and which didn't. Mann determined that in order to compete effectively, the club would need to shorten the Dome's deep fences to create a more normal playing field. "Tal didn't buy it, because he's from the pitching, speed, and defense school," Mann recalled. "I was preaching to the incontrovertible." Opinionated and abrasive, Mann also chafed Smith by lambasting the team's use of Enos Cabell and his low on-base percentage in the lineup's number two spot. Mann's stint with Houston ended in February 1980.

Having done all his analysis with pencil and graph paper, Mann decided to work on a grander plan: forming a company to computerize play-by-play data so that he could run studies wholesale, providing analysis to several clubs at once. He brought the idea to the most connected stats man in the biz, the Elias Sports Bureau's Seymour Siwoff, with the idea of perhaps working together. Siwoff all but brushed him aside. "It was very clear that he regarded himself as the keeper of the gate—the data gate that lets you into Major League Baseball—and he just wanted to hang on to that gate, protect it," Mann said. "I think he just had that simple, let's call it 'mercantile,' attitude: *This is my company, and if you think you're getting a piece of my action, well, you're wrong.*" (Of course, Siwoff had been selling his *Player Analysis* printouts on the hush-hush for years.) Mann approached the American League statistician, the Sports Information Center, about a joint venture, but that outfit had little interest in branching out into analysis. Calling SIC wasn't a total loss, though. The brains behind that operation's computer system, Pete Palmer, was a SABR member who knew statistics nuts all over the country. He suggested Mann call a friend from Philadelphia, a scientist and computer programmer named Dick Cramer.

Mann and Cramer hit it off from the start. They spent an entire October day at Cramer's house watching sports—the Eagles beat the Cowboys, and then the Phillies beat the Royals in Game Five of the World Series—but most of the talk concerned Mann's ideas for computerizing statistics. "I could program that," Cramer answered dreamily. "I could definitely program that." They talked for hours, bandying about ways to keep and distribute statistics like never before.

That night in Cramer's living room was the genesis of a company that would spend the next two decades revolutionizing the sports statistics business, a little outfit called STATS Inc. It launched three months later, but only after pushing Steve Mann out the door just before liftoff.

Plastics. They were no joke around the Cramer household—Richard Cramer was a research chemist for DuPont, and his son, Dick, was predestined to follow him to Harvard to study chemistry himself. Not that this stopped young Dick from growing obsessed with baseball and his local major league team. ("I decided that following the Phillies would be more fun and less costly than building and crashing model airplanes," he said.) In 1958, when he was 16, Cramer's parents went away for the weekend and left Dick $15 for expenses; he promptly mailed the cash to APBA for its baseball dice game. The Cramers were furious, but Dick was hooked. He figured out how to make his own cards from old-time players' statistics and replayed past seasons into the night. He indeed grew up to go to Harvard, get a Ph.D. from the Massachusetts Institute of Technology, and became a respected computer-oriented chemist for Smith Kline French (now GlaxoSmithKline), but baseball remained his true love. He joined SABR and invented new statistics of his own. When Steve Mann proposed in October 1980 they start a company to keep major league statistics with computers, Cramer signed right up.

As luck would have it, one club was already interested. The Oakland

A's were considering using statistics in a new way—to draw fans. The team barely had any. One of baseball's flagship teams after winning three straight World Series from 1972 to 1974, the A's had been run squarely into the ground by renegade owner Charlie Finley and finally unloaded. New owners had retained Matt Levine, a California sports-marketing whiz, to raise the profile of the suddenly sad-sack franchise. "When I first walked into the A's offices, the World Series trophies were being used as coat racks," Levine recalled recently. "You know the little gold flags? People had hung their coats on them. It was such a filthy mess." The A's drew just 3,700 fans a game during the 1979 season, prompting new club president Roy Eisenhardt to hire Levine's firm, Pacific Select, to devise new ways to sell the club to the public. One idea was to furnish broadcasters with more interesting statistics to use during games. "The team's no good, but fans are really into stats," Levine told Eisenhardt, citing surveys he had conducted for other clients. "Not just batting average, but performance in the clutch, against certain pitchers, the whole deal." Eisenhardt nodded in agreement.

So when Steve Mann later sat in Eisenhardt's office to pitch a new, computer-operated statistics system, it was an easy sell.

"Would you like a full-fledged record of every play-by-play event so we can see who does well in pressure situations?"

"Oh, yes."

"How about having a person in the press box track the direction of batted balls to determine hitters' tendencies?"

"Love it."

"How about we lay out the strike zone in a three-by-three grid and record where all the pitches go, and what type of pitches they are, so we can start looking at things like pitch patterns?"

"Definitely."

This was a perfect marriage. But Mann would not be around to witness it. As Levine looked past the A's and toward marketing a system to additional clubs, he saw Pacific Select handling sales. Dick Cramer would write the code. And Steve Mann . . . well, what would Steve Mann actually *do*? Levine and Cramer met in January 1981 and decided that the future of their venture would not include Mann. Mann naturally went nuts—he had hooked up Levine and Cramer in the first place, and much of this venture's conception had been his. He finally settled for $8,000 in compensation and moved on, never receiving another dime, or public credit, for his idea of this new statistics service. "It was Steve's vision,"

Cramer conceded recently. Asked if he and Levine essentially stole Mann's idea, Cramer sighed, "I guess that's true."

Levine quickly set up the new company as a subsidiary of Pacific Select, with Cramer as coprincipal, and then had to come up with a name. He wanted an acronym. He fiddled with "S" for "Sports" and "T" for "Team," and within seconds the name stared back at him: Sports Team Analysis and Tracking Systems Incorporated.

STATS Inc.

Now all Cramer had to do was build a system that actually worked. When STATS secured a $75,000 deal with the A's in January of 1981, they didn't even have a computer of their own; Cramer had to scribble out the Pascal programming code on paper. There were two halves to the system he envisioned: A club operator would input data onto an Apple II personal computer during a game and then send it over phone lines to a remote Digital Equipment mainframe, which had the power and memory to crunch the data into something useful before uploading it back to the Apple the following morning. The hardware was downright neanderthal by today's standards. Apple IIs had no hard drives, just floppy disks that held barely any data. The modems sputtered along at 300 baud, one-hundredth the speed of the dial-up connections that modern Web surfers curse as maddeningly slow. Cramer tackled the input algorithms. Pete Palmer, Cramer's SABR friend at the American League statistics house, wrote the FORTRAN mainframe code. The final system—hardware, software, modem, and all—was called Edge 1.000.

The A's loved it. Their Edge 1.000 spruced up their game broadcasts just as they had hoped, thanks to its wizardly operator, Jay Alves. A 26-year-old former sportscaster looking for a job in baseball, Alves was hired full-time to sit in the broadcast booth and input everything that happened in the game, from where each pitch crossed the plate to where batted balls landed on the field. The Apple compiled it all from there. The team announcers, Bill King, Lon Simmons, and Wayne Hagin, no longer had to rummage through reams of paper to ferret out some numerical tidbit; a few keystrokes by Alves and it would pop right up on the screen. Dozens of new statistics were suddenly at their disposal. They could tell listeners what slugger Tony Armas batted against curveballs, or whether pitcher Mike Norris struggled in day games at the Oakland Coliseum. If Rickey Henderson was having trouble in the clutch, the numbers would tell them. (The information never made its way down to the manager's office, where the cantankerous Billy Martin harrumphed that he didn't need it. "I've got it all right here," he would say, pointing at his head.)

Servicing Oakland gave STATS Inc. instant credibility, so Levine set out for more customers. The next team to sign up was the Chicago White Sox, whose vice president, Jack Gould, was more interested in using the new statistics in contract negotiations. Gould, a blunt former B-24 bombardier in World War II, put it thusly: "We wanted to find out if the players were worth what we're paying them." Heck, one victory in arbitration would save the team the system's $80,000 price tag right off the bat. Levine's sales pitch to club officials, with young manager Tony La Russa sitting in the front row transfixed, went perfectly. The White Sox jumped on board. To run their Edge 1.000, they assigned a twenty-two-year-old former college intern named Danny Evans.

Five-foot-nine and looking about half his age, Evans had grown up on the North Side of Chicago in a baseball-crazed household. His father, Dan, who answered 911 fire-alarm calls and dispatched equipment to emergency scenes, was a rabid White Sox fan; mom pulled for the Cubs. Danny would play pickup ball with his friends every day after school and go to about two dozen Cubs games a year at nearby Wrigley Field, but he loved the game's statistics just as much. His father taught him arithmetic

Dan Evans. (*Jeff Lowenthal/Newsweek*)

by having him figure batting averages and ERAs. When he would watch NBC's *Game of the Week* on Saturday afternoons, he would listen to Vin Scully quote a stat straight from the network's numbers man—Allan Roth, who had left the Dodgers for television—and think that keeping baseball statistics would be the coolest job. Soon enough, it became just that.

A summer intern with the Sox while at DePaul University, Evans was hired after graduation to run their new Edge 1.000. Evans had never used a computer before. But before he knew it he was flying to Oakland and Anaheim for his first road trip with the team, computer system in tow, lugging the big galoot everywhere. "We had these two huge blue cases, probably four feet high by three feet wide, about 200 pounds," Evans remembered. "Those two carried the Apple II, three disk drives, and a slow, slow computer with the old green-screen monitor. You'd go into some press boxes and people would give you these nasty stares. People couldn't understand why you were pushing these cases up the ramps at Fenway Park. Or sitting at Memorial Stadium in Baltimore with no ventilation whatsoever, sweating your butt off after getting those things up to the press box."

White Sox brass wanted to see every tidbit Evans could come up with; La Russa even allowed the kid into his meetings with pitching coach Dave Duncan. When the printouts showed that Rudy Law, a left-handed hitter, actually performed better against lefthanded pitchers, La Russa eased off pinch hitting for him in those situations. He learned the effects that a strong wind blowing in at Comiskey had on his flyball-oriented pitchers. The data on where grounders went through the infield suggested that putting Mike Squires at third base—despite being left-handed, which is verboten for the hot corner—would not be too costly, and Chicago played him there under certain conditions. The White Sox never mentioned the computer to players, assuming they would rebel against anything so impersonal helping to determine their playing time. "I don't always make the move printouts suggest," La Russa told a reporter, "but at least I'm aware of what the percentages say when I choose to ignore them."

Evans sought any stat that could help the club. After that first season of 1982, he noticed that of the 83 flyballs hit to Comiskey Park's warning track, more than 50 of them belonged to the White Sox. He suggested to general manager Roland Hemond that perhaps the club could rein in its fences to turn some of those flies into home runs, especially with young sluggers Ron Kittle and Greg Walker on the cusp of the majors. "I was absolutely sure of it," Evans said. "I must have double-checked the data three or four times because I knew I was a young guy." Owners Jerry Reinsdorf and Eddie Einhorn decided the kid was onto something. Comiskey Park's concrete fences could not be moved in, so the club decided to do the next best thing: move the plate forward, leaving the walls around 10 or 12 feet closer than before. The result? The White Sox, a good club in 1982 which had outscored its opponents at home by 51 runs, exploded in 1983 to outscore them by 126. "All of a sudden, balls that had been getting caught on the track were sneaking into the third row," Evans said. "I have to admit, I got a kick out of it for a while. I felt like I contributed something."

The Sox won 99 games that season and ran away with the American League West, making Evans want to dive deeper and deeper into the data. He talked with Dick Cramer, STATS's programmer and baseball guru, about the innerworkings of the game. Cramer showed how lacking batting average was, how slugging and on-base percentages were more important. They learned together how batters working deeper counts would lead to higher on-base percentages and opponents' pitchers tiring more quickly. This experience served Evans well: He ran Chicago's Edge 1.000 system through the 1985 season before graduating to higher-level club work and becoming one of baseball's hottest front-office minds of the 1990s. He spent several years as general manager of the Los Angeles Dodgers, one of the game's most prestigious positions.

STATS knew that the Edge 1.000 system would appeal mostly to hands-on, meddlesome owners, so it was just a matter of time before Levine approached George Steinbrenner of the New York Yankees. Levine will never forget the morning he was set to make his pitch, in the summer of 1982, when 25 top club officials crammed into a room in the bowels of Yankee Stadium for the 10 A.M. meeting. When 10 arrived, there was no George. Ten-fifteen, no George. Worried suits started calling around the stadium looking for George. At 10:25 Steinbrenner finally arrived, three yes-men at his heels. His first comment: "What's holding you up?"

"Uh, Mr. Steinbrenner," Levine stumbled. "We're waiting for you."

"Oh, well, let's get the damn thing going!"

Levine got two syllables into his presentation before Steinbrenner interrupted. "Wait a minute! Wait a minute!" he said. Steinbrenner pulled an envelope out of his pocket, opened it and unfolded a list he had prepared. "I want to know whether your system can do these 10 things. If it can do these 10 things, we'll buy it."

They were basic functions of Edge 1.000. Data to show where to position fielders? Check. Batter-versus-pitcher breakdowns? Check. Clutch situations? Check. Pitch counts for pitchers? Check. Everything was no problem . . . until number 10.

"Will your system tell our manager who to pitch every day?"

Levine knew that disappointing Steinbrenner was bad strategy, but had to be honest. "No."

"*What?*" Steinbrenner demanded.

"This is a *tool*," Levine answered. "This doesn't answer all questions. It doesn't diminish the importance of the manager. It gives him more information to work with to make better decisions. But the starting lineup and who pitches will always be a manager's decision."

Steinbrenner sat and pondered that silently for the longest 10 seconds of Levine's life. Then he looked over his shoulder at team treasurer David Weidler.

"Buy it."

And with that, George Steinbrenner walked out of the room.

I n its original incarnation, STATS Inc. was not a data company. It was a software, and to a lesser extent, hardware company. It supplied teams with the *means* by which to keep data themselves on their own players and opponents, and the Edge 1.000 system did this in greater detail than any device to that point. It could print the statistics out either numerically or graphically. Diagrams would show where batted balls were hit by batters or against pitchers, with different pitches and in different counts. It also gave the start to three lifelong front-office careers: Alves went on to become public relations director of the A's and now the Colorado Rockies; Evans became GM of the Dodgers; and the Yankees' first Edge 1.000 operator, Doug Melvin, is now GM of the Milwaukee Brewers.

STATS had a rival, though. Steve Mann didn't go away *that* quietly. "I wasn't out for revenge," he said. "I was out for *competition*." After being jettisoned from STATS, Mann started his own firm, the Baseball Analysis Company, and devised a "BAC-ball" system similar to the Edge 1.000. Rather fortuitously, Mann's old schoolboy pal, Dave Montgomery, had risen to become executive vice president of the Phillies, which helped him get that club and then the Atlanta Braves as BAC clients. (Atlanta's young manager, Joe Torre, was particularly taken with what the computer could teach him.) But baseball was not ready for revolution—Torre and other managers still chafed at the idea of confessing they used computers. As Phillies BAC-ball operator Jeff Eisenberg put it, "If the players smash water coolers, what'll they do to an IBM?"

The first manager to proudly admit his reliance on microchips was Steve Boros. After Billy Martin left the Oakland A's following the 1982 season, one of the first questions Boros asked club president Roy Eisenhardt during his interview was, "Will I have access to a computer?" Eisenhardt was thrilled. To that point the club's Edge 1.000 had been used only for radio and TV broadcasts. Now it might help the team on the field. Fitting baseball's stereotypes never suited Boros anyway: Back in the late 1950s, as a bonus-baby infielder from the University of Michigan, Boros was known as "Joe College," a kid who read actual books in the clubhouse, wore tweed sportcoats and attended Edward Albee plays on New York road trips. ("Most players think I'm weird," he told the *New York Post* in 1964.) While working his way back to the big leagues as a coach under Whitey Herzog and Dick Williams, Boros watched in reverence as those managers spent hours updating their own statistical charts with 12 different colored pencils. So when he got his first managing job in Oakland, right beside Silicon Valley, Boros embraced the possibilities of the computer. He called his Apple II "my predicting machine."

Steve Boros and his Apple II. (*Anthony Neste/Sports Illustrated*)

Boros used his Edge 1.000 openly, explaining to reporters after a puzzling pinch-hitting choice or removal of a pitcher that the computer statistics backed up the move. He juggled his lineup and rotation frequently based on its numerical suggestions. Boros never brought the machine into the dugout, but consulted it before the game for every decision that might arise. The press seized upon the renegade manager with his bits and bytes. Publications ranging from *Sport* ("Computerball is Here!") and *Sports Illustrated* ("It's the Apple of His Eye") to *Newsweek* ("The Computers of Summer") and *Psychology Today* ("The Microchipped Diamond") cried from the mountaintops as computers marched upon the national pastime. Soon, other managers were expressing interest in the device, such as Seattle's Rene Lachemann, who just happened to be a former minor league teammate of Boros and one Tony La Russa. Said Lachemann, "I'm going to take advantage of every tool I can to win."

Baseball's conservatives howled in horror. As 1984 neared, you'd think that George Orwell was in the press box: Almost every article on baseball and computers used a silly, futuristic lead, with machines replacing managers and robots turning double plays. *USA Today* suggested that the next Hall of Fame skipper would be the Apple II. Oakland players began to resent Boros's reliance on the information, taking him as a cold tactician who ignored the emotional side of the game. After A's center fielder Dwayne Murphy was thrown out in a rundown between second and third, he grumbled to his manager, "The *computer* made me do it." Traditional managers such as the Pittsburgh Pirates' Chuck Tanner rose up to protest the newfangled devices. "The computer can't tell you how a player feels on a given day," he said. "Sandy Koufax might beat a team 20 straight times but there's no way to guarantee he'll beat you the twenty-first. You don't know how he woke up that morning."

Steve Boros woke up one morning as the standard bearer of baseball's on-field information revolution. After one year on the job, having been profiled in dozens of publications and all but cast as a circus freak, he became unpopular enough in his own clubhouse that he was fired midway through the 1984 season. "[The computer] figured in less than 5 percent of our decisions last year," Boros tried to explain. "It was so overblown it became a problem." Sure enough, the backlash directed toward Boros made several clubs, who had been considering the purchase of either an Edge 1.000 or Steve Mann's BAC-ball, recoil in apprehension. One *Tank*

McNamara cartoon said it all: A downtrodden manager peered over his computer and asked, "But will it take the blame?"

The computer receded under baseball's turtle shell for several years, as far as its use in the dugout. But there was one place in which it kept whirring along at greater and greater speed, spewing out statistics like a leaf blower: salary arbitration, where statistics meant money, pure and simple.

S tatistics, of course, had been used to negotiate player salaries since the 1869 Cincinnati Reds first began accepting paychecks. As we saw earlier, nineteenth-century players would eschew sacrifice bunts to boost their batting average, which was their main selling point after the season. "A premium has been put upon clean hitting for so many years, by paying extra salaries to players who have great records in this respect," the 1891 *Reach Guide* lamented. "It has induced them to play for themselves instead of for their side." Then again, players weren't exactly rolling in options. They had no bargaining power for even most of the twentieth century; after Mickey Mantle hit .365 in 1957, Yankees general manager George Weiss tried to cut his salary. Only after Marvin Miller began to lead the fledgling Players Association in 1966 did new avenues to riches begin to emerge. Salary arbitration arrived in the early '70s, free agency soon thereafter, and the two made most contracts subject to legitimate negotiation. Those talks had more statistics flying around than flakes in a slow globe. As agent Bob Wolff once recalled, "When I negotiated Bob Stanley's contract with the Red Sox, we had statistics demonstrating he was the third-best pitcher in the league. They had a chart showing he was the sixth-best pitcher on the Red Sox!"

No setting encourages more statistical rhetoric than salary arbitration, which allows both player and team to argue its case, courtroom-style, before a neutral arbitrator. Each side submits one and only one salary offer, and a three- or four-hour debate ensues, with cases made and rebuttals offered as to why the player either deserves or does not deserve either figure. The arbitrator chooses whichever number he finds most reasonable given each side's arguments. From the first cases in 1974, it became increasingly clear that the judges were swayed far more by *facts*—charts that used statistics to compare one player to another—than the more plasticine *opinions* that major league executives traditionally preferred. A club general manager would plead to the arbitrator, "I know my player hit 22 home runs, but he can't hit to the opposite field," and get a disapproving look from the bench. They wanted hard information. "Arbitrators," Dodgers GM Al Campanis once complained, "went solely by statistics."

It was only natural, then, for the game's most skilled statistical mind to be lassoed into this process. After buying the 1979 *Baseball Abstract*, the Houston-based agent team of Randy and Alan Hendricks hired Bill James, still virtually unknown, to crunch numbers for their clients' upcoming arbitration cases. James was charged with devising comparison charts—"comps" in arbitration lingo—to support briefs for dozens of players. He got up to argue some hearings as well, often rebutting an opposing side's clumsy stat study that had more holes than the Indians' defense. James loved it. "What was so satisfying was that the arbitrator would *listen*," he remembered. "The rest of the year, nobody listened." In his first case in January 1980, representing Houston Astros pitcher Joaquin Andujar, James helped explain the hurler's second-half slump by showing how the club started using him as a reliever, hurting his subsequent starts. (This implied that Houston management had mishandled him.) Andujar won a $125,000 salary—$35,000 more than the club had offered. A few years later, James showed that White Sox pitcher Steve Trout's 9–16 record derived from poor offensive and defensive support. And in another case, he demonstrated how Mario Soto's posting a winning (14-13) record for a last-place team, the Cincinnati Reds, was incredibly rare in baseball history. Both pitchers won their cases.

Contrary to the image of arbitration hearings portrayed by the press, which has never been allowed to attend, the affairs are relatively tame and orderly. No one stands up and shouts, "That's crazy! My player has a 4.65 range factor and .287 isolated power!" In fact, while perceptive statistical categories and charts are vital, they must be kept simple for the arbitrator to understand and weigh them. It took a while for clubs to get the hang of all this. Even after James entered the ring, bringing a level of statistical sophistication the process had never before seen, team officials tended to cling to their subjective approaches, which didn't sway arbitrators. Recalled James: "I had grown up all these years listening to owners from afar, and general managers, thinking, 'These are not the brightest people in the world.' Then I get into a room with them and realize, yes, these are not the brightest people in the world. Multimillion-dollar decisions were being made on the basis of intuitive decisions by people who didn't have the slightest instinct for factual analysis." From 1979 to 1981, players posted a 34-25 record in arbitration, their best performance ever.

Ownership soon wised up in taking the statistics seriously—and countered with none other than Tal Smith. The former Yankee GM who later hired Steve Mann for the Astros, Smith had been shockingly dumped by Houston owner John McMullen in October 1980 after the Astros came within one win of the World Series. Smith's keen statistical sense was still very respected by his progressive peers, though, and A's president Roy Eisenhardt immediately enlisted him to help handle his club's two arbitration cases involving pitcher Mike Norris and slugger Tony Armas. The A's won both, saving $440,000, and word of Smith's talent spread quickly enough that he formed his own company, Tal Smith Enterprises, that soon became a one-stop arbitration clearinghouse for half of the 26 major league clubs. He and his nine-member staff built an exceptional database that mapped statistics to salaries and prepared graphic presentations that filled dozens of three-ring binders. When Smith stood up to argue a case, he took his statistical notes with him on index cards, just like Earl Weaver. Smith won 44 of 76 cases in his first six years. And just as STATS Inc. was launching the front-office careers of Dan Evans and Doug Melvin, two of Tal Smith's young number crunchers were Ed Wade and Gerry Hunsicker, now the general managers of the Phillies and Astros, respectively.

Young stat whizzes were soon being recruited by both sides of the arbitration wars. While the Hendricks brothers enlisted Bill James, Tal Smith Enterprises grabbed Mann. Mann helped Smith represent the Red Sox in two of the sexiest cases of the 1980s, those involving Wade Boggs after the 1984 and 1985 seasons. Boggs was one of the hottest commodities in baseball at that time, winning the American League batting title in his first full season, 1983, and finishing the next year with a .344 career batting average. Boggs and the Red Sox couldn't come to terms on a contract before the 1985 season and headed to arbitration, where Mann argued on behalf of the team. It did not go as Mann had hoped. A study from the player side listed the highest all-time batting averages among players' first 1,000 at-bats, and Boggs was the only modern player among the chart's Gehrigs and DiMaggios. That so impressed the arbitrator that Mann lost the case, and Boggs won a $1 million salary.

Boggs continued his hot streak in 1985 by winning another batting title and heading to arbitration again. His representatives naturally updated their chart to list the highest batting averages among players' first 1,500 at-bats, with Boggs moving even higher on the star-studded list. Recalled Mann: "If you're a bubble-gum-card stats arbitrator, Wade Boggs as far as

you're concerned is Ty Fuckin' Cobb. So we've got our work cut out for us."
Mann based his case on *conceding* up front that Boggs's batting averages
and on-base percentages were exceptionally high, but then investigating
whether Boggs ultimately made the most of them. Boggs had spent much
of the previous two seasons as Boston's leadoff hitter because of his on-
base ability. But his lack of speed, Mann explained, kept him from finishing his job; specifically, to score runs. Mann whipped out a chart that rated
several top 1985 leadoff hitters by Runs per Plate Appearance, and
demonstrated that Boggs's .146 was considerably below that of his contemporaries, Tim Raines's .160 and Rickey Henderson's .207. "He does not
bring home the bacon—he doesn't have the wheels to do it," Mann told
the arbitrator. "If you're going to be a leadoff hitter, if you're going to set
the table for the rest of the gang, you'd better be able to score, because you
sure as hell ain't knockin' 'em in. Boggs puts up wonderful, flashy numbers.
He's one of the better run scorers. But he's not *top of the line*, and he
doesn't deserve a top-of-the-line salary." Mann won the case, saving the
Red Sox $500,000.

Mann eventually left Smith's team and switched to the player side,
working with the Hendricks-James group for the 1988 arbitration season.
(Randy Hendricks spent a year making sure that Mann wasn't a spy for
the owners.) He soon helped Hendricks and James represent pitcher Bob
Milacki, a relatively average starter who in 1991 had gone 10–9 for Baltimore. Mann presented a standard study that compared Milacki to pitchers with three or four years of service time. The Orioles' side countered
with a chart that showed how he yielded a lot of stolen bases. Looking to
refute the impression that Milacki gave up bases willy-nilly, Hendricks
came back with a statistic he called Index of Self-Destructive Acts,
which showed that Milacki was in the American League's top 5 percent
in avoiding wild pitches, balks, and errors. Each side kept trying to trump
the other with new and impressive numbers.

The crescendo came when the Orioles tried to prove that Milacki
was "inconsistent," a real bugaboo among baseball folks. To do this they
trotted out a statistic called Game Score, which boiled down a pitcher's
entire performance in each game into one easy-to-access number, and
showed how Milacki varied wildly, up and down. Murmurs around the
room suggested that Baltimore had scored a key point.

Problem was, game score had been invented by none other than Bill
James, who was sitting right there, on the Milacki side. James just happened to have handy the game scores for Roger Clemens, the best pitcher

in the league, and showed the arbitrator how even the game's greats could be inconsistent, too. The Orioles were dead. Milacki won the case, thanks to James's at-the-ready game score sheets. "It was a stake through their heart," Hendricks crowed afterward. "Sabermetrics at its finest."

With teams realizing the value of statistical data, and with arbitration its perfect, lucrative setting, you'd think there would be plenty of takers for STATS's Edge 1.000 system. But by 1985 STATS was only gasping. The Oakland A's, the company's first client and entrée into the industry, dropped the service after the 1983 season because it cost too much ($100,000 by that time) and because some statistical studies needed for contract negotiations, particularly those involving Rickey Henderson's stolen bases, came out horribly buggy. Moreover, Pacific Select, STATS Inc.'s parent company, had diversified so far beyond its original sports marketing platform, adding such indulgent ventures as music videos, that it promptly imploded in debt. Facing personal bankruptcy in the summer of 1985, Matt Levine allowed Dick Cramer to take possession of STATS Inc.'s assets if he would fulfill its existing contracts with the White Sox and Yankees. Cramer agreed and broke off from Levine, the future of STATS in serious doubt.

Cramer could not keep STATS Inc. running by himself; he needed a capital investor, one who appreciated the potential economic value of baseball statistics. So he called the one person who probably understood that better than anyone: Bill James. James knew more than how to fiddle with statistics. He knew how to collect them, too. Project Scoresheet, his network of fans keeping their own statistics to circumvent the Elias Sports Bureau, had been running for two years now. Just for the love of it, people all over the country were keeping score of each game on a special scorecard that James had invented and sending them in to an executive director who generated the statistics. That person was a Chicago actuary named John Dewan.

Dewan was crazy for baseball statistics, always had been. As a boy he loved going to Comiskey Park to see the White Sox, most of the time with his father, John Drohomyreckyj, a South Side corrugated-box factory worker and first-generation Ukranian immigrant who quickly shortened the family name. Young John grew to love the Sox so much that at 14 he kept a game-by-game stat log of all their players, from Luis Aparicio all the way down to the benchwarmers. That same year, he got hooked on Strat-O-Matic, and soon became the commissioner and statkeeper of a league he started with his friends. (He came to be nicknamed "Bowie" after baseball's boss, Bowie Kuhn.) Even after earning his dual math and computer science degree at nearby Loyola University, Dewan loved Strat-O-Matic so much that he wrote a BASIC program to computerize that game, just for fun. Even after settling down as an actuary, Dewan was a natural volunteer for James's Project Scoresheet, scoring games of his beloved White Sox before taking over as the group's organized and officious executive director.

When Dick Cramer called James looking for a potential STATS partner, James heartily recommended Dewan, who jumped at the chance to invest. Having run Project Scoresheet and looked into various publishing deals (as well as seeing the rabid enthusiasm among the volunteers at his disposal), he saw from the inside that these stats could be worth well into six figures if leveraged astutely. Dewan and his wife, Sue, put up $30,000 for a 30 percent stake in the revamped STATS Inc. Bill James decided to chip in $5,000 for 5 percent, while Cramer controlled the rest. Most of that first year of 1986, the Dewans worked three jobs: their daytime employment, running Project Scoresheet (still on a volunteer basis), and getting the new STATS Inc. ready for business.

When that business arrived, though, all hell broke loose, causing a rift that forever changed the future of baseball statistics. In early 1987, a Florida entrepreneur named Floyd Kephardt was starting a Sports News Network that would give fans twenty-four-hour modem access to up-to-date box scores and statistics. Needing the raw data, Kephardt called the Project Scoresheet office, John Dewan answered, and eventually they worked out a $50,000 three-way deal where Project Scoresheet's volunteers would score games for roughly $20 apiece, and STATS Inc. would crunch and upload the numbers to SNN. Dewan, who was in the process of quitting his actuary job to focus on statistics full-time, would be paid $39,600 to run the entire operation. This didn't sit well with many worker bees at Project Scoresheet, who felt that Dewan had negotiated a sweet deal for himself while forgetting those below him. They raised one hell of a stink, James himself called Dewan's actions "an egregious conflict of interest," and then things got really ugly, eventually blowing Project Scoresheet apart.

Kephardt defaulted on most of the deal and, after the "Black Monday" stock-market crash that October, totally vanished. (Dewan hasn't heard from him since.) Project Scoresheet board members and scorers, upset about not getting paid, called for Dewan's head. During this period, the Dewans resigned from the Project to concentrate on STATS Inc.

Project Scoresheet was convinced that the Dewans were using their home phone, which doubled as Project Scoresheet's number, to steal scorers and business, and called up Illinois Bell to disconnect the line. (They even considered approaching the Illinois attorney general before cooler heads prevailed.) There were bitter fights over the data itself: Project Scoresheet said that Dewan had improperly taken possession of the 1984–86 play-by-play information for STATS's own commercial purposes; Dewan said he was entitled to do so after spending three years running the Project for virtually nothing—and besides, he had a contract authorizing him to do so. Project Scoresheet said, "Show us that contract." Dewan could not produce one.

At loggerheads through a 1987 holiday season that was anything but jolly, Dewan and Project Scoresheet decided to have the matter settled by arbitration. But who understood all sides of the issue, everyone's beefs and concerns? Why, Bill James, of course. Even though he owned 5 percent of STATS, James had started Project Scoresheet and wanted it to survive. He was stuck right in the middle and was seen as having a fair outlook on the entire mess. A hearing was set up for March 1988 at a hotel near the Kansas City airport. The Project Scoresheet side attacked Dewan for pilfering the company's assets. Sue Dewan argued her husband's case and ultimately broke down in tears. In the end James, whose goal all along had been to make information available to fans, reached the following compromise: The data belonged to both sides, but Dewan had to go it alone from that point forward, cutting his ties with Project Scoresheet forever. "Bill knew right from wrong the whole way," one Project officer recalls.

In fact, James was distraught about the whole affair. Friends who had once banded together to form Project Scoresheet to create something for the common good were now yelling and screaming and threatening lawsuits. No wonder he was in such a foul mood while writing that last, acerbic *Baseball Abstract* essay that same winter, when he basically told the entire statistics community to stick it. Once a source of fun and intrigue, baseball stats had become a big, corrosive business.

And John Dewan, finally free of Project Scoresheet and running STATS Inc. untethered, would show everyone just how lucrative they could be.

A ll of this rancor took place well under the radar of baseball's power brokers, who had no idea that fans—whether they be Project Scoresheet volunteers or the Cramer-Dewan-James troika that spun off from them—

were beginning to take the keeping of statistics into their own hands. And if they did know, they certainly didn't care. As far as baseball was concerned, it had two official statistics houses, the Elias Sports Bureau in New York (National League) and the Sports Information Center outside Boston (American League). The numbers that those firms churned out after each season were the ones that became part of history, each set fitted upon those from the past, building story after story upon baseball's sacred, statistical monolith.

Problem was, that structure, now more than 100 years high and so impressive to so many, was still far more unsteady than most anyone realized. Some of its most famous cornerstones—Ty Cobb's record 4,191 career hits, Hack Wilson's 190 RBIs in 1930, and many more hallowed numbers—were anything but firm. Many of them were shifting from one figure to another almost annually, as tiny to titanic mistakes were being discovered left and right by fans, mostly from the Society of American Baseball Research. Soon enough, the push and pull of one hit there and one RBI there would leave the entire building swaying to and fro, no one knowing if the entire thing would soon come crashing down in a pile of digital dust.

8

All the Record Books Are Wrong

Pete Palmer knew a smoking gun when he smelled it. He was more than just a computer whiz, a New England engineer who spun the mainframe code for STATS Inc.'s first Edge 1.000 system. Palmer was also one of the Society of American Baseball Research's top historical statistics buffs—"statistorians," as they called themselves. He didn't just know the American League caught-stealing leaders for every year; he could tell you when that became an official statistic and why. He could recite how batting champions were determined all the way back to 1871, and give you the play-by-play of how Taffy Wright got jobbed in 1938. (Don't ask.) If the subject turned to the record for one-hitters in a season, he would either know the answer off the top of his head or, perhaps more important, know how to find it.

Palmer had an advantage his SABR pals could only dream of. By helping out at Sports Information Center, the Boston-area outfit that kept and computerized the American League's official statistics, Palmer gained access to not just current stats but the entire league microfilm archives. He dove into those numbers like Norm Peterson would a swimming pool of Budweiser. One of Palmer's first projects was to research something he had always wondered about: He went through Babe Ruth's game-by-game stats and separated them into games in and away from Yankee Stadium to determine just how much the park's short right-field porch helped him. Palmer then examined Joe DiMaggio in Yankee Stadium, Ted Williams in Fenway Park, and dozens more players, as far back as Ty Cobb and his 1910 Detroit Tigers. Then, one night while Palmer stared at his microfilm screen, something explosive began to stare right back.

Pete Palmer understood how to scan the skies for bombs—the guy did it every day. As a programmer for System Development Corporation, a military contractor he worked for through most of the 1970s, Palmer developed radar-intelligence software to monitor Soviet missile tests beyond the western edges of Alaska. But nothing captivated Palmer more than baseball statistics. He built linear-regression models to assess the run values of doubles and stolen bases. He moonlighted on his company mainframe to build a bustling database of historical numbers. And, out of simple curiosity, he figured out the statistics of old-time players in their home park and away. It was here that Palmer discovered something fishy with not just one little number, but Ty Cobb's career total of 4,191 hits— a number that had become a sacred entry in baseball's lexicon, and an all-time record that Pete Rose was starting to threaten. When the mainstream press learned what Palmer had discovered, headlines across the country began to ask: *Has Cobb's record been wrong all along?* The resulting crisis unmasked baseball's record book as nowhere near the all-knowing tome its reputation suggested, but fallible—and fractious.

The Rose affair started during one of Palmer's leisurely strolls through the microfilm, breaking down the home-and-away statistics of "Wahoo" Sam Crawford, a Hall of Fame Tigers outfielder in the early twentieth century. (Palmer spent night after night in his Lexington, Massachusetts, home on projects like this, sitting at a desk that actually was a wooden door laid atop two file cabinets.) When he worked on Crawford's September 1910 statistics, though, he noticed something rather odd. Crawford had been given two lines on September 25 when, in fact, the Tigers had played only one game that day. Very strange. But as Palmer scanned further, it became clear that whoever kept the statistics back then must have realized his goof (the game actually was played on the twenty-fourth) and added a line for that date at the bottom. But he never erased the old one! This mistake wasn't discovered until an auditor, well after the season ended, noticed double entries for every Tiger player and crossed out the extra ones. *Except for Ty Cobb.*

Palmer immediately knew what he had stumbled across. As seen earlier in this book, the 1910 American League batting race had been one of baseball's most embarrassing episodes prior to the 1919 Black Sox scandal; the St. Louis Browns played their infield deep to let Nap Lajoie bunt his way to an eight-for-nine final doubleheader in hopes he would beat out the unpopular Cobb for the title and prized Chalmers automobile. AL president Ban Johnson quickly figured the final statistics and announced that Cobb still finished with a higher average, .385 to .384, thereby sidestepping further controversy. But now, almost 70 years later, Palmer had unearthed a fascinating new wrinkle. Cobb had gone two-for-three in the game that was listed twice. When the off-season auditor crossed out the extra games for every Tiger, he surely knew that doing so for Cobb would have meant lowering his average from .385 to .382—two points behind Lajoie. There's no question that either the auditor kept his mouth shut, or was told to by Johnson.

Palmer wrote to friends at *The Sporting News*, who spent three years secretly checking every last detail of Cobb's career. In the end they confirmed not only Palmer's discovery but two more games from 1906, in which Cobb went 1-for-8, that the American League had simply overlooked the first time around. The magazine finally unveiled its scoop in an immense exposé in April 1981. Cobb did not deserve the 1910 batting crown, they announced. The career statistics that so many fans had memorized were wrong, too. Cobb's .367 lifetime average was now .366. He didn't have 4,191 hits, but 4,190. This wasn't merely trivia; because of these discoveries, the Pete Rose countdown had to be adjusted. Rose was not 634 hits from tying Cobb, but 633.

Bowie Kuhn was furious. As baseball's longtime commissioner, he was thrilled to have Rose, a modern and popular star, threatening the records of a legend like Cobb. Everyone knew Rose was chasing 4,191—monkeying with it now would only confuse the issue, and dilute the record's majesty. In lambasting the magazine for running the story, Kuhn announced: "The passage of seventy years, in our judgment, constitutes a certain statute of limitation as to recognizing any changes . . . The only way to make changes with confidence would be for a complete and thorough review of *all* team and individual statistics." (Emphasis added.) This was an extraordinary pronouncement. Kuhn himself had empowered a special Baseball Records Committee in 1975 to investigate questions such as these, and had only one year before green-lighted 21 corrections in the statistics of Hall of Famer Tris Speaker. Now, Kuhn was deciding that Cobb's numbers were too important to mess with. As far as baseball's official records were concerned, Cobb's total was 4,191 and would stay there—which indeed it did, up to and through the night in September 1985 when Rose passed it forevermore.

The truth was, by this time, baseball's historical statistics had been caught in such a tug-of-war between the SABR researchers who found

Bowie Kuhn. (*National Baseball Hall of Fame Library, Cooperstown, N.Y.*)

mistakes and baseball traditionalists who wanted to ignore them that all of baseball's records were beginning to get shockingly fuzzy. Rogers Hornsby, Walter Johnson, Cy Young, and other long-deceased legends gained doubles or lost wins every few years, to the point where no one knew the correct numbers or where to find them. Major League Baseball considered two different sources "official"—the Elias Sports Bureau and *The Baseball Encyclopedia*—but their accounts grew to agree about as often as the Hatfields and the McCoys. Most of the discrepancies flew under the radar of all but the most fervent stat freaks. The Rose episode, however, threw all of baseball's records into public question. As the leader of a sport that always sold its past as much as its present, Kuhn tried to make the matter just go away.

It wouldn't. By the early 1980s, the most ardent fans of baseball statistics had grown just as zealous about getting the statistics *right*. Whether Bowie Kuhn liked it or not.

Macmillan was a mess. The first edition of *The Baseball Encyclopedia*, hailed in 1969 as the greatest book of sports statistics ever compiled, had printed updated editions in 1974 and every few years after that, ascending to the status of icon. Players wanted to get into that book more than St. Peter's; upon reaching the major leagues, players would comment that finally, after all those bus rides in the minors, they'd be listed in *The Baseball Encyclopedia*. But despite Macmillan's growing majesty, behind the scenes, its foundation of accuracy was cracking worse every year.

David Neft was no longer in charge. The spiritual and organizational leader of the late-1960s effort to create the book, to sift through the mountains of play-by-play logs and conflicting box scores to create a new database, Neft had left Information Concepts to join Sports Illustrated Enterprises, where he devised a series of sports dice games. (The roots of the baseball version went all the way back to the playing-card game he invented in childhood summer camp.) Without Neft, Macmillan broke from ICI and hired a new editor for the book: a Major League Baseball flack named Joe Reichler. Reichler had once made a considerable name in journalism: As the Associated Press's top baseball writer for most of the 1950s and 1960s, he broke stories on Joe DiMaggio's retirement, the Dodgers' move to Los Angeles, and other scoops. Everyone in baseball knew Joe Reichler. He was so well connected that in 1966, commissioner Spike Eckert hired him as baseball's official press liaison, giving Reichler a comfy spot in the baseball hierarchy that he enjoyed the rest of his life.

Unfortunately, by the time Macmillan hired Reichler to edit the 1974 edition of *The Baseball Encyclopedia*, his journalistic instincts had been nudged aside by a desire to please his bosses at MLB, who had not been entirely thrilled with the first 1969 *TBE* when they left the Mamma Leone's party and actually leafed through it. Some of the game's most sacred numbers had been changed—by *outsiders*, no less. Ty Cobb's all-time career hit record had been bumped up from 4,191 to 4,192. Cap Anson, the first member of the 3,000-hit club, suddenly had just 2,995. It didn't matter that these alterations followed thousands of man-hours of research to correct errors from tiny to grievous in baseball's early, horrendous record-keeping. Never mind that ICI used sophisticated double-entry correction systems to make sure totals reconciled. One of baseball's top selling points was its statistics. Hall of Fame plaques literally cast players' numerical accomplishments in bronze, sanctifying the statistics for generations; those plaques couldn't have numbers that were *wrong*, for heaven's sake. Baseball was in the business of selling legends, not admitting mistakes. So what did Reichler do when he took charge of *The Baseball Encyclopedia*, and all its controversial numbers? *He changed them back.*

This on its own was a specious decision, one never explained, but only made worse by the slipshod manner in which Reichler went about reversing time. First, he adjusted totals just for star players, and then only when it meant *adding*, not subtracting. He gave back Hall of Famer Fred Clarke three hits and five points on his 1899 batting average, and made similar fixes for other top players. Heinie Zimmerman, a Cubs third baseman who lost his 1912 triple crown when ICI discovered three too many RBIs on his official sheets, found his triple-crown status summarily restored. Reichler's adjustments to Anson were downright laughable: The nineteenth-century star received 46 hits—all singles!—to put him back over 3,000, while getting just 20 at-bats, and not one run or RBI. Reichler simply boosted totals where he saw fit, and made matters even worse by not adjusting their teammates downward to compensate. The double-entry balancing of the first book was completely lost, scratched out one number at a time by Reichler and his pencil. This process continued with every successive *Baseball Encyclopedia* that came out under Reichler's reign. (He died in 1988.) The numbers fluctuated madly, with little or no justification, to the point where the statistics for dozens of stars—including Jack Chesbro, Rogers Hornsby, Walter Johnson, and Rube Waddell— changed at least five times in six editions.

Different record books cited such different numbers in the 1970s and 1980s that no one knew whom to believe anymore. A perfect example came in 1975, when Hank Aaron was chasing Babe Ruth's all-time RBI record. (He had passed Ruth's 714 home runs the year before.) Aaron opened the season with 2,202 RBIs, seven behind the Babe's 2,209—or so people thought. On May 4, three days after Aaron stroked a third-inning single for his eighth RBI and the record—presumably—the *New York Times* giggled, "How many runs batted in did Ruth have in his career? Nobody really knows . . . Depending on which record book you read or which official you talk to, Aaron either broke Ruth's major league RBI record last year, broke it Thursday, or will break it soon."

The writer wasn't kidding. *The Baseball Encyclopedia* listed Ruth at 2,217. *The Sporting News*, which published a popular and "official" record book, had him at 2,199. An unnamed source in the commissioner's office claimed it was 2,209 but couldn't explain why. And then, most amazingly, the Elias Sports Bureau's *Book of Baseball Records*, published by baseball's official statistics house, claimed that Ruth's mark *could never be known*, because RBIs were only Ernie Lanigan's personal tallies, and not official statistics, before the Elias brothers started counting them in 1920. "I had no alternative but to ignore Ruth's RBI before 1920," Seymour Siwoff explained, adopting an Elias-or-nothing smugness with which he would vex

researchers for decades. While all this was going on, Aaron kept on hitting and beat every Ruth career total there was. So it all became somewhat moot.

But not to everyone. The Society for American Baseball Research
was adding hundreds of members each year, surpassing 5,000 by the early
1980s, and no historical quandaries piqued them more than those involving questionable statistics. A growing subculture of fans and researchers
uncovered more and more mistakes in the record books every year and
strived to have them corrected. As the baseball establishment—Bowie
Kuhn, Joe Reichler, Seymour Siwoff—tried to ignore SABR's discoveries,
baseball's screwed-up statistics were becoming less and less of a secret,
confidence in their keepers eroding at every turn.

By the late 1980s, it became clear that the guts of *The Baseball Encyclopedia* had become tangled beyond repair; a new book would have to
take its place. Only a person who had built his own data archive, one un-
corrupted by politics, could start from a credible base. He would have to
be from within SABR, inclined to view its members as historians rather
than crackpots. He would have to respect the new statistics, such as Bill
James's runs created, and be open to incorporating them. He would have
to have a researcher's eye, a bookkeeper's bent, and a child's enthusiasm.

He would have to be Pete Palmer.

R emember the old Miller Lite beer ads? The ones where Boog Powell,
Billy Martin, and other retired beanbags would sit around a bar arguing "less filling" and "tastes great"? One of those spots, scripted in 1981,
was supposed to have a brainy trivia geek giving Powell and some other lug
a baseball quiz. Palmer got a call to try out for the ad, got a paid trip to
New York, and auditioned—right after Seymour Siwoff—but the Miller
folks changed their mind and went with three ballplayers instead. Too bad.
One, Palmer knew his stuff—he pointed out that one question about
Harvey Haddix's perfect game was actually wrong. (To which the ad guys
groaned, "We don't care.") Second, if anyone were born to play a nasally
baseball nerd on television, it was Pete Palmer.

Baseball was his lifelong love. Born in January 1938, Edgar Polle
Palmer Jr.—"Pete" was inevitable—tried to play on various youth teams
in Wellesley, Massachusetts, but was pretty much terrible, and resigned
himself to enjoying baseball from the outside. He collected Bowman bub-
ble gum cards and, with his obsession for completeness forming early,
filled every set from 1948 through 1952. He bought the new Turkin-

Thompson encyclopedia when he was 13 and decided that its listing of players alphabetically wasn't enough, so he manually pieced together every team's roster from 1900 onward. (The 1927 Yankees would have Lou Gehrig at first, Tony Lazzeri at second, and so on.) He typed these out in his parents' basement, on their Smith Corona, his electric trains sitting wholly ignored.

Young Pete liked statistics, and because Turkin-Thompson listed only games played, batting average for hitters, and won–lost record for pitchers, he collected all the *Who's Who in Baseball* books all the way back to 1912, and built an entire statistical archive on index cards. He made lists of every player with 200 hits in a season, 25 wins, and other groups. After going to Yale, graduating with an electrical engineering degree in 1960, and working for technology giants Raytheon and Sylvania, Palmer was still hooked on baseball statistics and ready to tackle some serious analysis. Using play-by-play data from the 1956–60 World Series and using no computers—just a slide rule, pencil, and paper—he constructed probability tables similar to those of Earnshaw Cook, Eldon Mills, and Harlan Mills, years before their books were published. And when he read those books, Palmer would write the authors 10-page harangues, critiquing their theories on an atomic level and suggesting tweaks throughout. After several years of such pestering correspondence, Cook finally wrote back to Palmer, "I regret that I just do not have the strength of character to argue all the details with you."

Palmer got his hands on his first computer in 1971 when he joined Mitre, a think tank that automated flight-formation and bombing strategies for the U.S. Air Force. That wasn't, however, the most exciting part of his job. "It was great," Palmer said, "because I had the use of this million-dollar mainframe that I could put all my stats on!" The Air Force used the computer during the day; at night, Palmer would load the database he had built from Turkin-Thompson, *Who's Who*, and other sources. He also moonlighted at the Sports Information Center, helping that outfit computerize the American League statistics.

With computers still young, this wasn't exactly a snap. Palmer would type box scores into a Digital Equipment microcomputer (what we now call a desktop) that would upload the data into a PDP-11 mainframe housed in a room down the hall. (The ventilation fans around that monster were so loud, workers pretended they were stadium fans cheering.) The mainframe would compile the statistics in the early morning after each night's games, but not without help from Palmer; he would have to swap out several 14-inch hard drives to keep the galoot running smoothly. Fifteen minutes later the mainframe would finally deign to spit out a long paper tape that would be read into a teletype machine and fed into another central computer. "Each of the teams could then call in each morning and get their stats off of the teletype," Palmer said, laughing. "That's what computers were in those days."

As if Palmer had much free time, whatever he could find was spent on his most solemn project: working on a grand, unifying theory of baseball. The equations he had fiddled around with in the 1960s were now blossoming into a comprehensive system. They incorporated not just batting, which was relatively straightforward to model by determining a run value for each offensive act (home run, caught stealing, and so on). Palmer also managed to translate pitching and fielding accomplishments into the common currency of runs, either saved or allowed. Pitchers' runs would derive from how their earned run averages deviated from the league norm. Fielders' runs came from comparing their total chances to other players at the same position. Every measure compensated for whether the player's home park was large or small. The entire system was called Linear Weights, but Palmer didn't share it with many people. It was his own toy, one he would play with into the Massachusetts night, his adult set of model trains.

Then he met John Thorn. A noted baseball author, Thorn had the opposite gift: to put into words what Palmer saw in numbers. He ran into Palmer while covering SABR's 1981 summer convention in Toronto for *The Sporting News* and was immediately taken by Palmer's fresh way of looking at the game. But the statistics bug had bitten Thorn long before. Growing up in New York City, Thorn learned at age five that he had a photographic memory when he found himself reciting off the top of his head entire backs of Topps baseball cards: all the players' batting averages, home runs, wins, and losses for every season. "It seemed normal to me," said Thorn. (He also had a Rain Man–type ability to count hundreds of matchsticks instantly, just by looking at them.) But then his incredible mind blew a fuse. Thorn suffered a stroke when he was just nineteen that cost him some personal memory, left him blind in one eye, and unable to drive. The stroke also forced him to walk with a cane for 18 years. He earned a master's degree in English literature but as his condition worsened (he still tripped over curbs so often, he arrived home bruised and bloody) that he gave up his dreams of being a big-time New York editor and figured he'd better focus on something he could do from a wheelchair in his home, writing. Luckily, in the mid-1970s his condition improved enough that he began to lead a reasonably normal book-writing life, including a fortuitous assignment from *The Sporting News*.

After meeting Palmer in Toronto, Thorn wanted to do a new baseball encyclopedia, one considerably different from Macmillan's Reichler-riddled mess. Palmer's database would soon be the most accurate around. He could expand it to include the new statistics, such as runs created and his own linear weights. And Thorn, who craved a literary aspect to the book as well, would handle the inclusion of scholarly articles to make the book a true encyclopedia. Thorn's proposal so wowed Simon & Schuster in 1982 that the publisher offered Thorn and Palmer $120,000 to do the book. The catch: The publisher wanted a finished manuscript in just nine months, so it could come out in time for the 1984 season. There was no way they could pull that off. So they turned down the huge advance, shelved the project, and wound up tackling something far more doable: A short history of baseball's statistical methods past and present, before the unfurling of Palmer's linear weights model. They called it *The Hidden Game of Baseball*.

Whereas Bill James's *Baseball Abstract* series was then at its height of giving fans oodles of new statistical gizmos, *The Hidden Game* was a more comprehensive manifesto, looking at all of baseball's traditional statistics and examining possible replacements. The previous decade had seen an explosion in new statistical widgets; James's were the most famous, but were by no means alone, thanks to SABR's growing community of weekend analysts. In 1972, Dick Cramer (the future STATS Inc. cofounder) and Palmer collaborated on an article in *The Baseball Research Journal* that introduced the Batters Run Average, obtained by multiplying players' on-base and slugging averages. In the same publication four years later, David Shoebotham discussed his Relative Batting Average, which rejiggered batting averages to reflect their distance from the *typical* batter; in 1979, Merritt Clifton expanded a similar method in his self-published book, *Relative Baseball*. Others invented ways to compensate for large or small ballparks. And around this same time, two different men—Barry Codell, a lecturer on religion and poetry for the Chicago Public Library, and Tom Boswell, a baseball reporter for the *Washington Post*—introduced virtually identical statistics, essentially dividing batters' bases earned (by hits, stolen bases, and so on) by outs. Codell actually came up with his Base-out Percentage first, while Boswell got the renown through self-celebratory articles on his

Total Average in *Inside Sports*. The resulting spat for credit became saber-metrics' version of Philo Farnsworth and David Sarnoff fighting over who invented television.

Thorn and Palmer's *The Hidden Game of Baseball* described every method and spent more than 100 pages explaining linear weights in a manner that could take root with the more general fan. It sold a very strong 33,000 copies, including one to a particularly influential reader. Adam Clymer was the assistant to the executive editor of the *New York Times*, in charge of the paper's polling operation; he picked up the book at a Manhattan store. He inhaled it like ambrosia. "I thought it made a hel-luva lot of sense," Clymer said recently. He had been a huge baseball fan all his life, particularly of statistics—as a kid growing up on the Upper West Side, he would devour newspapers' leader lists every Sunday. He eventually made statistical thought his profession as the *Times's* polling ed-itor, read Bill James's early *Abstracts*, and thought *The Hidden Game* could be brought to the masses.

Clymer convinced the *Times's* sports department to run two of the new statistics in a weekly "By the Numbers" box: on-base plus slugging percentage (OPS) and Palmer's Earned Runs Prevented. "Combining on-base and slugging was manageable—there was no multiplying, no square roots, and people could do it in their head," Clymer said. "I also thought it would give fans, most of whom loved statistics, something more to argue about." The feature ran for four years. While Bill James was still a some-what fringe phenomenon (his *Abstracts* became bestsellers among hard-core fans), *The Hidden Game* was being legitimized in the Paper of Record every week. Sabermetrics was getting its intellectual seal of approval.

Thorn and Palmer never tabled their encyclopedia idea, though. They spent most of the 1980s refining Palmer's database—the one he had begun as a kid on index cards. Most important, they gave safe home to the hundreds of statistical corrections that SABRites kept finding, and base-ball officials kept resisting.

For a sport that revels in record chases, baseball has always had an odd bent toward protecting its legends' accomplishments from the tram-plings of modern interlopers. When the American League joined the Na-tional as a major league in 1901, traditionalists carped that talent was being diluted, making it easier for players to break records. (Similar protests followed the abolition of the spitball 20 years later.) The most celebrated episode came in 1961, when Yankees sluggers Mickey Mantle and Roger Maris began to threaten Babe Ruth's standard of 60 home runs in a season. Because the schedule had been extended from 154 to 162 games that year, commissioner Ford Frick, Ruth's former biographer and friend, ruled that Mantle or Maris would have to break the record in the *first 154 games* to be considered the official record holder, to avoid having the record listed separately from the tried-and-true 154-game lists. (Two-thirds of baseball writers supported the decision, including the influential *Washington Post* columnist Shirley Povich, who called any 162-game rec-ords "artificial" and "synthetic.") Sure enough, Maris hit only 59 home runs through 154 games, ending the pursuit as far as Frick and Ruth's other embalmers were concerned. When Maris did hit number 61 against Boston on the last day of the season, just 23,154 fans came to Yankee Sta-dium to watch. The chase sapped of its drama, the game might as well have been an exhibition.

Baseball officials and fans eventually got over their willies regarding the 162-game schedule; essentially, the sport grew up. It also began to grudgingly accept that some of its statistics, even belonging to its stars, were flawed. Kuhn appointed his Official Records Committee in 1975 to weigh the merits of various findings and in fact supported some clarifica-tions. Babe Ruth's career RBI total of 2,209, the one that caused all the confusion when Aaron broke it—several times—was fixed to 2,211. (Cler-ical errors, such as miscarried ones, at the old Howe Baseball Bureau had left the Babe short by two.) Walter Johnson's 1913 ERA was officially changed from 1.09 to 1.14 after it was learned that the Big Train had made a brief relief appearance on the last day of the season that originally went unrecorded. But the thirteen-member committee tended to move only on the most glaring and incontrovertible mistakes. A few of its members— such as Seymour Siwoff of the Elias Sports Bureau and Cliff Kachline, the Hall of Fame's official historian—understood the issues, but others, mostly league public relations people and former players, had no clue. "Ralph Kiner didn't have the vaguest idea what statistics were about and how they were even compiled," recalled Kachline, the committee's chairman. When the Cobb and Rose career-hits matter came to the fore in 1981, the group shuddered at the idea of changing something that people actually cared about. "It frightened everybody on the committee," Kachline said. After Kuhn went nuts at *The Sporting News* and said he would ignore any changes to Cobb's record, MLB's Official Records Committee was useless. It never met again.

But SABR researchers kept on finding mistakes. Drawn by the scent of inaccuracy (and surely because baseball officials disapproved!) they dug deeper and deeper to find statistical screwups. These were people, mostly middle-aged men, who had regular jobs during the day—doctor, lawyer, even one furrier—but made these quests their hobby. Frank Williams, a Connecticut accountant, went back and looked at every American League game from 1901 to 1919 to confirm the winning and losing pitchers. Someone discovered that Dutch Leonard's 1914 ERA of 1.01, the lowest of all time, actually deserved to be 0.96, because he pitched two more innings and gave up one fewer earned run than previously believed. Other members uncovered one game in which the batting statistics for early-century stars Eddie Collins and Buck Weaver were switched by a shockingly inept American League office. They even found "phantom" players who never existed: Lou Proctor, who had a line in *The Baseball Encyclopedia* for having walked in one plate appearance for the 1912 St. Louis Browns, turned out to be a Western Union telegraph operator who apparently wanted some immortality and inserted his own name while transmitting a box score. From top players to the decidedly arcane (putouts and passed balls were considered as significant as home runs and wins), SABRites found hundreds upon hundreds of mistakes. But Major League Baseball had decided not to bother with any of it.

Thorn and Palmer did. In 1989, they published their long-awaited encyclopedia, *Total Baseball*. The 2,294-page anvil was a mammoth manifestation of how far baseball statistics had evolved over the past two decades: Old statistics were corrected, and new statistics celebrated. Ty Cobb had 4,190 hits, not 4,191. Dutch Leonard's ERA record was 0.96, not 1.01. Walter Johnson had 417 career wins, not 416. Cap Anson fell back out of the 3,000-hit club, with just 2,995. And poor Lou Proctor was no longer a major league player. ("There can be no statute of limitations on historical error," Thorn explained.) And just as the book looked backward with a keener eye, it looked forward to the world that baseball statistics was entering. The register portion of *Total Baseball* included for every player not just his regular statistics for every season, but the new sabermetric ones, as well. Bill James's runs created. Tom Boswell's total average. Even Wins Above Team, the pitcher rating Ted Oliver had invented in his little self-published book in 1944, got a column to itself, as did Palmer's linear weights and other measures that normalized for eras and ballpark size. Though some of its categories were downright bizarre— notoriously average second baseman Glenn Hubbard in 1985 scored the best season ever with 62 Fielding Runs—*Total Baseball* sold 75,000 copies. It was a resounding hit.

Though not with the Macmillan folks, of course. By this time *The Baseball Encyclopedia* was in the hands of Rick Wolff, a former minor league second baseman who had entered publishing and risen to take charge of the project. Wolff knew that despite robust sales *TBE's* credibility had drastically eroded. From the outside, he himself had wondered why, for example, Honus Wagner's lifetime batting average had risen from .327 in the book's first 1969 edition to .329 in 1988. "The guy was a good hitter, I know, but he was dead!" Wolff said. "Finally I got someone to figure out this mess and find out what was going on." All roads led back to Joe Reichler, the book's longtime editor who had died earlier that year. Wolff continued: "We wanted to know, 'Where did these changes come from? If Honus Wagner got 15 more hits, didn't someone else lose them?' But there were no handwritten records. Nothing existed to tell us what had happened. Reichler had added the things willy-nilly." Wolff decided that with *Total Baseball* having raised the bar on accuracy, the 1990 edition of *The Baseball Encyclopedia* would have to start over, revert to its original database, and adjust totals only where evidence called for it.

Jerome Holtzman went ballistic. The longtime voice of the *Chicago Tribune* and one of baseball's most respected baseball writers, Holtzman lambasted Macmillan, Wolff specifically, and SABR's "amateurs" for a long list of statistical crimes. They were "tampering with baseball's most sacred text." Wagner (whose hit total was trimmed from 3,430 to 3,418) and Nap Lajoie (3,251 to 3,244) were "the victims of a statistical grave robbery." Holtzman called it "a baseball Watergate." And he wasn't alone. Tom Barnidge of *The Sporting News* wrote, "There is no sport on this planet [which] treats its records with greater reverence than baseball . . . Macmillan violated the trust bestowed upon it when it unilaterally changed existing accepted statistics." And Seymour Siwoff, quoted in *Baseball America*, said, "It's a disgrace. The best thing to do is let the statute of limitations exist and let written records stay. How dare Rick Wolff and the amateurs he deals with arbitrarily change the records of Hall of Fame players?"

Never mind that Reichler had done this for years before anyone cared to notice. Suddenly, baseball writers all over the country were ripping into Macmillan for changing records that had bounced up and down for more than two decades. Cap Anson's hit total at various times had been 3,013 or 3,509 or 3,081 or 3,423 or 3,418 or 2,995 or 3,022 in all sorts of sources. (Including, that contentious spring of 1990, four different numbers in four different record books.) Honus Wagner's hits, Christy Mathewson's wins, and dozens of other listings had fluctuated with little explanation. But this time around Wolff faced such fire that he found himself squaring off with Holtzman over live radio on New York's rough-and-tumble WFAN:

> WOLFF: "You don't understand—no one knows WHY Honus Wagner's batting average went up from .327 to .329. It's probably wrong. We want it to be accurate."
> HOLTZMAN: "You don't understand. It's baseball history . . ."
> WOLFF: "Don't you want it to be accurate?"
> HOLTZMAN: "But who gives you the right to change these things?"
> WOLFF: "It's OUR book, Jerome!"

This public fiasco led Major League Baseball to stop endorsing *The Baseball Encyclopedia* as its "official" historical record. Not that MLB took its imprimatur very seriously—it simply sold it to Macmillan for about 20 grand per edition, cashed the check, and gave it little thought. But the secret was out. Baseball's records, so important and so revered, were hopelessly screwed up, and the average fan now knew it. Soon enough, MLB decided to endorse the fourth edition of *Total Baseball* as its official encyclopedia. It was the ultimate triumph of research over reverence, of the outsiders over the establishment.

Before the Macmillan debacle, before Pete Palmer's Cobb discovery, and before baseball's records mess had come to light, a letter arrived at the offices of *The Sporting News* in the fall of 1977. It came from a reader in Chicago named James Braswell, a student at Northwestern University who, out of curiosity, was researching the record for most consecutive games with a run batted in. The handwritten note read:

Gentlemen:

I believe if you check Hack Wilson's record from July 24 thru August 5, inclusive, of 1930, you will find Wilson knocked in at least one run in 11 consecutive games, and should be listed in your Baseball Record Book—along with Mel Ott—as the co-holder of this N.L. record.

TSN got these kinds of notes all the time, but this one begged some looking into. It just so happened that 1930 was the season in which Wilson had 190 RBIs, the well-known all-time record. Unless this Braswell guy was a wacko, he might have found something pretty darned important. Cliff Kachline, the historian at the Hall of Fame, looked at the NL's 1930 official sheets, kept by the old Elias Baseball Bureau, and found RBIs listed for only 10 of the 11 games. But the Associated Press box score did, indeed, show an RBI in that eleventh game, the nightcap of a July 28 doubleheader. Kachline checked the box scores and play-by-plays in four Chicago papers—the *Tribune*, *Herald-Examiner*, *Times*, and *Daily News*— and discovered that sure enough, in the third inning that afternoon, Wilson had singled home Kiki Cuyler from second base. But the RBI was somehow given to Charlie Grimm on Elias's official sheets. Kachline brought the matter before Bowie Kuhn's Official Records Committee that December. He was told, mostly by Seymour Siwoff, that every single one of Wilson's RBIs—those of *every* Cub, for that matter—would have to be checked before the 190 could be altered.

A SABR member with a particular interest in Hack Wilson decided to do just that. Bob Soderman, a former vice president of advertising for the Jim Beam Distilling Co., was so into this stuff that one year, just for the heck of it, he determined that one Tommy Thevenow held the major league record by going 3,347 consecutive at-bats without a home run. Soderman dove into the microfilm and prepared a 27-page package that documented every one of the 1930 Cubs' RBIs, game by game, with Wilson coming out at 191. But it was too late. By the time Soderman had finished, commissioner Bowie Kuhn had ruled on the Ty Cobb two-extra-hits issue, saying all historical records would stand forevermore, evidence or not. Kuhn's attitude eventually snuffed out the enthusiasm for checking into Wilson's record. "When the Kuhn administration ends," one *Sporting News* interoffice memo read, "perhaps we'll have better luck with a reorganized Records Committee."

Better luck took more than a decade. The Hack Wilson affair receded into the background until 1998, when at SABR's national convention, Kachline mentioned to some friends that Wilson probably had 191 RBIs, not 190. Their ears immediately perked up. Two nearby ears belonged to a writer from a small paper near Cooperstown, Oneonta's *Daily Star,* who wrote an article that July headlined WILSON'S LOST RBI HAS HISTORIANS BOTHERED. This caught the attention of the Associated Press, whose digest of the story got printed in papers around the country. After all, Juan Gonzalez of the Texas Rangers had 101 RBIs at the All-Star Game break that year and in a few months would possibly challenge Wilson's record, known to everyone as 190. And the 190 was wrong?

As baseball's coronated official statisticians, Siwoff and the Elias Sports Bureau were deluged with media phone calls wondering what was going on. Siwoff told SABR they would need to provide him with play-by-plays from every one of the Cubs' 156 games (two ended in ties) from that 1930 season. This they did—a dozen SABR members from all over the country, from California and Chicago to Delaware and St. Louis—banded together to resurrect Soderman's old research and supplement it beyond dispute. After a year of reviewing the evidence, Siwoff and Major League Baseball had no choice. On June 22, 1999, MLB issued a press release conceding that the researchers were right: The official major league record for RBIs in a season belonged to Hack Wilson not at 190, but *191.* "I am sensitive to the historical significance that accompanies the correction of such a prestigious record, especially after so many years have passed," commissioner Bud Selig sighed. "But it is important to get it right." After 25 years of fighting with baseball to be taken seriously, SABR's sensibilities, valuing fact over fiction and accuracy over myth, had won out.

All the record books became a little less wrong than they had been. Numbers—even the biggest ones—*could* be changed. The 25-year quest of Northwestern students, whiskey execs, and countless other zealots had proven that the hallowed Hall of Fame plaques hanging in Cooperstown were not sacredly all-knowing, but actually stood for two things: not just the players' greatness, but also baseball's old, sloppy record-keeping. The Hall now even admits it. Fans entering the Hall of Fame gallery to look at the plaques today are met with another bronzed tablet that cautions them about the numbers they'll soon read: "The data on all players," it coughs, "was taken from reliable sources at the time the plaques were made."

For all the work done by SABR researchers—hundreds of hours in library microfilm rooms to find one little box score that could solve a mystery—there was little money in it. They derived no financial benefit, and even the folks printing the record books were finding a tougher and tougher road. (Macmillan ceased printing *The Baseball Encyclopedia* in 1996, and the parent company of *Total Baseball* eventually went bankrupt.) Tending baseball's garden of historical statistics became far less business than hobby.

Current statistics, though, were always a vastly different matter. The numbers that players were accumulating *today*, in games every evening during the season, were becoming more valuable every year. *USA Today* came along in 1982 with the specific goal of tapping fans' desire for more statistics. A new phenomenon called Rotisserie League Baseball created huge markets for numbers, with thousands and ultimately millions of fans running to the box scores every morning, their emotions rising and falling with their players' RBIs and ERAs. When the 1990s arrived, the sweeping spread of the Internet allowed statistics—the instant players were putting them up—to be delivered almost intravenously to an audience that only clamored for more.

No outfit foresaw the financial potential of baseball statistics more than STATS Inc. and its new co-owner, John Dewan. He knew it from the moment he invested with Dick Cramer in 1985. To that point, baseball statistics had only enriched Dewan's life. They would soon make him *rich*, period, beyond his wildest dreams.

9

The Arms Dealer Goes to War

John Dewan couldn't believe his eyes. He knew he and his redefined company, STATS Inc., were keeping data that could change how people enjoyed and understood baseball. But he never imagined *this*. As he watched Danny Cox fall apart on the Candlestick Park pitcher's mound, the new world of STATS Inc. was coming together.

It was Game Four of the 1987 National League Championship Series, St. Louis versus San Francisco. One of the Cardinals' top starters, Cox was sailing along with a 2–1 lead entering the fifth. But NBC, which was broadcasting the game, knew something about Cox that no one else did, not even the pitcher himself. The network had hired STATS Inc., which for the first time in baseball history had kept detailed pitch-by-pitch records of every single major league game that season, to come up with some statistical tidbits that announcer Vin Scully could refer to as the game progressed. In sifting through it all, Dewan had found a doozy. So even when Cox appeared in control of Game Four, as he prepared to throw his 70th pitch with one out in the fifth, Scully narrated as this graphic went up on viewers' TV screens:

DANNY COX

Pitches 1–70: .268 batting average

Pitches 71+: .345 batting average

As if following a script, Cox immediately lost it. On pitch number 73, Kevin Mitchell lined a double. Jeffrey Leonard slammed Cox's next pitch to left for a home run to put the Giants ahead, 3–2. Cox then gave up two more sharp hits. He lost the game 4–2. "Boy, that 70-pitch mark that we talked about has really become prophetic!" Scully yelped, almost falling out of the booth. Cox couldn't have disintegrated any faster if Dewan had stuck pins in a voodoo doll.

This was the future of the new STATS Inc. The first version that programmer Dick Cramer and marketer Matt Levine had founded in 1981 failed four years later in large part because it was only a software and hardware company: Its sole product was the Apple II system with which clubs could keep their *own* statistics, and only a few progressive organizations— the A's, Yankees, and White Sox—ever bought it. STATS needed a complete change of focus. It had to become a *data* company, one that kept the statistics from every game, collated them quickly, and packaged them not just for teams (a limited market) but for media and other outlets (a practically unlimited one). It was all about the data. They had to have the data. And if anyone knew how to get that data, it was John Dewan.

Dewan's departure from Bill James's Project Scoresheet after the 1987 season, however acrimonious, at least led to some definition in the stat world: Project Scoresheet was keeping statistics for fun. STATS Inc. was doing it for money. The company bought four Digital Equipment Micro VAXes and built a modem network to link their own web of scorers, many lured away from Project Scoresheet, and forge a streamlined gathering and delivery system. "We had to be timely," Cramer recalled. "We had to do this stuff *overnight*." Soon enough, STATS Inc. would find so many markets for baseball statistics—media, video games, fans, and an emerging technology called the Internet—that it would make millions exactly that way.

Overnight.

Until the 1980s, the word *rotisserie* referred to a kitchen appliance popular with humans but less so with pigs and other animals: a slab of meat would be skewered and rotated over an open flame, broiling or barbecuing or otherwise making life very uncomfortable for the critter soon to be consumed. This drool-dripping culinary style was attractive enough for a restaurant in Manhattan, on East 52nd Street, to call itself La Rotisserie Française. In early 1980, the joint was so tasty that a group of Philadelphia Phillies fans would meet there once a week for lunch and talk baseball. One of them just happened to be Dan Okrent, who a few blocks away, at the *Sports Illustrated* offices, was furiously trying to get his profile of Bill James past the fact-checkers.

One day, Okrent came in with an idea he had sketched out on an airplane flight a few months before. Having spent much of his adult breath arguing with his buddies about the relative merits of Denny Doyle and Ross Grimsley, Okrent had come up with a game where they all would construct teams of their own, with pitchers and shortstops straight off major league rosters, and determine the end-of-season winner by adding up the players' real-life statistics. Okrent had already done this with his beloved Strat-O-Matic game, shuffling player cards into new teams whenever he wanted, but this was much better: Friends could root for their favorite players during actual games at night, and read the box scores every morning to see how their menagerie had done. It was the perfect antidote for the new era of free agency; as fans watched their favorite players waft around major league rosters like dandelion spores, now they controlled rosters as they saw fit. Okrent got several of his lunch friends to join up, recruited some others, and staged the first draft of players in April 1980. They named the circuit in honor of their old haunt: Rotisserie League.

Just like Jamesian statistical analysis and teams' use of computers, which were beginning to flourish at the same time, Rotisserie (a.k.a. fantasy) baseball was not entirely new; its roots stretched back for decades. New York tabloids had long run games in which readers would win prizes by predicting which major leaguers would score the most runs. Earl Weaver, while managing the Orioles, every day would square off against a local newspaperman, each choosing three players for that night's games and keeping score of their home runs. Okrent's game was far more intricate, but its direct ancestry dated back to 1960. That year, a Harvard University sociologist named William Gamson started something called the "Baseball Seminar," in which colleagues would have rosters of players who scored points based on their final standing in batting average, RBIs, wins, and ERA. Gamson later brought the league to the University of Michigan and some of its younger professors. (It became known as the Assistant Professors League or, depending on their state of employment, the Untenured Faculty League.) During the 1968–69 school year, one of those teachers, Bob Sklar, taught an American Studies seminar in which one student never forgot the weird baseball-stats game his professor played. That student was Dan Okrent.

Okrent had the old Michigan league in mind when he gathered nine friends to start his Rotisserie League Baseball Association. He made the rules delightfully realistic, instituting salaries for each player, a $250 cap on club payrolls, 22-man rosters, trades, free agency (naturally) and, of course, elaborate statistics.* Okrent chose eight measures—batting average, homers, RBIs, and steals for hitters; and wins, ERA, saves, and a base runners-allowed ratio (hits and walks per inning) for pitchers—because they were popular, important, and easily determined from the stat sections in most Sunday newspapers. The owners of the 10 teams met for a seven-hour draft on the season's first Sunday and auctioned off the players' rights onto squads like the Fleder Mice, the Sklar Gazers, and the Okrent Fenokees. Then the season began.

With most of Okrent's co-owners also connected in the New York media—Rob Fleder was an associate editor at *Esquire*, while Bruce McCall (the McCall Collects) was a freelance illustrator and writer for *Playboy* and *The New Yorker*—the disease flashed into epidemic. Within a month the *New York Times* ran a large feature on the Rotisserie League; a few weeks later some owners appeared on the *Today* show and then the *CBS Morning News*. Fans everywhere took notice. After Okrent wrote a long primer on how to play the game in the May 1981 issue of *Inside Sports* (entitled THE YEAR GEORGE FOSTER WASN'T WORTH $36), new leagues sprouted by the thousands in boardrooms and classrooms all over the country. Fans became more statistic-oriented than ever, scanning the morning box scores like stock listings, their moods determined as much by one as the other. Many wound up caring more about their fantasy team than the one for whom they used to root. "So what if the Yankees lost? *My shortstop went 5-2-3-2 with two steals!*"

Fantasy league baseball drove home how a .275-18-75 statline was good for a catcher but bad for a first baseman. It ripped the game from its regional moorings, encouraging fans to follow players from out-of-town markets. And at a time when real-life players and owners were staging strikes and lockouts, it gave fans a welcome sense of ownership and control, stoking their passion for baseball when it otherwise might have flickered out. By the late 1980s, 1-900 telephone services were giving advice on roster moves to panting owners for $2 a minute; dozens of stat-keeping services, with names like "Statman," "Bar-B-Que Stats," and "Walter Mitty Sports," served leagues that didn't have the time to crunch all the numbers themselves. Some dictionaries eventually added *Rotisserie league* to their pages; a lesser-known term, *Rotisserie rage*, came to define the fury fans felt when their players struggled or teams made controversial roster

---

*The $260 cap and 23-man roster that became popular came one year later.

moves. (The White Sox were once barraged by angry callers after putting slugger Frank Thomas on the disabled list for a minor injury.) Major leaguers felt Rotisserie players' indignation yelled directly from the stands: Ace pitcher David Cone once recalled, laughing: "One guy said, 'You're killing me! You walk too many guys, and strikeouts don't count in my league!'"

By 2003, according to the Fantasy Sports Trade Association, fifteen million adults were playing in some fantasy sports league, whether in baseball, football, basketball, even NASCAR auto racing. Some of those adults have run into Okrent and all but genuflected to him as their religion's founder. "People come up to me and interrupt my life to tell me about their fucking team, as if I could give a shit," said Okrent, clearly comfortable with his status. "There's nothing more interesting than your own Rotisserie team, and nothing less interesting than somebody else's. Once a guy followed me into a bathroom—I'm trying to take a dump, and he's outside the stall talking about the trade he made for Champ Summers or whoever. I feel like Robert Oppenheimer having invented the atomic bomb: If only I had known the horrible things I had unleashed on the world."

One outfit for which this was anything but horrible was STATS Inc., as it pursued markets for its statistics beyond major league front offices. At first, Dewan, a die-hard Strat-O-Matic man, bristled at the idea of catering to fantasy players, to him the great unwashed. "I just didn't think it was something for a professional company to be involved with," Dewan said with a chuckle. But before the 1988 season, a friend convinced him to try co-owning a team. Their closer, Oakland's Dennis Eckersley, came out of nowhere to save 45 games with a 2.35 ERA and won them the league title. Dewan was hooked. He got Bill James to design a game with more advanced statistics (like runs created, naturally) that attracted close to 1,000 players, forming an important revenue source for the company. And in a conscious effort to *not* be the Elias Sports Bureau and to make its statistics openly available, STATS allowed any fan with a computer and telephone to access updated player stats through an early online service for 25 cents a minute. At last, an intravenous stat drip.

STATS wasn't the only company catering to numbers freaks. *USA Today* began daily publication in September 1982 with an express raison d'être to print comprehensive sports statistics, especially baseball, and particularly in light of ever-growing Rotisserie masses needing to figure stats for their leagues. "It's an immediate hook to get people into the paper," sports editor Henry Freeman once said of USA Today's statistics section. "It is to the paper what the sun is to Miami." Page upon page of USA Today's broadsheets began being covered with the warm glow of player-by-player statistics. Full league leaders in dozens of categories were updated every day. And of course, there were the box scores. Nothing characterized USA Today like its short, just-the-facts stories, and nothing encapsulates facts more quickly and efficiently than a baseball box score.

Ever since Alexander Cartwright codified the first baseball rules in 1845, box scores invigorated fans as much as the morning coffee sipped over them. They have been compared to language, to music, to drugs, to sex . . . whatever a baseball fan considers vital must first compete with box scores for ultimate loyalty. Every era of baseball history has had its own form of box scores, shrink-wrapping the game into whichever statistical categories were valued at the time. Old Henry Chadwick spent most of Reconstruction arguing for sacrifices and stolen bases to be included in box scores; he died in his sleep no doubt dreaming of how to squeeze his beloved Runners Advanced in there, too.

Having been around for more than 150 years, old box scores testify to the game's slow evolution, fossils pressed into permanence by layer upon layer of change. Nothing has spoken louder than the stats considered important enough to be listed for every player in columns next to their names. The first box scores, owing to baseball's cricket roots, presented only players' outs and runs. Dozens of other experimentations followed through the nineteenth century—every newspaper seemed to have its own format—but through the first decades of the twentieth-century convention developed to where every player got five columns: at-bats and hits on offense, and putouts, assists, and errors on defense. (A paragraph below would list any extra-base hits, steals, and the like that had occurred, as well as pitchers' totals of hits allowed and strikeouts.) The devotion of three categories to defense but just two for offense, even as sluggers such as Babe Ruth and Hank Greenberg pounded into prominence and glove advances rarefied errors, shows how slowly box scores reacted to the changing game. And pitchers! Even as they emerged in the first half of the century as the most important single players on the field, their own IP-H-R-ER-BB-SO listings, which we now take for granted, did not become commonplace until 1958.

Around that same time, rising paper costs led newspaper editors to want a narrower box score. The Associated Press complied, trimming the columns down to four by trading the antiquated putouts, assists, and errors for a different pair of categories that reflected the modern game: runs and RBIs. (This snubbing of defensive stats naturally caused a firestorm among the traditionalists, with the ever-stodgy *Sporting News* calling it "a joke" and "absurd.") But this new AB-R-H-RBI box score stuck, and wound up weaning more than 30 years of fans. Subsequent changes were only minor: In 1964, not long after Roger Maris broke Babe Ruth's record with 61 home runs, players who went deep got their season homer totals listed in parentheses; in 1982, Rickey Henderson's 130 steals did the same for stolen bases. But as baseball metamorphosized after 1960—with expansion, the designated hitter, free agency, labor strife, and cable television—the box score remained staunchly stagnant.

USA Today wanted something different as it gained momentum in the late-1980s. (By then it had five million readers, more than any daily newspaper in the United States.) It approached the AP about expanding its box scores, but given how the wire service still collected its information by having stringers read it all over the phone—"Raines, 4, 1, 1, 0 . . ."—adding to that clunky process was out of the question. *USA Today* needed a more nimble, modern operation. It needed an outfit that was just as iconoclastic and wanted to make a splash. It needed STATS Inc.

STATS contracted with *USA Today* to replace the AP, and in 1990 the paper unfurled the most comprehensive face-lift that baseball's box scores had ever seen. The tight and taut ledgers suddenly went on steroids, bulking up to the delight of stat-crazed fans and Rotisserie players alike. The standard four columns for batters were boosted to eight, adding men left on base, walks, strikeouts, and—this was the biggest advance—the player's batting average updated through that game; no longer would fans have to wait until the Sunday leaders to see what players were hitting. (Pitchers' ERAs were kept current as well.) Speaking of hurlers, they also got a slew of new categories to analyze issues that the Bill James revolution was bringing to light. To monitor whether pitchers were overused, there was the number of pitches thrown; to gauge whether a sinkerballer was keeping the ball down, the number of groundballs and flyballs each gave up; and blown save opportunities. Some pitchers reputedly gave up more stolen bases than others? The STATS box score listed each steal and its victims. RBIs not enough for the clutch-hitting devotees? How about a listing of two-out RBIs? Middle relievers didn't get enough recognition? Dewan came up with a statistic called a Hold, marking when setup men protected a lead but didn't qualify for a save. "What a

thrill," recalled ESPN's Jayson Stark, then the national baseball writer for
the *Philadelphia Inquirer*. "Box scores always told stories, but they were
more like elementary school. Now we were getting novels. We went from
Spot and Jane to Tolstoy."

The new STATS/USA *Today* box score was overload for some, orgas-
mic for others. But it would only grow larger as STATS brainstormed new
categories to add. A perfect example: Dick Cramer was driving home in
St. Louis one night listening to the Cardinals game. Ozzie Smith hit a
ground ball that advanced a runner from second to third, to which announcer Mike Shannon reflexively commented, "You won't see that in
tomorrow's box score!" That's all Cramer needed to hear. "I can fix that!"
he said to himself, and soon he programmed the listing of Runners Advanced in every STATS box score, and in every *USA Today* across the
land.

Somewhere, Henry Chadwick was smiling.

STATS was picking off new clients left and right. Bill James, a minori-
ty investor, helped get a deal with *Sports Illustrated*. Video game leader
Electronic Arts bought STATS statistics for Earl Weaver Baseball, the
most realistic game on the market. ESPN began broadcasting Major
League Baseball in 1990, and as the newcomer to the baseball biz chose
STATS—over the Elias Sports Bureau—to provide hipper statistics for its
young audience. (So did *The National*, the daily sports newspaper unveiled
in 1990 by Frank Deford—who, 26 years before in *SI*, had introduced the
world to Earnshaw Cook.) The ultimate victory came in 1991: The
Associated Press, after a year of watching STATS humiliate their traditional, skinny box scores like weaklings on the beach, bagged their own
network and started buying their box scores from STATS.

A company awash in numbers soon had its biggest ones in the revenue column. In Dewan's first year with STATS in 1986, revenues from
Yankee and White Sox contracts amounted to about $50,000. Like the
transistors that kept squeezing onto their computers' silicon chips, that
figure soon doubled every year, to the point where STATS raked in $2
million in 1992. The next year, STATS ranked 144th on *Inc.* magazine's
list of America's fastest-growing privately held companies (the highest-
ranked sports firm on the list). Baseball statistics weren't just fun anymore. They were big business. "Everything was very intense," Cramer
said. "All of a sudden you realize, *This hobby I've been farting around with,
it's making money, for God's sake!*"

The company expanded its offices and hired more manpower, but nothing confirmed the arrival of STATS Inc. as a business more than the interest showed in it by Paul Allen. The billionaire cofounder of Microsoft had started another company, Starwave, that aimed to provide sports scores and statistics via a burgeoning network of personal computers connected all around the globe called the World Wide Web. Starwave recognized the attraction and strategic value of STATS's content, and in early 1994 invested about $800,000 in the company, in return for data and a Starwave seat on the board of directors. (Starwave's initial sports Web site, satchelsports.com, would later be bought by Disney and evolve into ESPN.com.) But Paul Allen's money did more for STATS than add to its bottom line. It allowed Dewan to tackle the one project he knew would shoot the company into orbit like nothing else: going live.

Through its entire first decade as a statistics provider, STATS had supplied its numbers just after games had ended—quicker than anyone had before, but only at the conclusion of the game. The Internet, though, was allowing a new method of information delivery: not soon, not quickly, but *instantly*, in "real time." How about box scores updated after each batter? Fantasy-team owners would salivate like Pavlovian dogs. How about a scoreboard of all 14 games at once, updated pitch-by-pitch? What fan

John Dewan. (*Copyright © 2004 Chicago Sun-Times*)

wouldn't want that? Dewan's mind was whirring faster than the computers that would make his visions come true. "This was just at the time that interactivity was starting," Dewan recalled. "We thought that people who would be interested in information after the game would be interested in information *during* the game. I envisioned a system where you could follow your team, get a box score for your players, as it's happening."

STATS made the bet of its life, a cool $1 million, before the 1994 baseball season started to upgrade its computers, databases, and communications network. It set up its network of stringers, who followed the games on television and radio while entering the plays into computers, to gather the play-by-play so efficiently that scores and statistics could be updated on computers in Chicago and broadcast immediately in real time, either through STATS directly or via an emerging phenomenon called America Online. STATS's promotional materials swooned: "You can catch every game as it happens around the country—pitch-by-pitch! It's your link to the most accurate, up-to-the-minute baseball information available. You can 'watch' any game in progress, or even ALL the games, via real-time game accounts."

Real-time statistics blew fans off their computer chairs. With the Internet just beginning to boom, particularly as a news source and particularly as a *sports* news source, statistics both archived and in real time became one of the Net's hottest commodities. STATS was positioned perfectly—tech-savvy, great data, superb packaging, a deft communications system—to outfit every new Web site (there were dozens) with the goods it needed to compete; STATS would just sit back and see who won. Dick Cramer joked that they weren't statisticians anymore. They were arms dealers in a war.

Not surprisingly, all this money flying around brought a war of its own inside the STATS offices. The company had become so powerful that Gannett, the parent company of *USA Today*, and Disney, which owned ESPN, began bidding to buy STATS outright. Disney came forward with a $7 million offer that Dewan was ready to accept, before it was trimmed to $4 million plus incentives. Allen's Starwave representative still wanted to take it, and ultimately recruited Dick Cramer in a surreptitious attempt to strong-arm John and Sue Dewan, who together owned a plurality of the company, into selling. The maneuver backfired, Dewan retained control, and after learning of Cramer's activities severed Cramer from all STATS business, even disengaging his computer password. "Everything I did, I did for the good of the company and its shareholders," Cramer said. "John didn't take it that way." Cramer was out. STATS's original cofounder, who had programmed the old Apple II's for the A's back in that first spring of 1981 and had helped run the company ever since, would contribute nothing to the operation again.

That dispute, though, was nothing compared to what STATS's real-time bonanza ultimately brought. In late 1995, STATS began providing Motorola with up-to-the-minute basketball data for a pager-like device called SportsTrax. The little gizmo, about the size of a cigarette lighter, used radio waves to display the real-time state of every NBA game every night: its score, player statistics, time remaining, and more. No longer would fans—at least those paying the $200 annual subscription fee— have to be connected to a television, radio, or computer to follow every game in the league. They could wear it on their hip.

STATS's own dial-up service and site on America Online displayed similar information. Everything seemed dandy before Dewan opened his mail one morning in February 1996 and found a letter from NBA attorneys:

> The NBA has learned that Stats, Inc. recently began to supply companies including America Online and Motorola, Inc. with minute-by-minute accounts and descriptions of NBA basketball games and constantly updating player statistics which these companies then resell to their subscribers or customers . . . All of these uses of NBA Properties' valuable intellectual property assets, none of which are authorized by the NBA constitute, *inter alia*, (i) infringement of the copyrights in NBA games and broadcasts, (ii) misappropriation of commercial property belonging to NBA Properties, (iii) unfair competition in violation of the U.S. Trademark Act . . . In view of the foregoing, the NBA hereby demands that Stats immediately cease and desist from further advertisement, distribution and sale of the NBA Programming . . .

If STATS wanted war, it had certainly found one: a fight that placed the future of the company, and sports news delivery in general, right in the crosshairs. The NBA contended that it, and only it, had the right to distribute statistics of games in real time. Motorola did not. America Online did not. And STATS was breaking the law by selling them the goods. That silly disclaimer fans had tuned out for decades during every game telecast—"The accounts and descriptions of this game shall not be disseminated without the express written consent . . ."—was about to step out of the shadows and become the crux of a dispute that would play out in federal court. What do sports leagues own? Do real-time scores and statistics violate broadcast licenses? Are sporting events news or entertainment? What portion of them are copyrightable, and which parts are fair game?

STATS Inc. suddenly found itself pitted against the most legally potent sports league in the world. The NBA filed for a permanent injunction to put a stop to STATS as quickly as possible. Dewan thought to himself: "They're gonna kill us."

As futuristic as "real-time scoreboards" sounded in the mid-1990s, baseball's version of them is so old, it predates television and even radio. Baseball and the telegraph grew up around the same time, and worked side-by-side as they matured.* Many ballparks featured a telegraph operator who would transmit scores and other information as the game progressed to newspapers for their afternoon editions that went to press around 3 P.M.; by the late 1880s, some of those papers, not wanting to wait for the presses to run, would put a large chalkboard outside their offices that displayed to passersby the score, current batter, count, base runners, and even direction of batted balls. One report from outside the New York *World* in 1888: "The spectators followed the [Giants] game with considerable satisfaction and almost as well as if actually present at the grounds. The excitement aroused by the contests attracted tremendous crowds to the neighborhood and necessitated the attendance of a squad of police to keep traffic from being blocked altogether." One scoreboard that introduced light bulbs to display the information became such a technological wonder that *Scientific American* profiled it, complete with diagrams of its electrical innards. As the scoreboards grew to up to 20 feet square, they attracted throngs of up to 10,000 fans for World Series games either outside newspaper offices or in armories and concert halls from Newark to Salt Lake City, with fans cheering for tallies and groaning for outs as everything went up on the scoreboard. And not just in the United States: In 1918, the YMCA arranged for news to be sent to Army infirmaries throughout Europe and Asia. One soldier told *Baseball Magazine*, "Being a bed patient in a ward at the hospital was the next best thing to having a seat in the bleachers."

*As a matter of fact, Theodore N. Vail, later the head of American Telephone & Telegraph and the visionary behind the United States' first coast-to-coast telephone system, had played ball for Iowa's Waterloo Empires in 1866, often against Marshalltown's Cap Anson.

Chicago fans jam-pack the Loop District to watch a mechanical scoreboard (above bridge) during Game 1 of the 1929 World Series. (*National Baseball Hall of Fame Library, Cooperstown, N.Y.*)

Radio entered baseball in 1921, and for a time, teams encouraged many stations to cover games, not just one. The Chicago Cubs were soon on five different stations in Chicago and countless others outside the city; broadcasters who couldn't be at Wrigley Field or the away park would interpret Western Union Morse code—"B2L" meant "ball two, low" for instance—and call the games as if they were there. (Ronald Reagan was one such announcer for WHO in Des Moines.) But many club operators banned radio from its ballparks, fearing that fans wouldn't bother coming anymore; the same concern stunted television when it arrived in the 1940s. Even Branch Rickey, one of the game's most progressive thinkers, believed broadcasting games into living rooms would cannibalize their audience. Television manufacturers such as RCA begged teams to allow broadcasts to bring the games to those who wouldn't experience them otherwise. "All the club sponsors had to come up with all sorts of charts and proofs that this would help them," remembered Bob Wolff, the Washington Senators' TV and radio voice from 1947 to 1960. "TV was getting people talking about the team." Club owners eventually warmed up to radio, then television, to the point where broadcasting became a vital revenue source; rights packages were auctioned to networks for millions of dollars, then billions. Leagues protected that lifeblood whenever possible—hence the disclaimer heard on every broadcast warning against any "use of the descriptions or accounts of these games"—to discourage outsiders from diluting their most valuable property.

That boilerplate became so widely known it developed an air of impregnability. Seymour Siwoff of the Elias Sports Bureau, who bowed to the leagues instinctually, so blanched at the idea of disseminating real-time scores and statistics that when he saw a STATS ad promoting its services, he sent the following fax to William Nix, NBA Properties' vice president of business affairs:

To: William Nix
From: Seymour Siwoff—Look at this!

How can they offer a service while a game is in progress?
Every sport has a disclaimer which states "Any rebroadcast or transmission is prohibited without express written consent etc."

At your convenience phone me.

Seymour

Then again, just because the league *says* you can't copy and disseminate information doesn't mean you can't. (Similarly, a sign in a parking garage that claims "Not responsible for damage" carries no legal weight whatsoever.) Only the courts determine what rights belong to whom. And the legal roots to the real-time issue stretched back as far as the telegraph.

The seminal case in this arena came in 1918 when, during World War I, the International News Service (INS) simply took news from Associated Press bulletins and disseminated it over their own wires. The Supreme Court created what became known as the "hot news" doctrine, which held that a news provider must have protection against freeloading, or misappropriation, by another. New York state courts thereafter built a philosophy loosely based on the INS case that gave event proprietors (i.e., professional sports leagues) property rights to the facts within their broadcasts, deeming the instant reselling of those facts "commercial immorality." (For example, in 1953 and 1954 a New York entrepreneur named Martin Fass listened to radio broadcasts of several teams' baseball games and instantly teletyped play-by-play data to other radio stations, who put the information on the air. The court ruled that his actions "jeopardized the value and marketability" of the teams' broadcasting rights.) Federal copyright law played little role in these affairs until 1976, when Congress' sweeping new Copyright Act strongly stated that facts are not copyrightable; it afforded copyright protection to the live broadcasts of events, such as the audio and video feeds, but *not to the events themselves*. The problem was, did the Copyright Act supercede all of New York's hot-news and misappropriation doctrines? Could enough scores and statistics, strung together in real time, constitute a taking of what sports leagues lawfully owned?

The NBA certainly thought so, particularly in the mid-1990s, when wireless pagers and the Internet made real-time data delivery not just futurism, but economic reality. The NBA maintained that it possessed the federal copyright to the games' goings-on—the scores, the statistics, and every other tidbit of information were the league's "original works of authorship" that it controlled exclusively. Up to that time the NBA, like other sports leagues, had restricted the in-game reporting of scores (by radio stations and wire services) to a fixed frequency, say three times per quarter; to learn more as the game was live, fans had to turn to the officially licensed radio and TV broadcasts. As the Internet made its push into the national consciousness in the mid-1990s, those broadcasts were

worth well into the billions. How did the NFL react to the real-time Internet issue? When the young Web site sportsline.com began disseminating up-to-the-minute football scores and statistics, the league got it to
stop by suing it within an inch of its life. As one NFL executive told the
Wall Street Journal: "This is part of the mad scramble to redefine intellectual property. Just as we control the rights for the game in television and
in radio, we intend to control the way the game appears on the Internet."

STATS decided to fight. The NBA filed its suit on March 5, 1996,
claiming that the actions of Motorola's SportsTrax service, and STATS's
supplying it with data, constituted "a flagrant taking of extremely valuable property rights belonging exclusively to the NBA parties." The
league sought a permanent injunction and, citing the immediacy of
harm, asked for and received expedited proceedings. The battle attracted
bigwigs on both sides. Major League Baseball and the other two major
sports leagues filed amicus briefs supporting the NBA. (Motorola had, in
fact, marketed a baseball version of SportsTrax as early as 1994, with little stick men denoting runners on base and electronic "charge!" music for
rallies. But MLB, not exactly on top of new media in the first place, had
enough legal headaches with its eight-month player strike and didn't
protest.) Meanwhile, media powerhouses such as America Online, the
New York Times, and the Associated Press supported STATS as it took on
the NBA's legion of lawyers.

STATS's main representative was a New York attorney named An-
drew Deutsch, a recognized expert in intellectual-property and copyright
law who had worked on several key cases that went as high as the Supreme
Court. He took an original approach to the 1976 federal copyright law by
claiming that it said "just as much about what you *could* copy as what you
couldn't." This didn't always find sympathetic audiences. "We're taught
early on, in second and third grade, that 'copying is bad,'" Deutsch said.
"Some people really take this to heart. These people grow up to be judges."

One of those judges was Loretta Preska. Fairly new to the federal
bench, Preska had a strong track record on First Amendment issues but
was somewhat miscast in hearing this case. A sarcastic sort already, Preska
gave strong clues after the trial opened on April 15 that she did not care
for or even understand sports, which became problematic in evaluating
what appealed to sports fans. (When she was given a SportsTrax to take
home and use during that night's basketball games, she chuckled, "My
kids thank you.") While she clearly sympathized with Deutsch's argument
that STATS's gathering information off of radio and TV had not violated

copyright law (the broadcasts' audio and video were copyrighted, but the facts contained in them were not); she was just as clearly a judge stuck in the grade-school mindset that copying in itself was inherently wrong. During the proceedings, Preska likened STATS's data-gatherers to the INS "flunkies" (her term) who stole from the AP bulletins back in 1918. She scowled impatiently when Deutsch claimed that games were actually news. Throughout the trial's four days, Deutsch became increasingly concerned that STATS was about to lose.

He was right. On July 19, Preska issued an injunction against STATS and Motorola, ruling that real-time data effectively constituted a simultaneous broadcast of the game, violating league rights. She did dismiss the NBA's copyright claim. But she strongly upheld the argument that the NBA's property had been taken unlawfully. "I find without hesitation," she wrote, "that [SportsTrax] crosses the boundary from mere media coverage of the NBA games into competing commercial misappropriation of these games." She held that in sufficient amounts, data equaled drama. "By disseminating to fans the changing scores and leads on a real-time basis . . . defendants have appropriated the essence of NBA's most valuable property—the excitement and entertainment of a game in progress." She evoked language straight out of the 1918 INS case: that the NBA should be able "to reap where it has sown." Ultimately, she devised a "partial preemption" doctrine of her own, claiming that while the federal Copyright Act rendered facts contained in game broadcasts up for grabs, that was partially overridden because the facts at issue here were created through the "skill, expenditure, and labor" of the NBA. Case closed.

STATS was in big trouble. John Dewan could feel the future of his company—real-time scores and statistics—being snatched away. Colleagues remember him getting withdrawn and paranoid, occasionally walking around the company's suburban Chicago offices "like a zombie," one staffer recalled. But his lawyer was less concerned. STATS was procedurally assured an automatic appeal, and Deutsch understood that the legal scaffolding on which Preska's decision rested was rickety at best. Deutsch called her partial-preemption approach "legally unsound, unworkable in practice, and unconstitutional," and wondered how Preska could have judged the root of games' excitement after never having experienced it herself. "The fact was that everybody in the courtroom, except the judge, understood what sports was about," Deutsch recalled. He immediately filed his appeal to the Second Circuit.

Appeals to federal circuit courts are heard not by one judge but by a three-judge panel, and STATS was encouraged that three older men, probably with a greater understanding of sports than Preska had, would hear the case. They were still far from a slam dunk. Making matters more complicated, one of the judges was Ellsworth Van Graafeiland, a bizarre, 81-year-old lifer who presented a unique challenge to counsel. "Frankly, he is a cranky old man many times," one New York attorney said, requesting anonymity because Van Graafeiland is still a sitting judge. "I've seen him where, if he doesn't like something that a lawyer says to him, he will turn his hearing aid off and turn his chair around during the balance of the argument. All you see is the back of his chair."

Deutsch navigated this obstacle course deftly when the appeal was heard on October 21. He argued that Preska's partial-preemption approach relied far too heavily on the old INS case, which should be seen as a "reporters and wire service protection act" only, every other interpretation of it superceded by the 1976 federal copyright law. "Facts are available for copying once they are published," he told the court. "States can't take this public-domain information and return it to the status of private property." In effect, scores and statistics were *news*—moreover, news gathered by STATS's own stringers at the company's own expense.

During his turn at the podium, NBA lawyer Jeffrey Mishkin played the "reap where we have sown" card to which Preska had been agreeable. "We spent last year about $700 million just on players' salaries and benefits in order to get the players to 'create' these 'facts' the defendants want to take without any contribution to the presentation of NBA games," he said. "*That's* the evil here." But he soon discovered during the open debate of circuit court proceedings, particularly with the cantankerous Van Graafeiland, that these judges were far less open to his approach than the last one was.

> MISHKIN: "It depends on how much they're repeating, Your Honor . . . what they're doing is, they're making a systematic, continuous transmission of every single NBA game from start to finish."
> VAN GRAAFEILAND: "All they're doing is repeating facts."
> MISHKIN: "Yes Your Honor, but . . ."
> VAN GRAAFEILAND: "No matter how often you say that, that's all they're doing."

MISHKIN: "Yes, but they're taking enough of those facts that what they're doing is appropriating the entertainment or the economic value . . ."

VAN GRAAFEILAND: "No, no. All they're doing is repeating facts."

VAN GRAAFEILAND: "Suppose I had listened to the radio, and I hear the score of some NBA game and my next-door neighbor says, 'How's the game going?' and I say, 'Well, I just heard that New York is losing as usual by 50 to 49.' Would that be a violation of your rights?"

MISHKIN: "No of course not, Your Honor."

VAN GRAAFEILAND: "Well, why not? What's the difference?"

VAN GRAAFEILAND: "They're not taking anything, counsel—all they're repeating are facts that are present, public knowledge."

MISHKIN: "But we have created those facts."

VAN GRAAFEILAND: "Are they public knowledge, or are they not public knowledge? Once they are broadcast over the radio and television, are they not public knowledge?"

MISHKIN: "They are public knowledge, Your Honor, and what the Supreme Court said in the INS case is . . ."

VAN GRAAFEILAND: "I don't care what the Supreme Court said."

The courtroom burst out in laughter at that one, but Deutsch smiled silently, knowing that old Judge Van Graafeiland had indeed kept his hearing aid on and heard STATS's arguments loud and clear. But there still were no guarantees (particularly with an eccentric like Van Graafeiland). A loss at the circuit level would be far more devastating than the first; if the U.S. Supreme Court didn't find grounds for another appeal, a distinct likelihood, any decision against STATS would be final and binding, killing its real-time operation for good. Deutsch, Dewan, and all of STATS Inc. endured a long winter of waiting for a decision. Then, on January 30, 1997, Deutsch was about to step into a partners' meeting when an associate stopped him and said, "You have a call from the Second Circuit."

Deutsch got on the phone and was told by a clerk, "They reversed in part and confirmed in part."

What the hell does that mean? Deutsch yelped.

It meant that STATS had won. The Circuit Court confirmed the original decision holding that no copyright laws had been broken, and reversed—strongly—the holding that STATS had taken NBA property by broadcasting scores and statistics. The NBA was not a news-gathering service on which STATS was free riding, and therefore did not warrant INS-type protection. And while the video and audio broadcasts of sports events are protected under copyright law, the facts contained in them are not. "We hold that Motorola and STATS have not unlawfully misappropriated NBA's property by transmitting 'real-time' NBA game scores and statistics taken from television and radio broadcasts of games in progress," the decision read. "We therefore reverse on the misappropriation claim and vacate the injunction."

Deutsch called Dewan in Chicago and told him the news. Dewan fought back tears of relief, and afterward walked out into the large, open data-collection room of the STATS offices to tell his dozens of staffers. "We won," he said, to a whooping round of hollering, applause, and high fives. They sent out for champagne and toasted the future.

The celebration didn't last long, though. There were 12 NBA and NHL games scheduled for that night. They all had score changes, statistics, box scores, and more that needed to be processed in real time; all those numbers bouncing off satellites and through phone lines to fans around the world.

Legally.

STATS's triumph over the NBA burst open the next frontier. The real-time landscape was clear for providers to devise all sorts of new ways for sports fans to keep up with scores and statistics: over the Internet, on their wireless handheld PDAs, through their cellphones. Baseball games began being covered in a level of detail once thought unimaginable. Web sites recorded not just every at-bat but presented where each pitch crossed the strike zone, and exactly where on the diamond each batted ball was hit. Statistics for every situation were available instantly. Having wrested the numbers from the grabby hands of the leagues, STATS's victory became one for the fans as well.

It also confirmed STATS Inc. as the major player in the burgeoning real-time statistics business, and made the company more valuable than ever. Dewan had always resisted intermittent offers to purchase the firm (like to Disney in 1995) but they now came so often, and at such dizzyingly high amounts, that he had to consider them seriously. "Our goal was never to worry about the money and to try to make the company successful," he said of STATS, which grew to 70 employees. "But then the money became everything." That can happen when three companies are bidding against themselves to purchase you. Rupert Murdoch's News Corporation (whose Fox broadcasting network was MLB's over-the-air rights-holder), Broadband Sports (a portal intent on becoming sports' next big thing), and Total Sports (the multimedia parent of John Thorn's and Pete Palmer's *Total Baseball* encyclopedia) all put in bids during 1999, with News Corp. and Broadband pulling ahead in November.

Broadband offered $53 million in stock, which Dewan didn't trust, anticipating the eventual tech crash. He called James Murdoch, Rupert's son, who was handling this transaction, and said, "If you can pay us in cash not much less than 53, we've got a deal." Two days later, Murdoch phoned back with an offer of $45 million, cash. Dewan took it. The man who had resurrected STATS Inc. with Dick Cramer back in 1985, navigated a nasty break from the Project Scoresheet volunteers in 1987, spent the early days operating STATS out of the bedroom of his home, pioneered Internet delivery of real-time box scores and statistics, and successfully beat back the NBA a decade later, was suddenly worth upwards of $20 million. "It was incredible," Dewan recalled. "It was at the top of the market. It was the perfect timing for that sort of thing."

Dewan remained as CEO of the reorganized STATS but, no longer in ultimate charge of the operation, soon resigned to pursue other interests, specifically Christian book publishing. But he didn't last long away from baseball statistics. Missing what he had always known to be his life's calling, Dewan made some overtures to buy back STATS Inc.'s publishing division from News Corp., which had quickly realized it had drastically overpaid, given the almost immediate Nasdaq avalanche. Repurchase talks never got far, though, so Dewan instead looked elsewhere. In 2002, he became the prime financial backer of a Pennsylvania startup named Baseball Info Solutions, which is basically a modern equivalent of what STATS Inc. was almost 20 years ago, recording play-by-play, crunching numbers, and thinking of new ways to package them to teams and media outlets. "The most fun time of my life was the early days of STATS, when we were a smaller company just trying to make it," Dewan said from his Chicago home. "It's funny. I guess deep down I'm still Bowie Dewan, keeping statistics for Strat-O-Matic."

This inner child, the one who scratches out and plays with baseball statistics just for the fun of it, has existed in every man who has ever made his living in the field: Al Munro Elias, Seymour Siwoff, John Dewan.

Writers such as Ernie Lanigan, F. C. Lane, and Bill James turned their adolescent hobbies into long, legitimate careers. But this fascination with baseball stats has always been shared by thousands more who never make a dime, many of them notable academics, for whom tinkering with all these numbers remains a simple quest—an intellectual call to devise the ultimate statistic, to write the perfect simulation program, to solve the mystery of clutch hitting. And beat their fellow Nobel Prize winners to the answer.

10

Luck and Where to Find It

C arl Morris really does have better things to do. He is a Harvard University professor, former chairman of the Statistics Department, and one of the nation's experts in the quantitative analysis of health care policy. His papers have appeared in more than a dozen scholarly journals over some 35 years. Late at night, when his Cambridge neighbors are asleep, Professor Morris's light remains on as he pores over numbers, graphs, and mind-bending formulas. But the scribblings on his legal pads are not cost-benefit studies of various universal health care proposals. They are not hospital patient-recovery ratios. They are baseball statistics.

Oh, the unfulfilled dreams of youth. While growing up in San Diego in the 1950s, Carl Morris so adored baseball and its numbers (he was drawn to the Boston Red Sox by their high Fenway Park batting averages) that while his friends longed to be the next James Dean, he plotted to be the next Allan Roth. Baseball statistician not being the safest career route, though, he eventually migrated to aeronautical engineering and then formal mathematics, which led to professorships at the University of Texas and then Harvard. But he continued to view his world of formal statistics, its Markov chains and Gaussian distributions, through the eyes of a baseball fan, and used these new tools to probe mysteries of his favorite sport. Do slumps and streaks evidence anything about a batter's talent, or are they just the residues of randomness? (Binomial theory is tailor-made for that.) Was Ty Cobb ever a *true* .400 hitter? (Trot in Bayesian analysis from the bullpen, and you can find out.) The list went on. Morris loved x-raying baseball's numbers in ways only a statistician could, but as a grown man always felt a little embarrassed about it, like it

Carl Morris. (*Jim Harrison*)

was some childish affinity for Ring Dings. "I don't go out of my way to advertise my baseball work," he said with a laugh, "for fear people will have
nothing to do with me as an academic."

The thing is, more of Morris's academic colleagues, at Harvard and at
universities around the world, have liked Ring Dings than you'd ever believe. Even Nobel laureates have whiled away their free time banging on
baseball statistics, contributing some of the field's most significant and
useful work. In 1972, two members of the Stanford University statistics
department, working under a National Science Foundation grant, used
sophisticated Markov analysis to devise a new batting statistic called Offensive Earned Run Average. The growth of free agency prompted Dr.
Thomas H. Athey, the chairman of the Information Systems Department
at California State Polytechnic University, Pomona, to examine how a
team's winning percentage varied with its payroll, for the *Journal of Systems Management*. And if Morris ever feared that Hahvahd considered

itself above this sort of thing, all he had to do was look around campus, where several of Cambridge's most prestigious faculty played in the sandbox of baseball statistics. Stephen Jay Gould, one of the nation's preeminent paleontologists and the author of two dozen books on ontogeny, phylogeny, and several other ogenys that no one had ever heard of, spent years investigating whether his theories of evolution applied to batting averages. And Ed Purcell, who won the 1952 Nobel Prize in physics for his work on the magnetism of atomic nuclei, was himself viscerally drawn to the mystery of hitters' slumps and streaks. Said one of Purcell's Harvard collaborators, Dudley Herschbach, "We may be pointy heads, but we're also human." When Herschbach won his own Nobel, in 1986, he wore a Red Sox cap to the press conference.

Scientists see things in baseball statistics the way astronomers do in the deep, night sky: connections, evolution, meaning. They use their telescopes of equations and theories to explore which statistic—home runs, on-base percentage, or some gadget of their own devising—might share an orbit with runs and wins. And they wonder if various constellations of statistics, so jumbled to the untrained eye, could be found to have some grander order. Ed Purcell, who died in 1997, was one of these. "My father was always working on baseball stuff—it was his hobby, because of the dreaminess of the statistics he encountered there," said Purcell's son, Dennis. "Baseball was his laboratory. It was a lab where an experiment was going on all summer long at Fenway Park." Of all the experiments Purcell conducted in that lab, none captivated him more than those involving perhaps statistics' greatest mystery: luck.

Luck—the dispassionate governance of randomness—has always been one of baseball's most underappreciated concepts. The weight and meaning given to the game's feats are, of course, astronomical: Joe DiMaggio's 56-game hitting streak, Reggie Jackson's three home runs in a World Series game, Ted Williams's .406 batting average . . . each strengthens the fans' belief that the most special players can virtually *will* their way to these accomplishments, digging deep within themselves to summon one more amazing performance. (Or, in the tragically opposite worlds of the Red Sox and Cubs, crush their fans' hopes every season.) But academia's brightest minds could sense that something else might be at work here—something, no matter what the press and public thought, beyond the control of athletes playing a game. Scientists suspected that all of baseball's hitters and pitchers and base runners might actually be connected by tiny, invisible strings to a far greater power that controlled them high up from the rafters, a force from above that the players and managers were in no position to see.

These scientists and professional statisticians didn't just wonder—they had the tools to truly explore. And what they discovered is that luck plays far more of a role in baseball than anyone before had cared to understand or admit. Hitters used to hitting .300 didn't hit .182 in May and .416 in July because of a new stance or extra batting practice or "seeing the ball well," but because of the pure, inescapable vagaries of chance. How did a nondescript pitcher for the 1953 St. Louis Browns, Bobo Holloman, throw a no-hitter in his first major league start but flame out soon thereafter? Because if enough nondescript pitchers break into the big leagues—and let's face it, we've all seen too many of those—one of them is going to debut with a no-hitter sooner or later. Other examples abound, all of them testifying to how if you wait long enough in baseball, if you roll the Strat-O-Matic dice or spin the All-Star Baseball spinner enough times, they will create for us our legends.

While also modeling nuclear fusion and tracing the development of life on earth (meaningless little tasks like that), these scientists made distilling luck from baseball statistics one of their most passionate quests. Their discoveries about the ubiquity and power of chance in baseball are routinely met with a mixture of horror and disbelief, not unlike when Darwin's theories were first explained to the British aristocracy. ("Descended from apes!" one woman shuddered. "Let us hope it is not true, but if it is, let us pray that it will not become generally known.") Baseball fans felt the same way when pointy-headed brainiacs—guys who might know why a curveball curves but couldn't hit one to save their lives—used the statistics that baseball holds so dear to dispel the some of the game's most cherished truths.

Lineup order? Inconsequential. Batters' hot and cold streaks? Misunderstood and meaningless. And don't get these guys started on clutch hitting, the greatest myth of all. So much of baseball comes down to randomness, and these scientists followed its statistical footprints to find the wizard and pull the curtain on him. Said Ed Purcell's son: "My father was always suspicious of humans' excess tendency to form patterns where they did not exist. Baseball was a good way to attack that problem. Besides, it was fun!"

It isn't surprising that the formal understanding of luck, of defining what it is and detecting where it lies, came late to baseball. It did to the rest of the world, too.

Civilizations as far back as ancient Egypt were intrigued by the capriciousness of chance. The Egyptians played with a precursor to dice, a vaguely cubic animal bone called an astragalus, but believed that their randomness was controlled by a deity; the astragali were windows into God's will, used merely to eliminate the possibility of human interference. The church similarly controlled most of the thinking in this area through the Dark and Middle Ages. Those who tried to wrest randomness from religion were deemed witches and sorcerers, labels not much worse than those slapped on sabermetricians today.

The sweeping scientific curiosity of the Renaissance allowed Galileo to investigate gambling, particularly six-sided dice. A more formal logic and language of probability—throwing a one with a conventional die has an underlying chance of 1 in 6, so throwing a snake eyes is 1 in 36, and so on—soon followed with Frenchmen Pierre de Fermat and Blaise Pascal around 1650, allowing for more informed inquiries into what owed itself to luck and what did not. (If a pair of dice came up snake eyes once in three total throws, this was nothing remarkable; if they came up that way 10 times in 30 throws, flying squarely in the face of their underlying probability, there was almost certainly something else at work, like the dice being fixed.) By the early 1700s, French mathematician Abraham de Moivre was able to make this pronouncement, blasphemy a century before but a guiding light for thinkers after him: "We may imagine Chance and Design to be as it were in Competition with each other for the production of some sorts of Events . . . We may learn in many Cases how to distinguish the Events which are the effect of Chance, from those which are produced by Design." It took until the twentieth century for an entire discipline by which one could investigate what was luck and what was not—formal statistics—to fully develop, arming its practitioners with confidence intervals, r-squareds, and other mathematical stethoscopes.

It was only a matter of time before statisticians and other scientists, taking a break from more serious work, applied these instruments to baseball's stacks of numbers and listened to what was going on deep inside. And what they have invariably found, after examining all the box scores, batting averages, and play-by-play logs, is that in baseball, randomness rules—whether we choose to believe it or not. Home run heroes and strikeout goats have been cast, generation after generation, often due to nothing more than the serendipity of their spinner. This unavoidable conclusion, a somewhat disappointed Stephen Jay Gould once wrote, "is easily and swiftly summarized. Nothing ever happened in baseball above and beyond the frequency predicted by coin-tossing models."

For the 95 percent of readers no doubt allergic to probability: Coin-tossing sounds frivolous, but is actually quite powerful and an easy-to-grasp pillar of formal statistics. The deeper theory and equations will be skipped here to avoid any epileptic fits, but the simple fact is that while everyone knows a nickel has a half-and-half chance of falling heads or tails, flip one a hundred times and you're liable to see everything: some alternating heads and tails, some tails in groups of threes followed by heads in fours, and sometimes even six heads or seven tails in a row. You can't predict where they will appear, but long runs *will* almost certainly be there, begging for some explanation yet truly having none at all. The application to baseball comes in how, just as the nickel has a 50 percent chance of landing heads, a batter also can be seen as having a constant, inherent chance of getting a hit, say 27 percent (owing to a batting average of .270). Assuming this figure stays fixed for every game, year, and season can be unrealistic, but it still allows statisticians to investigate questions like: How often will that .270 hitter over a two-week span bat under .200 (a slump) or above .400 (a streak) simply out of randomness? Do no-hitters (every batter going 0-for-3 or 0-for-4 in one day) happen as often as they should? And what are the chances that a .300 hitter will get "hot" and rap out at least one hit in 20, 30, or 56 consecutive games?

Sure enough, it was that last number, 56—the legendary length of Joe DiMaggio's hitting streak—that captured the boyish fascination of Gould and Purcell, two of Harvard's most prestigious faculty. Gould had grown up playing stickball on the streets of Queens, a breathless DiMaggio fan, dreaming of someday inheriting center field from the Yankee Clipper. (Alas, Mickey Mantle stole the job from under him.) Purcell was born in Illinois and became a Boston Braves fan upon arriving at Harvard as an instructor in 1938; he also came to love the Red Sox after discovering that he and Ted Williams were born on the exact same day. Gould and Purcell became fast friends as Harvard professors through the 1970s and 1980s, frequenting Fenway Park and discussing the science of baseball as often as physics or evolution. Recalled Herschbach, who often joined them, "We all loved talking about baseball statistics. People of science have the urge to recognize in them some underlying complexities, in hope of finding an ultimate solution." The ultimate solution they arrived at was shocking.

Stephen Jay Gould and Ed Purcell. (© *President and Fellows of Harvard College*)

Gould wrote several articles on this, and while never publishing the calculations (a relief to current readers, no doubt), claimed that almost every one of the statistical records that baseball held dear—a .424 season batting average (by Rogers Hornsby), two consecutive no-hitters (Johnny Vander Meer), three home runs in a World Series game (Babe Ruth and Reggie Jackson), and so many others—could be explained by randomness alone. The fact that they were accomplished by Hornsby, Vander Meer, Ruth, and Jackson *specifically* was obviously notable. But *someone* doing these things was bound to happen sometime, given the 11 million batter-pitcher confrontations in more than 150,000 games since the major leagues began. They were natural by-products of the process, nothing to get so surprised at if you watch the proceedings from above. (Similarly, when a woman wins the Pick 6 lotto, she wonders how she got so lucky; the lottery commission, meanwhile, doesn't bat an eye.)

Even though 28 real-life Hornsbys had gotten hot enough to bat .400 over a season, and 16 Don Larsens were unhittable enough on one given day to pitch perfect games, those totals were so close to what simple chance prescribed that Gould had little choice but to decide, contrary to our view of sport as unscripted, that they were effectively predestined to occur. "We believe in 'hot hands' because we must impart meaning to a pattern—and we like meanings that tell stories about heroism, valor, and excellence," Gould wrote. But most of what baseball revered was the result not of valiance, but *variance*. There was only one, single feat that

Gould and Purcell found to be outside the realm of happenstance, one record that was too freakish to be explained away by chance: DiMaggio's 56-game hitting streak, which he extended a full eight to ten games longer than chance should have taken him. "Joe DiMaggio," Gould reported, "beat the hardest taskmaster of all, a woman who makes Nolan Ryan's fastball look like a cantaloupe in slow motion: Lady Luck."

Just as Earth seems flat to a human but is clearly round to an astronaut, luck is commonly misperceived by those in direct contact with it: the players and managers whose livelihoods depend on where the millions of spinners come to rest. Hitters, for example, roll their dice four or five times every night, the results easily varying from 0-for-5 with three strikeouts, after which the press asks them what went wrong, to two homers and a double, after which they're hailed as a hero. This is one of baseball's great ironies: Games are played every day, with explanations for everything sought after every one, when most of the time the primary explanation is luck. And we wonder why baseball players are superstitious; Trevor Hoffman, the star reliever for the San Diego Padres, doesn't wash his socks during a streak of successful saves. Red Sox slugger Nomar Garciaparra always places his glove in the same spot in the dugout between innings. These players, and countless others, are grasping for some (however silly) feeling of control over their destiny. They need something to grab onto during luck's roller-coaster ride. The media also flail around for rationales, citing extra batting practice or a tinkered-with pitching motion, because attributing the game-winning hit or strikeout to randomness day after day don't exactly sell newspapers. "You try not to take it too seriously," said Yankees pitcher Mike Mussina, "but it isn't easy."

Luck's ubiquity shapes the culture of baseball in how its players, particularly compared to athletes in other sports, show strikingly little emotion. They cannot get as worked up about the game's ups and downs as do the fans and press; there are so many trials, so many coin flips, that overreaction to either good or bad luck would quickly drive them insane. Players who strike out walk back to the dugout stoically. Home run hitters often round the bases with their heads down, their celebrations limited to a few high-fives. The awful cliché, "I'm just taking things one day at a time"? That's Joe Ballplayer's grudging resignation that he can't let luck get to him, whether the microphone likes it or not. Even the worst of slumps can't deter him. In 2003, White Sox slugger Paul Konerko hit just .197 with five home runs in the first half, leaving writers wondering what was wrong. But he knew that baseball's randomness was more powerful than any antidote he could devise himself, and simply stayed his course. "Over the long haul, things have a way of evening out," he told me calmly. Sure enough, he hit .275 with 13 home runs in the second half, much closer to his career norms. Players call it "the law of averages"; statisticians call it regression to the mean. Either way, the force is there, hard as it may be to detect or trust.

You can never be sure what you're watching on the baseball field—talent or luck. It's like looking at air and trying to distinguish the oxygen from the nitrogen. But boy, do statisticians love trying. In 1977, Carl Morris co-wrote an article for *Scientific American* that wondered, "Was Ty Cobb ever a true .400 hitter?" This is a perfect example of how statisticians see the game: Just because Cobb hit above .400 in three seasons (.420 in 1911, .409 in 1912, and .401 in 1922) doesn't mean his inherent probability of getting a hit was actually 40 percent; it might have been 38.5, and his spinner simply got a little lucky. Conversely, when he narrowly missed .400 (.390 in 1913 and .389 in 1921) he might indeed have been a .400 hitter but gotten unlucky. Morris relied on page upon page of complicated Bayesian analysis and hierarchical modeling to get his answer. Sure enough, while we can never be sure, Cobb did have an 88 percent chance of being a *true* .400 hitter for some season—but not necessarily the ones in which he actually reached the mark. "Pursuing questions like that must be like climbing Mount Everest," Morris said. "No one had asked the question that way before. The thrill is very personal."

Morris's *Scientific American* article on something as frivolous as batting averages might have made some academics blush, but it helped legitimize baseball as a subject worthy of formal statistical intrigue. Jim Albert, a 24-year-old at Purdue University, was at that time working on his doctoral thesis in Bayesian applications, and was inspired to allow baseball statistics into his own work. "It showed that we could take baseball seriously," said Albert, who had played All-Star Baseball and Strat-O-Matic growing up outside Philadelphia, playing entire seasons and keeping full statistics. It wasn't long before Albert dove into the issue of slumps and streaks himself, with an approach somewhat backwards from the others. Rather than demonstrate that hot and cold stretches are natural byproducts of coin-flipping, Albert studied the real-life performances of players, their daily box-score lines of 0-for-4s and 2-for-5s, and measured the fluctuations to see if players did better after good days or worse after bad ones, making streaks longer than what randomness would otherwise ensure. Very little showed up at all.

"There may be something going on, but it's such a small effect—most of it is just noise," Albert reported. "I would be amazed to find any player who is actually streaky year after year. There's no pattern. But that's what makes baseball so exciting—you can never make accurate predictions. You can't know what's going to happen."

Among all the discoveries that professional statisticians have made about baseball, the most significant is this: What's *going to happen* and what *has happened* are vastly different things. Through the 1980s and 1990s the Elias Sports Bureau, and then STATS Inc., kept on publishing more and more statistical categories—breakdowns for games at home and away, by month, on grass and turf, and so on—and sold hundreds of thousands of books crammed with this information. Fans loved learning that George Brett had hit .388 in July of 1990, and that Greg Maddux was lights-out in 1993 day games, posting a 1.91 ERA. The problem occurred when everyone (especially writers and blathering broadcasters) used this information to imply or outright declare that Brett *is* a good July hitter and Maddux *is* strong in day games. Not only did real life prove these leaps to be false—players usually reverted to their normal levels the following year—but almost every formal statistician to look at the issue, whether it was Stephen Jay Gould, Jim Albert, or countless others, showed that most of these stat splits were little more than trivia. They described players' past performance, sure, but told nothing about their inherent skills, their ability to do it *again*. This was particularly true for one of baseball's most fabled concepts, the most renowned and controversial stat split ever conceived: clutch hitting.

Baseball statistics have spent most of their 150 years trying to reward batters who come through when it matters most. Runs batted in made its first brief appearance in 1879 before being resurrected by Ernie Lanigan in 1907. Allan Roth helped Branch Rickey set the Brooklyn Dodgers' lineup in the late 1940s by keeping track of batting average with men on base. In 1957, Charles F. Mullen, a district manager of a Milwaukee water-softener company, devised a system by which players would get assigned points (+200, −50, and the like) depending on whether they succeeded or failed in important situations. It was this system that Harlan and Eldon Mills perfected with their 1970 book *Player Win Averages*, where every event was rated by how it might alter a team's probability of winning the game. The most notorious of clutch-hitting statistics was the Game-Winning RBI, which became an official statistic in 1980 and highlighted, in every box score, which player drove in the winning run. But two major problems made it the fodder for hundreds of angry sports-writer columns and fan letters: First, middle-of-the-order hitters such as Mike Schmidt and Eddie Murray had far more chances at GWRBI than players on the lineup edges; and second, since the GWRBI was defined as the RBI that put the team ahead for good, it often came in the early in-nings when little tension existed at all. Alas, the GWRBI was euthanized in 1989.

Leonard Koppett couldn't understand what all the fuss was about. One of the top sportswriters for several New York papers from the 1940s through the 1980s, in addition to writing a weekly column in *The Sport-ing News*, Koppett was one of the first nationally recognized columnists to write seriously about statistics. He would rail against the ERA and try in-venting measures of his own, such as batting average when not striking out. (This didn't necessarily endear him to his crusty colleagues; Jimmy Cannon once sneered that Koppett's briefcase was "full of decimal points.") Koppett believed that the only way to approach the problem of clutch hitting was to not only keep track of runs batted in, but also of RBI *opportunities*, and figure out the percentage of chances the hitter converts. "There is a fundamental flaw in the way statistics are kept," he wrote in his 1966 book, *A Thinking Man's Guide to Baseball.* "They record *how much*, but not *when*—and in the winning and losing of ball games, the *when* is all-important."

But even that wasn't so simple. Try as we might, no statistic, Koppett continued, could ever take into account of all these *whens*: the score of the game, the number of outs, the type of pitcher on the mound, the speed of the base runners, the hitter's fight last night with his wife . . . all of the things that baseball managers had to assess at every moment of every game. Too much was happening, too many things that even chance could never explain. Koppett decided that the only way to look at the matter was this: If a hitter comes through in the clutch, then he's a clutch hitter, pure and simple. If he strikes out with the bases loaded, he choked. This longtime bias among baseball writers is natural: So close to the ac-tion, attuned to every detail of what takes place before them, they must describe how Batter A's hit-and-run or Fielder B's error led to a win or loss. How could anyone call those luck? *He did it, didn't he?*

The scientists looking at baseball statistics from a far greater distance, though, could see how baseball's planet was not so flat, but curved toward randomness. In the mid-1970s, Dick Cramer, still a chemist and years away from starting up STATS Inc., took on the issue of clutch hitting by demanding the following: If the ability to rise to the occasion were an innate trait for some hitters (such as Yankee Tommy "Old Reliable" Henrich) then they would have hit in the clutch not just one year, but many years in succession. Yet Cramer found little evidence that this ever happened. ("So fades a legend," he wrote.) Around the same time, Pete Palmer took a similar approach: By running sophisticated linear regressions on the data he got from the official American League play-by-play logs, Palmer discovered that clutch performance didn't correlate very well with any clutch hitting from the past. Overall slugging percentage, say, was a far better indicator of who would deliver with the game on the line. In other words, what happened in the clutch had more to do with a player's inherent *overall* skill than any ability to summon his best at any particular moment.

This conclusion was so counterintuitive, so contrary to the public's view of baseball, that detractors, particularly those close to the spectacle and the league offices themselves, fell all over themselves trying to dispel it. Much of this came from the Elias Sports Bureau, whose 1985 through 1993 *Baseball Analyst* books were bursting with statistics to describe clutch hitting, who was good at it and who wasn't. Every regular player had his performance broken down by more than a dozen clutch-type scenarios, Koppett's all-important *whens*: with runners on base, runners in scoring position with two out, late-inning pressure situations, and more. These numbers showed that some batters were coming through in tight spots better than others, and that some even did so for a number of seasons. To the Elias folks, these were in effect Bigfoot's footprints, proof that the clutch-hitting beast indeed did exist, and was roaming batter's boxes around the majors. "A small group of shrill pseudo-statisticians," the 1988 *Analyst* sniped, "has used insufficient data and faulty methods to try to disprove the existence of the clutch hitter. But . . . the trends are undeniably apparent except to those who choose not to see."

Sufficiently provoked, more professional scientists, who might have been shrill but were anything but pseudo, jumped into the fray to take care of this matter once and for all. Harold Brooks, then a Ph.D. candidate in atmospheric sciences at the University of Illinois, examined Elias's method and determined its conclusion to be utter nonsense. Yes, some batters showed good clutch performance several years in a row. But with so many players out there, some were bound to. (Just as our coin flipped 1,000 times will almost certainly have a streak of seven heads in it somewhere.) Brooks then went in for the kill. "The signal is clear," he wrote, "that their definition [of a clutch hitter] is simply a statistical artifact with no predictive value, and that its distribution is random . . . Clutch hitting, as presently defined, is a mirage at best."

It was only natural for computers to be summoned to help tackle baseball's most nagging statistical questions. That call came early, before Bill James used his first slide rule.

In the early 1960s, those who had access to the behemoth machines—mostly military men—began writing programs to simulate the playing of baseball games, using random-number generators to roll the dice that make for at-bat after at-bat and see what happened. Even children got into the act: A 16-year-old from Philadelphia named Larry Rafsky wrote a program on the University of Pennsylvania's famed ENIAC computer that helped him become a finalist in the prestigious Westinghouse science talent search. The kid told astounded newsmen: "We fed various kinds of statistical and other information into the computer and caused it to play 10,000 games in 10 minutes—games it would take the big leagues 65 years to play!" Rafsky programmed the computer to try different strategies, such as stealing bases and juggling lineups, to see if they could improve run scoring. They didn't. "Most managers, when they have a man on first with nobody out, will call for a bunt," the boy explained. "We're finding out that that's not so good a deal." The theoretical work done by George Lindsey and Earnshaw Cook with pencils could now be tested, and corroborated, by transistors.

Baseball was perfectly suited for computer simulation, for the same reason it appealed to Lindsey in the early 1950s: The game's methodical nature, its built-in stoppages of play, allowed the computer to move one step at a time, applying the proper probabilities at each stage. The chances of any specific batter hitting a double, striking out, or anything else could be assigned at the start, just like Strat-O-Matic, but with the computer able instantly to roll the dice millions of times; entire games and seasons could be played with the push of the <ENTER> button, with statistics spewing out by the reamful. This allowed for the kinds of experiments that academics in statistics and computer science departments had always dreamed about conducting. No one wanted to make that dream a reality more than a Stanford University graduate student named Art Peterson.

Growing up in the 1950s outside Washington, Peterson once thought his life had ended when his beloved Senators moved to Minnesota and became the Twins, but he recovered well enough to attend Cornell University and graduate in 1965 with a degree in nuclear engineering. He spent five years in the Navy designing nuclear reactors, during which time he happened upon a book written by a fellow military man: Earnshaw Cook's *Percentage Baseball*. "I was just fascinated how he took a scientific interest in the game," Peterson said. "I had to go meet him." After his discharge, Peterson did just that, making the pilgrimage to Cook's Baltimore home, talking baseball with him into the night. The torch passed from old to young, it was baseball statistics' version of Bob Dylan visiting Woody Guthrie.

Fascinated by formal probability, Peterson entered the statistics Ph.D. program at Stanford, where over the summers of 1970 to 1972—just for the hell of it—he wrote a 2,260-line FORTRAN program to simulate baseball games with unprecedented complexity. "I had to wait to do it at night," Peterson recalled with a laugh, "before the mainframe could free up enough memory to run the program." When it finally got up to speed in October 1972, spitting out 100 seasons worth of data in 10 seconds, Peterson was able to examine dozens of luck-related questions that only speedy simulations could answer. By how many runs, for instance, did a team's offensive output vary from season to season strictly due to chance? (Sure enough, the same lineup would fluctuate up to 70 runs from one year to the next, solely because of randomness.) How about individual players? Did they also swing back and forth from good year to bad? A loyal Twins fan, Peterson programmed a version of slugger Harmon Killebrew, and it turned out ol' Harmon, through no fault of his own, would see his RBIs each season bounce from 119 to 138 to 90 to 115 with no possible explanation but simple chance. No nagging injuries, no "just trying to stay consistent," no marital squabbles to rationalize it. The statistics for Killebrew and other batters *had no choice* but to be inconsistent. Baseball prescribed it.

Peterson took special interest in two issues: lineup order and the designated hitter, which the American League in 1972 was considering as a way to boost offense. As for ordering batters in a particular way—Cook, for example, had contended that putting the best hitters first would increase a team's production by 11 runs a season—Peterson's simulation program proved that the difference was almost always negligible; it simply didn't matter much what order hitters batted in. This was utter heresy among veteran baseball observers. (Not all of them, though. While he surely would have likened Peterson's 83-page paper to kindling, Detroit

Tigers manager Billy Martin tried a randomizing test of his own one day in 1972 by literally pulling hitters' names out of a hat to order his lineup against Cleveland. Plodding slugger Norm Cash led off and anemic short-stop Eddie Brinkman hit cleanup. Poetically, Brinkman was in the middle of the afternoon's key rally, doubling home the game-tying run and scoring the winning one in the Tigers' 3–2 victory.)

While lineup order didn't matter much, the designated hitter was a vastly different story. Replacing the weak-hitting pitcher in Peterson's program with a considerably stronger batter resulted in eye-opening statistical jumps: league batting average (nine points); slugging average (22 points); and an overall leaguewide rise of about 70 runs per team. This was exactly what the offense-starved American League was looking for—AL lineups in 1972 scored just 3.5 runs per game, their second-lowest output since the deadball days of 1909—so Peterson wrote to Yankees general manager Lee MacPhail in November 1972 to explain his findings. MacPhail forwarded the study to commissioner Bowie Kuhn. Two months later, the American League adopted the designated hitter and in its first season saw even larger jumps in offense than Peterson's program had predicted. The DH has been a fixture of the junior circuit ever since. Peterson never found out how much his paper influenced MacPhail or Kuhn, but whatever amount it did, he harbors no guilt. "I'm OK with the DH," he admitted. "Even if a lot of others aren't."

The computer changed the face of statistical baseball analysis. Whereas the George Lindseys had to do everything with pencil and slide rule, more and more academics, with access to mainframe power, summoned the new machine as simulation tool and tireless number cruncher. Dick Trueman of California State University, Northridge, who as early as 1959 had written "A Monte Carlo Approach to the Analysis of Baseball Strategy" for *Operations Research*, 15 years later wrote a simulation program to computerize his investigations. In 1977, Mark Pankin of Marshall University developed a way to rate hitters called the Offensive Performance Average, using a computer to refine how well it would correlate to real-life run scoring. Dozens of other papers employed the digitization of their Markovian and chi-squared microscopes to peer ever more deeply inside baseball's statistics. The obsession has grown to be self-perpetuating: Many university statistics departments across the United States today use baseball to teach formal statistical theory, with students spinning off to conduct projects of their own.

The community of stat-crazed professors has grown so large that the

American Statistical Association has formed a division and annual publication devoted solely to the study of sports statistics. In the fall of 2002, Harvard's Carl Morris packed the house during a Boston chapter meeting to discuss his new Runs Per Game statistic that, by using Markov modeling to determine what a lineup of nine of the same batter would score, rated Barry Bonds as having just posted a 22.5 RPG—the best season of all time. As it turned out, Bonds himself did not share the reverence for Dr. Morris that the scientist had for him. "He's from Harvard?" Bonds harrumphed to a San Francisco reporter. "There's some true idiots at Harvard."

Vörös McCracken has never met Barry Bonds, and doesn't particularly care to. Being a baseball outsider never bothered him. Growing up in Chicago a marginal ballplayer at best, McCracken was weaned on Bill James's *Baseball Abstract* series; each book provided an intellectual jolt of adrenaline, empowering the teenager to view baseball how *he* wanted, not how the players and managers and writers told him to. He could play with the statistics to learn whether clutch hitting existed or not. He could see how defensive numbers might be interpreted in more meaningful ways. And he could investigate just how luck—far more than anyone had ever suspected—wreaked utter havoc within pitching statistics. People had started to appreciate how chance was intertwined in batting averages, but ERAs, too? By the time he had finished his investigation, McCracken had discovered something about pitching statistics that shook even the sabermetric community.

The instinct to look into this matter didn't arrive until years after Vörös—a Hungarian family nickname meaning "Red," for his hair—more or less found himself frittering his life away after high school. He dropped out of Butler University after his freshman year and spent five years as a paralegal and bicycle messenger in downtown Chicago. He joined a punk-rock band called the Clams. He also joined a baseball Rotisserie league, and was so thirsty to win his first season of 1999 that he pulled his old *Abstracts* down from his closet to relearn ways to more accurately rate players. One issue nagged at him: separating a pitcher's statistics from the defense that played behind him. Everyone knew that a Roger Clemens could have a 3.10 ERA or a 3.40 ERA depending on how many good plays his fielders made, but no statistic measured that. A mediocre pitcher with a 12-14 record could actually have performed quite well, but been snakebit by plodding outfielders. Standard sabermetric dogma held that no unraveling of these two could ever be found. "This seemed like a stupid approach to the problem, to give up," McCracken recalled. So he tried something else.

McCracken decided to examine two groups of at-bat outcomes: the ones that a pitcher determined by himself (strikeouts, walks, home runs, and hit batsmen) and those in which he allowed the ball to be put into play, subject to impact by the defense (singles, doubles, groundball outs, sacrifice flies, and so on). What he found was astonishing. Using Microsoft Excel spreadsheet tools he had learned as a paralegal, and the statistical theory he had sat through at Butler (those math classes were sure coming in handy now), McCracken discovered that while there was a strong correlation between good performance in the first group and a pitcher's year-to-year talent, the second found no relationship at all. This didn't make any sense. Almost all hits and outs were in that second group—didn't Pedro Martinez, the slingshot fireballer for the Boston Red Sox, succeed because he surrendered so few hits? Weren't the best pitchers, like Greg Maddux, the ones who induced easier groundballs and flyballs instead of scorching line drives? Sure, it was obvious that any pitcher can be occasionally victimized by a bloop hit or a lumbering left fielder, but suggesting that their "stuff" didn't consistently impact the fate of their batted balls—that this part of the game basically boiled down to luck—was simply preposterous.

That's what McCracken thought. But no matter how hard he looked, how many times he tried to avoid this conclusion, it kept plowing into him. He devised what were essentially two new types of batting average. One measured how often a pitcher kept the ball *out* of play:

$$\text{Balls kept out of play} = \frac{(\text{Home Runs} + \text{Walks} + \text{Hit Batsmen} + \text{Strikeouts})}{\text{Total Batters Faced}}$$

And another that measured how often balls put into play eventually fell in for hits. This formula read:

$$\text{Hits per ball hit in play} = \frac{(\text{Hits} - \text{Home Runs})}{(\text{Outs} + \text{Hits} - \text{Strikeouts} - \text{Home Runs})}$$

McCracken found that pitchers needed to fare well at both to have an outstanding season. But while the perennial all-stars such as Martinez,

Maddux, and Randy Johnson were, year after year, among the best at the first average (they whiffed a lot of batters, walked very few, and gave up almost no home runs) they generally had very little control over the second; their rates of watching batted balls turned into outs by their fielders bounced around with no rhyme or reason. One year they could be among the top 10, the next the worst 10. It was all but random. For decades, people had been trying to dampen the effects that luck had on pitchers: Ted Oliver's *Kings of the Mound* in 1944 compensated for how good a pitcher's team was; in the late 1970s, Bill James started keeping track of how many runs of offensive support a pitcher received each game; and 20 years later, a young Oracle software developer named Keith Woolner invented his Composite Opposing Pitcher rating, which monitored how good each pitcher's *opposing* pitcher was. (Effectively, to borrow a term from football, his strength of schedule.) But McCracken's discovery, which he refined into what he called Defense Independent Pitching Stats (DIPS), left him able to hack through the sagebrush of conventional pitching statistics to isolate what really mattered.

Mostly, DIPS presented a fascinating opportunity to use readily available numbers to predict pitchers' future performance. For example, consider two lefthanders from 1999 through the conventional pitching statistics of won-lost record, ERA, and base runners allowed per nine innings:

	W-L	ERA	BR/9IP
Omar Daal, Diamondbacks	16-9	3.65	11.5
Chuck Finley, Angels	12-11	4.43	12.6

The average onlooker, looking at these numbers, would determine that Daal pitched better and probably would again the next year. More wins, lower ERA, fewer base runners—they all pointed toward better pitching talent. Not only that, Daal was younger, just entering his prime at age 27, while Finley was on the back end at 36. So Daal certainly could be expected to be better as time moved on. But by running DIPS, McCracken noticed that in fact Daal had been lucky where Finley had not: Of the balls that Finley allowed into play, 30 percent fell in for hits, a high rate, while Daal's figure of 26 percent was, on the other end, quite low. (That might not sound like much, but over the course of a season it can be the difference between a great and gruesome year.) This is what their 1999 records looked like when McCracken infused them with normal, equal luck:

	W-L	ERA	BR/9IP
Omar Daal, Diamondbacks	12-11	4.62	1.47
Chuck Finley, Angels	14-10	4.11	1.36

It was clear that Daal probably owed much of his success, and Finley much of his mediocrity, to chance—and with more standard luck the next year, each would find his fortunes somewhat reversed. Sure enough, in 2000, Finley went 16-11 with a 4.17 ERA, more along his career norms, while Daal's luck happened to swing far in the other direction, leaving him with a disastrous 4-19 record and 6.14 ERA.

The reward for McCracken? In his Rotisserie league, for which he originally had invented DIPS, he finished in first place all three years.

That wasn't McCracken's only fantasy result. In January 2001, his long explanation of DIPS was posted on the popular sabermetric Web site, baseballprospectus.com. Monster sports portal ESPN.com picked up on it and ran a story of its own, heralding a new era of pitching statistics. "All hell broke loose," McCracken recalled. He received 950 e-mails the first day, 750 the next. Some called him a genius, others a loon. But Vörös McCracken became an instant sabermetric celebrity. Going through thousands more such e-mails over the next two years was a whopping pain in the ass, but one in August 2002 stopped McCracken's eyeballs dead in their sockets. It was from the Red Sox. *Would you be interested in working for us?*

The thought had never occurred to McCracken. A stathead who hadn't picked up a bat since high school suddenly on the payroll of a major league team, and one with its feet as cemented in tradition as the Sox? His batted-balls stuff had made more sense at first, for crying out loud.

But the Red Sox weren't the only club ready to try walking down new statistical paths. Although few would readily advertise it, by 2002 most major league organizations had someone either on staff, or retained as a consultant, to conduct sabermetric studies to evaluate players and other moves. Many were spurred by watching the Oakland A's, who, despite operating with one of the majors' lowest payrolls, were reaching the playoffs year after year. The A's made no secret of how they were moving away from the subjective opinions of old-time scouts—the brick-by-brick foundation of guesswork on which baseball decisions traditionally rested—toward the more objective answers found in numbers. And it worked. Whether through their belief in on-base percentage, defensive efficiency ratings, or several unique calculations of their own, the A's became a force in large part because they sat down and *did the math*. In 2003 this became common knowledge even outside baseball: When celebrated author Michael Lewis published *Moneyball*, his bestselling profile of the A's and their reliance on statistics, it made their general manager, Billy Beane, a bone fide business celebrity.

The thing was, for all the fuss being made about the modern A's, the rampant talk of the team reinventing baseball through sabermetrics, their approach was not new—not by a longshot. First, teams had been employing statistical analysts for the past 20 years. And even to the extent that the current revolution did start in Oakland, it was not the Billy Beane revolution. It was not even the Bill James revolution, his logic and writings having finally crowbarred open the game's iron door of conservatism.

No. The A's revolution had a clear starting point: spring 1982. Its Paul Revere was a virtually unknown, former aerospace engineer named Eric Walker.

11

The March of On-Base Percentage

In baseball, some numbers are known, some are not, and the meaning of most can be debated. But there's one number everyone knows and agrees with: three. Three outs and you're gone. Period. The end. All runners cancelled, all theories moot, all probabilities zero. That number must, in any rational evaluation of the game, dominate planning.

—Eric Walker
The Sinister First Baseman, March 1982

Sandy Alderson was an outsider. When the Oakland A's hired him as in-house counsel in October 1981, the native Californian had virtually no ties to baseball. He had never played college ball, let alone the pros. A Dartmouth graduate who later got his law degree at Harvard, Alderson instead served as a Marine infantry officer in Vietnam from 1970 to 1971, emerging from combat in Da Nang with such a steadfast look at the world around him that his face literally became that of the Marines. (He starred in a recruitment poster that asked for a few good men like him.) He became a top-notch San Francisco Bay area attorney, and caught the eye of baseball only when another baseball newcomer, A's president Roy Eisenhardt, was revamping the entire Oakland operation. Alderson was retained as counsel, did some arbitration cases, and offered an altogether fresh look at the baseball business. Heck, the guy even listened to National Public Radio.

It was during his NPR-accompanied drives to the Oakland Coliseum during the spring of 1982 that Alderson particularly enjoyed the baseball commentaries of a freelance correspondent named Eric Walker. Walker tended to talk about how screwed up baseball thinking had become. Managers didn't realize how precious outs were, instead squandering them on sacrifices and steal attempts that usually hurt their teams. A deeper look at defensive statistics showed how small a contribution glovemen actually made to the winning and losing of games. And no one, not anyone, was giving the walk its due as an offensive weapon. As he listened, Alderson, still a hunk of malleable clay as a baseball man, wanted to learn more.

One afternoon, while perusing a San Francisco bookstore, Alderson got that chance. He happened upon a small paperback that Walker had just published called *The Sinister First Baseman*, a collection of essays and other ramblings about baseball. Long before it was cool to camp out and read in bookstores, Alderson dove in:

- "[Managers] allow their judgment to be blown this way and that by each and every short-term run of luck. . . . Like the shrewd and winning player at any game involving odds, the successful baseball manager must discover the optimum long-range strategy, grit his teeth, and STICK TO IT, in ALL situations. Poker players who just know that THIS is the one inside straight it pays to try filling are always welcome at my house."

- "Fielding is dramatically overvalued. Most—the vast majority, in fact—of all plays will either be executed by virtually any man at the position or will be unmakeable by anyone."

- "What are the cumulative odds of a runner on second with one out eventually scoring? What of those for a runner on first with none out? If you don't know those things to a nicety, you're not making decisions, you're making guesses."

- "The big-inning manager has intuitively or intellectually arrived at the correct conclusion. By always playing for the most runs, he will indeed sometimes get none at all, and probably even lose some games he could have won with that one run. He will, however, GAIN BACK MORE than he loses that way, by the winning of games that a run or two would NOT have taken . . . Lacking a crystal ball, a manager CANNOT decide for himself which game is of which type, for the whole complexion of a game can change with two out in the bottom of the ninth."

Alderson reading Walker was like King reading Gandhi. That day in the bookstore, Walker started giving Alderson a comprehensive philosophy by which to build the A's, the first and single most important commandment being *Thou shalt not waste outs*. This was diametrically opposite to how baseball men conventionally viewed the sport. For more than a hundred years, runs were caused by *hits*. Walker turned that strategy backwards and claimed that runs were scored not by hits, but by *avoiding outs*. Outs were the true coins of baseball, with hitters hoarding them, pitchers grabbing them, and fielders plucking them out of the air. This took root with Alderson because at heart he was an Earl Weaver man, never particularly impressed by traditional one-run stratagems like the bunt and steal. Alderson was also open to new ideas: He had bought Bill James's early, self-published *Abstracts* through *The Sporting News* and, after joining the A's, dispatched some Stanford Business School students to run a linear regression model to determine which conventional statistic correlated best with runs scored. They came back a few weeks later with an answer: on-base percentage, the same one Eric Walker had been saying all along.

Every baseball fan has heard of the "On-Base Revolution"; dozens of newspaper articles have reported it, while Michael Lewis's *Moneyball* introduced the world at large to A's GM Billy Beane, the movement's modern leader. But its genesis has drowned in a brew of hype and misunderstanding. Beane carries the torch today, yes. And Bill James played his role. But from the inside, within baseball's conservative front offices, it was an NPR radio guy whose belief in on-base percentage taught a very old dog some very new tricks.

Those trampled in recent years by the march of on-base percentage wonder where in the world this thing came from. The statistic has become baseball's version of rock and roll, scaring the old and galvanizing the young—the ousted generation blaming it for everything gone wrong, wondering what happened to the world they used to know. For a century, batting average was easy. It was Americana. And then suddenly it was mocked as hopelessly passé, quaint but silly, pushed into irrelevance like big band music and show tunes.

Little do these folks know, the roots of on-base percentage, the effort to quantify and appreciate the skill not of getting hits but of avoiding outs, stretch back all the way to Henry Chadwick. In the 1860s, Father Chadwick would keep a statistic he called Outs Per Game as a measure of batting failure. Walks were relatively rare in the National League's early years; they originally required between five and nine balls, and waiting that long for better pitches was considered unsportsmanlike. But appreciation for getting on base in any way possible existed enough that, in 1879, the NL introduced a statistic called Reached First Base, rewarding batters for every time they got on base by a hit, walk, or error. (Not hit by pitch, as getting plunked didn't give the batter first base for another decade.) Providence outfielder Paul Hines led the league in reached first base in 1879, the stat's lone year of existence, as it was dropped for 1880. The season of 1887 provided the ultimate respect for walk-takers like New York's Roger Connor and St. Louis's Yank Robinson: to create more .300 hitters who would draw fans to ballparks, bases on balls officially counted as full-fledged hits, morphing all batting averages essentially into what we today call on-base percentage. Connor and Robinson saw their averages jump about 100 extra points apiece, while Robinson's teammate, Tip O'Neill, posted the highest batting average ever, .492 (since corrected to .490). This inflation so devalued batting averages, though, that the next season walks reverted to their status as neither hit nor out nor at-bat, and have stayed that way ever since.

Despite F. C. Lane's many efforts to explain walks' value in *Baseball Magazine*—in 1917 he called them "the orphan child of the dope sheets"—it took until the 1940s and 1950s for a batter's ability to take a base on balls to receive true respect, in part due to Ted Williams's spectacular success at doing it. (Besides hitting .340 or higher every year, Williams also walked about 140 times a season.) Allan Roth and Branch Rickey used on-base percentage to evaluate batters for the Dodgers, while Yankees manager Casey Stengel, more on instinct than hard data, occasionally batted the slow-footed Bob Cerv and Elston Howard leadoff because of their tendency to walk. Three years later, as *Sports Illustrated* presented a package of newfangled statistics to analyze the 1956 season, the first was on-base percentage, which the magazine listed in true percent form: Duke Snider of Brooklyn had led the National League with a 39.94 on-base percentage.

OBP had only a small cult following until computers allowed researchers to prove just how meaningful the statistic truly was. Pete Palmer ran correlation studies in the 1960s that showed how it was far superior to batting average and even slightly more important than the more widely known slugging percentage. He reported in SABR's 1973 *Baseball Research Journal:* "There are two main objectives for a hitter. The first is to not make an out . . ." Palmer personally figured OBPs and inserted them into the Sports Information Center's American League statistics reports through the 1970s. Earl Weaver began espousing the value of protecting outs on offense while managing the Baltimore Orioles around the same time, but it remained the province of the stat-absorbed. One precious example came in the classified advertising pages of *The Sporting News* in April 1979, when Barry Codell used Pete Rose to sell his booklet of base-out percentage statistics. Rose was one of the most revered players in baseball because he always hit .300, but he also wouldn't take a walk if it jumped into his doubleknits. That failing cost his teams dozens of outs a year, as surely as silently. Codell's ad featured the headline, PETE ROSE: BASEBALL'S STEADIEST OUT-PRODUCER? This was heresy, but the stat guys knew what Codell meant.

The on-base enthusiasts have always understood that for all of baseball's reputation as the only major sport without a clock, its strolling leisurely through summer afternoons without the cuticle-fraying countdown of time, it *does* have a clock. The timepiece simply measures the game's remainder not in minutes and seconds, but in its own unit: outs. The team whose defense (pitchers and fielders) make those outs tick down fastest for their opponent will probably win; meanwhile, an offense wants to slow down the clock by preserving its outs. This elevates on-base percentage, as well as the ability to avoid outs through foolish attempts at sacrifice bunts and stolen bases, as vital concepts—perhaps the most important in the game.

Contrary to popular belief, Bill James actually wrote very little about walks and on-base percentage. He railed at the National League and its official statisticians, the Elias Sports Bureau, for not making batters' bases on balls available during the season, and used walks as a major component of his runs created formula, but never cited OBP as a gaping hole in baseball understanding.

But Eric Walker sure did. He built his entire approach around it, and intrigued Alderson enough that after Alderson was promoted to general manager in 1982 he asked Walker, for a commission of $500, to submit a report detailing how respect for the out could improve the A's roster. The document arrived on September 22, 1982. Walker suggested moves based on improving the team's OBP. He rated pitchers by a personal PX statistic that looked like ERA but examined the pitcher's tendency to limit base runners while inducing outs. Alderson loved it and hired Walker as a consultant. "I'm sitting there, an outsider in baseball, and I have to develop a philosophy, a basis for decision making," Alderson recalled. "I was searching around for ideas. I was ripe for these kind of things." The A's already had STATS Inc.'s Edge 1.000 system and was about to hire the computer-minded Steve Boros as manager. Those two received tremendous press coverage, but Eric Walker, working behind the scenes with little notice at all, ultimately had far more impact than both.

Growing up in an Italian neighborhood of the Bronx in the early 1950s, Eric Walker originally followed his beloved New York Giants by clipping the box scores and National League standings from the *New York Times* into a notebook for posterity and ready reference. He eventually outgrew baseball, though. After earning an engineering degree from Rensselaer Polytechnic Institute in 1963, he embraced the Sputnik challenge and joined RCA's Space Center in Heightstown, New Jersey, doing classified government work on satellites. Bright and loquacious, Walker eventually tired of that, and decided to try his hand at radio broadcasting. This led to some syndicated NPR work out of San Francisco in the mid-1970s, when out of the blue his wife suggested they go to a Giants game.

Sitting in the upper deck of Candlestick Park, Walker realized how much he had missed baseball. But rather than look at the game as he did as child, he found himself examining it through an engineer's eyes. He scratched out notes on his scorecard, fiddling with equations for player value and stolen-base risks. Figuring he might not be the first person to goof around with these things, he decided to go to the San Francisco Public Library to search for some older literature on the subject, and pulled out from the stacks a musty old copy of Earnshaw Cook's *Percentage Baseball*. "It was one of those Reader's Digest moments," Walker recalled. "It changed my life. It was a revelation."

Cook's text was barely decipherable, of course, but sparked so many ideas in Walker's head that he wound up scribbling page after page of thoughts and formulas on an 8-by-14 yellow pad. Every approach he took led him to one conclusion: Outs and on-base percentage ruled the roost. He developed his ideas fully enough to start building some radio segments around them. He eventually devoted significant portions of his daily five-minute baseball morning reports to espousing these new statistical outlooks, his rhetorical proofs going out nationally through, poetically, San Francisco's KQED.

Needless to say, Walker figured his approach would do the most good for an actual major league team. In March 1981, through some reporting connections he had at the ballpark, he convinced Giants GM Tom Haller to read his 200-page report on the perennially mediocre club and how to improve it through respect for on-base percentage. (It led with a quote from noted sabermetrician John Locke: "He that judges without informing himself to the utmost that he is capable, cannot acquit himself of judging amiss.") Haller hired Walker as a consultant for $1,500 a month. But while he was smart enough to give Walker's ideas a shot, he wasn't smart enough to put them into practice. Few moves were made along Walker's lines, perhaps due to Haller's overwhelming reluctance to admit Walker existed. "He was *adamant* that I not let anybody know I was working for them," Walker said. "He was ill at ease using this stuff. He was casting about for anything that might help him out a little, and he didn't want that to be known." The Giants let Walker go after six months.

Walker took his ideas across the bay to the Oakland Coliseum, where Sandy Alderson, newly promoted from counsel to GM, was considerably more receptive. He knew Walker's work from NPR, had read *The Sinister First Baseman*, and was intrigued to see how the approach might help the A's become contenders again. It didn't matter that Walker was a bit of an odd duck, speaking a hundred miles an hour while quoting obscure philosophers. His ideas made too much sense to be ignored.

Walker's method became Oakland's method. The purest manifestation of this was how the club rebuilt itself around Walker's favorite stat: Rather than look for hitters who got a lot of hits (batting average), the A's went after hitters with high rates of *not getting out* (on-base percentage). This placed tremendous, and to that point unappreciated, value on the base on balls as an offensive weapon. Walker didn't attend meetings with the A's front office ("I probably made a conscious decision at that time that one outsider in this organization was enough," Alderson said) but every winter, for $3,000, he prepared a 100-page report on A's players that suggested moves for the upcoming season. A slugger with seductive home runs and RBIs but a low walk rate would be dumped on other clubs. Meanwhile, free agents with high on-base percentages could be had inexpensively. Alderson completely reworked his lineup along Walker's ideals of maximizing offensive output through walks and home runs:

- June 1984: Drafted pure slugger Mark McGwire tenth overall rather than two more speed-oriented players, Shane Mack and Oddibe McDowell.

- Winter 1986: Let go slugger Dave Kingman (35 homers and 94 RBIs the previous season) because he rarely walked, posting a pathetic .258 OBP. Signed Reggie Jackson (.381 OBP) as new DH.

- December 1987: Finally dumped Alfredo Griffin, a flashy shortstop who drew few walks with no power, on the Dodgers in return for all-star pitcher Bob Welch. This also allowed Griffin to be replaced by prospect Walt Weiss, who had decent OBPs in the minors and became Rookie of the Year.

- December 1987: Signed powerful but defensively poor center fielder Dave Henderson as a free agent.

- February 1988: Signed Don Baylor, a power hitter who got on base in large part by getting hit with pitches quite willingly.

- July 1989: Traded with the Yankees for Rickey Henderson, who besides being a top-flight base stealer drew walks and hit homers spectacularly often.

- August 1989: Traded with the Yankees for Ken Phelps, an OBP machine with power.

- August 1990: Traded with the Rangers for DH Harold Baines, who knew how to take a walk, too.

Not every deal worked perfectly, of course, and the development of other players (Jose Canseco foremost among them) played a role in helping the A's improve. But Alderson made few roster moves outside the sphere of Walker's philosophy, and the results justified it: The A's became the most successful franchise of the period, winning four division titles and three American League pennants from 1988 to 1992. "Eric allowed us to work with the concepts, and allowed me to more fully understand the ideas," Alderson said. "It was an educational process." Along the way, Walker also was asked by Alderson to indoctrinate a former player who was just joining the A's front office. Walker put together an updated manifesto, a 62-page packet titled *Winning Baseball,* which spelled out the math behind building a roster. The young executive's eyes all but popped out of his head when he read it. His name was Billy Beane.

As Eric Walker was starting the modern on-base revolution, he was by no means the first stat maven to bang on customized numbers for a major league club. Travis Hoke and Allan Roth introduced new methods to Branch Rickey in the first half of the century. Bob Whitlow, a retired Air Force colonel who had been in the running to become an astronaut in President Kennedy's budding space program, instead joined the Cubs in 1963 as a high-level executive and found himself sitting in the Wrigley Field stands and logging every pitch to find any patterns that could help his team. "Only about one batter out of 11 will swing at a first pitch if it's a breaking ball," he bubbled to *The Sporting News*. The Yankees had a full-time stat man for most of the 1960s, Bill Kane, who dug up tidbits at the request of manager Ralph Houk and general manager Lee MacPhail, while also funneling interesting stats on Yankee players during radio broadcasts to announcer Mel Allen. ("Let's see what Bill Kane's got for me here . . ." Allen would say.) The first statistical analyst in the mold that we find today, one who comes up with more sophisticated ways to evaluate players, would wait until Tal Smith briefly hired Steve Mann for the Astros in 1979. But it would take another few years before a club employee would stay on long enough, and with enough industry acceptance, to carry team business cards with his name and "Sabermetrician" as his title. That person was Craig Wright.

Ever since he'd been a kid in the early 1960s, growing up in Lansing, Michigan, Wright had loved detective stories—tales of investigators walking into a situation, surveying the facts, and dusting the furniture for clues that might lead to greater truth. This catalyzed Wright's interest in science, even thoughts of a career in forensic criminology, but then, at 16, a different siren called to him: the baseball dice game APBA. Similar to Strat-O-Matic, APBA allowed Wright and his friends to form a league and pretend they were running actual major league teams, trading players and experimenting with new strategies to maximize the probabilities of winning. The mix of baseball and science proved intoxicating. "It was like handicapping the future instead of the past—detective work in the other direction," Wright recalled. "It became clear to me, watching big league teams operate, that they didn't take a scientific approach. It hit me that I could make a living doing that if I so chose."

Wright put those thoughts aside for about a decade, during college and then four years of high school teaching, but in early 1980 decided to take his shot. He sent out letters to all 26 teams offering his services and was rejected by every one. He wasn't surprised. Rather than pester the same people again, Wright prepared for each club a long, statistical study specifically designed for that organization, what he called "hook" projects.

For the Reds, who had blown out several young pitching arms from over-use, he presented data to help safeguard pitching prospects. He analyzed the effects that Fenway Park had on Boston hitters. And for the Texas Rangers, who often played on sweltering ninety-degree summer evenings, Wright examined which players tended to succeed in such heat. These studies in wait, Wright watched the wires for whenever a team had a change in ownership or general manager, and phoned what he hoped were more open minds.

"I'm sorry, we don't have any openings, Mr. Wright," they invariably said.

"You don't know you *need* the opening," Wright responded. "And I am the person to fill it."

One day he spoke with Eddie Robinson. The Rangers' GM was an old-school sort, but one receptive to new ideas. (He had green-lighted the use of computers to keep statistics while with the Braves in the 1970s.) Robinson was intrigued enough to be willing to see more, so Wright sent along adaptations of a half-dozen of the studies he had originally done to entice other clubs. After surveying them, Robinson said: "OK. Let's do a one-year trial."

The trial evolved into a four-year hitch. Wright became an official member of the Rangers organization from midseason 1981 through late 1985, complete with his "Sabermetrician" business cards and a listing in the team's official media guide. He sat in on meetings with Robinson (and his successors, Joe Klein and Tom Grieve) while the club discussed trades, arbitration, free agency, and more. Many of the moves he suggested paid off. One statistical study found that knuckleballers, such as Rangers reliever Charlie Hough, were much better suited for the starting role; the club moved him into the rotation and watched him average 16 wins over the next seven years. When Wright's numbers showed that reliever Danny Darwin was pitching particularly poorly with men on base, it tipped off the pitching coach to a fault in Darwin's follow-through out of the stretch, which helped straighten him out. Wright examined minor league prospects for statistical signs of improvement, and in 1983 recommended trading for an unheralded Triple-A righthander in the Dodgers system whose walk and strikeout rates compared to other pitchers in the Pacific Coast League indicated he was on the upswing. The Rangers didn't get the guy, but the baseball world soon did: It was Orel Hershiser.

While the Giants' Tom Haller and the A's Sandy Alderson kept their use of Eric Walker a relative secret, Wright was anything but one. He

Craig Wright. (*Tony Avelar Photography*)

would stride his wiry six-foot-one frame into meetings dressed nothing like a baseball executive, wearing jeans, a flannel shirt, and sandals. "At first you were like, 'Who the hell is this guy?' He looked kind of like a hippie," recalled Sandy Johnson, the Rangers' scouting director at the time. "I didn't want to pay attention to him. But in the end I liked having him around. You respected his love for the game, and he had very strong and valid opinions on players." Those opinions mattered. When asked to write a report on the skills of manager Don Zimmer, Wright's unflattering analysis contributed to Zimmer's firing in July 1982. Zimmer spat to reporters: "Craig Wright is the laughingstock of this organization and he's a disgrace to this organization." Zimmer left town, but Wright stayed on, his position ironically bolstered by Zimmer's broadsides; the on-field lifer was out, and the new stat guy stayed. Recalled Wright: "Folks began to really take in the idea that mine was a real job, and had to be taken seriously."

By late 1985, Wright found his statistical work funneled more toward player contracts and arbitration cases, something he didn't particularly enjoy, so he broke off from Texas to start an independent consulting practice and branch off into other arenas. Wright joined John Dewan and Bill James at STATS Inc.—Wright had been a Project Scoresheet volunteer, contributing Rangers scoresheets during his time in Texas—and helped them serve their major league and media clients. (Including ESPN's debut 1989 baseball coverage, for which Wright added to each hitter's regular average-homers-RBIs stat graphic an additional number to indoctrinate the masses: on-base percentage.) Wright also wrote a book with Rangers pitching coach Tom House, *The Diamond Appraised,* in which the two debated their baseball philosophies. (For example, Wright showed statistical evidence for how excessive workloads led to pitchers' injuries, while House argued that proper physical training could prevent them. Wright was proven correct, as the Rangers blew out so many young pitchers under House that they wound up with fewer arms than the Venus De Milo.) Wright worked for the Dodgers, the Colorado Rockies, even the Hanshin Tigers of Japan, before calling it quits after 21 seasons in 2001. He now lives near Monterey Bay in California, not involved in baseball at all, instead spending his days as a Christian Science practitioner. "For a long time my work in baseball was in line with my desire to be where I can do the most good. Now it is not," Wright explained recently. "For example, I'd really like to change the way that pitchers are developed and used. But my ideas are pretty radical. I think they'd scare off a lot of people in the game today."

The Rangers' public use of a statistical analyst in the early 1980s helped make other clubs less skittish to do the same. In 1986, the Orioles asked Eddie Epstein, a young government economist, to provide hardcore statistical reports on Orioles players. Growing up in Baltimore, Epstein had learned the game three ways: watching Earl Weaver manage the Orioles, playing APBA and Strat-O-Matic, and reading Bill James. When his report on Baltimore's 40-man roster used statistics to make several correct predictions—low strikeout rates indicated that the Orioles rotation would slide, and a player the scouts liked, outfielder John Shelby, would never hit in the majors because he couldn't walk—the club hired him full-time in December 1987. Epstein explained to general manager and baseball lifer Roland Hemond methods to predict major league performance from minor league statistics and how on-base percentage was vital to a batting order. Epstein recommended trading for Red Sox prospect Brady Anderson because of his high walk rate. He bristled at the club's thoughts of dealing for slugger Cory Snyder, who had all the tools (power, great body, and more) that scouts looked for but had no eye at all—and eventually imploded as a player because of it. Epstein didn't hide any confidence in his methods. He told the *Boston Globe* in 1990: "If you've got a guy who's 23 or 24 [years old], and has been a professional player for four or five years, I don't care what the scouts think. I can look at the numbers."

Epstein's ego around the office eventually led to his firing in January 1994. "Eddie would have been better off not being on the scene," Hemond recalled recently. "He was a very good supplement. But he was like the inventor who can come up with great ideas but has no ability to market them." Luckily for Epstein, he had one staunch supporter, Orioles president Larry Lucchino, who, after leaving Baltimore and taking the reins of the San Diego Padres, hired Epstein in 1995 as director of baseball operations, the first time a statistics expert had been given such a mainstream title. (With the Orioles, Epstein was director of research and statistics.) Epstein had input in every move the Padres made, including the ones that helped the team reach the 1998 World Series, but ultimately he chafed at not having more power and resigned in 1999. He now consults for several organizations. "If I had the same skills I do now but had played a month in A-ball, I would be a strong candidate for a general manager position," Epstein said. "But there's not a snowball's chance in hell."

Sure enough, many baseball insiders retained their willies for people who hadn't played the game professionally, viewing the stat guys as pocket-protected, over-opinionated weirdoes. Their exhibit-A became a Brooklyn eccentric and one-time Red Sox consultant named Mike Gimbel.

Gimbel, an employee of New York City's Bureau of Water Supply, was so upset at Bill James's ending his *Baseball Abstract* series in 1988 that he decided to enter the field himself, and thereafter published his own annual books of player ratings. One customer happened to be young Montreal Expos executive Dan Duquette, who after ascending to general manager in Montreal was impressed enough to hire Gimbel as a stat analyst. After Duquette moved on to the Red Sox in 1994 he brought Gimbel with him, and used his custom numbers—generated by Gimbel's personal computer algorithm—to help evaluate players just as Walker, Wright, and Epstein had for other clubs. Duquette consulted with Gimbel almost exclusively by phone and, being a clandestine sort already, never divulged his role to the press. Then, one day in March 1997, Gimbel showed up at the Red Sox' Florida spring training site. A T-bone might as well have descended into a puma cage.

The Boston writers ridiculed Gimbel as a "Rotisserie-inspired stat geek" and a "statistics psycho, typical of his sick breed." The papers revealed that Gimbel was, in fact, a community college dropout whose Brooklyn loft had recently been raided by police, who found six pet alligators in a homemade pond, living amiably with five turtles and an iguana. (Gimbel confirmed this gleefully.) Dressed for the Iditarod in eighty-degree weather, Gimbel enjoyed this moment in the spotlight. He called himself "half-Jewish, half-gypsy," cast himself as the "secret power behind the Red Sox throne," and said Duquette never made a move without him. Duquette actually defended Gimbel at first, claiming to value his input, and fondly compared him to Boo Radley, the spooky shut-in of *To Kill a Mockingbird*, which only invited more ridicule. The Boston media fed on the story for almost a week, whipping New England into a stat-fearing hysteria. It was a public relations disaster for Duquette, who let Gimbel's contract lapse after the season, and for statistical analysts all over baseball. Today, one club's numbers man still refuses to acknowledge his employment publicly. Why? "I don't want to be Gimbelized."

If it was bad to be Gimbelized, it was downright fantastic to be Aldersoned. Working under Sandy Alderson during his tenure as A's general manager, from 1981 through 1997, basically punched your ticket to success in a major league front office. A's executives routinely graduated to top-notch big league jobs: Walt Jocketty (St. Louis), Ron Schueler (White Sox), and Billy Beane (A's, as Alderson's successor) all have won division titles as GMs themselves, while J. P. Ricciardi is rebuilding the Toronto Blue Jays. Bob Watson, an A's hitting coach, became GM of the 1996 World Series-champion Yankees team that kick-started their modern dynasty. Dusty Baker, Don Baylor, and Dave Stewart all played for Oakland in the late 1980s before moving on to management roles elsewhere. The A's under Alderson were a bustling executive petri dish. Everyone there was influenced by Eric Walker, either indirectly through Alderson or directly through Walker's manuals, which were circulated throughout the operation. No one bought into the philosophy more than Billy Beane.

In his previous baseball life, Beane had been one of the United States' top high school prospects during the spring of 1980, becoming a first-round draft pick of the New York Mets but never blossoming into the star scouts had foreseen. He bounced around several clubs and compiled a paltry .219 batting average (and even worse .249 on-base percentage, much to his future embarrassment) before landing with the A's, where he played for a bit before abruptly retiring in early 1990 to become a scout and pursue his true dream: being a general manager. As good as he once had been, Beane's heart had never really belonged to playing. The desire to run a club, not play on it, dated all the way back to high school, when almost every afternoon and weekend Beane would stay inside and play in a Strat-O-Matic league with his friends. (Fifty-two game season, playoffs, statistics, the whole deal.) Even today Beane bounces out of his chair when he remembers how Rudy York's card mauled lefties and that the all-time Indians squad of Bob Feller, Early Wynn, and Shoeless Joe Jackson was his team of choice. Beane took Strat-O-Matic so seriously as a teenager that when the dice didn't land his way, he would heave them down the street. "Not out *to* the street, but he'd walk out there and throw them *down* the street," a friend of his recalled. If a player choked too often, it wasn't unheard of for Billy Beane to literally immolate his card.

Playing Strat-O-Matic baked into Beane a respect for baseball's probabilities. That grew only stronger when Alderson promoted him to A's assistant general manager in 1993 and handed him a copy of Eric Walker's *Winning Baseball*, which mathematically proved how an organization, particularly one entering tough economic times like the A's, could remain competitive by relying on undervalued statistics such as on-base percentage. "Billy was smitten," Alderson recalled. When Beane succeeded Alderson as GM in 1997, Beane printed up *Winning Baseball* and distributed it to every minor league manager, coach, and scout in the organization. The lessons became so ingrained that the A's stopped contracting Walker's services in 1998 (Walker today runs a lawyer-placement business in eastern Washington) and ran the numbers on their own. Beane wasn't the one who sat behind the spreadsheets, of course. For that he needed an assistant.

Enter Paul DePodesta, baseball's new breed of baseball executive. A student of Bill James's *Abstract* series, DePodesta never played a day of professional baseball. He played only briefly in college. But that college was Harvard. By the late 1990s, baseball was starting to recognize the value of pure intelligence—after spending two decades frittering away millions of dollars on free agents who your average Strat-O-Matic player knew would flop, it could hardly afford not to. The Indians hired DePodesta as an intern in their scouting department, where he learned how to evaluate players more traditionally, by sight. After two years in Cleveland he became such a well-rounded package that Beane hired the 25-year-old to be his full-fledged assistant GM, handling contract negotiations, balancing budgets and, yes, doing sabermetrics. "If we make a move," Beane said, "it won't be done without research proving why it's correct."

With formulas and spreadsheets that would flummox older executives, DePodesta and Beane made running a club less about athletics than actuarial science. They determined the relative risks of taking raw 18-year-olds versus more polished collegians in the amateur draft. They resurrected the three-by-eight, base-out combination matrix pioneered by George Lindsey in the 1950s to calculate how the value of any in-game strategy might change from year to year. They surveyed the Internet for any new ideas cropping up in the sabermetric community. And, of course, they used on-base percentage as the starting point for any player evaluation. To suggest that the Oakland front office relied solely on statistics is ludicrous—a strong group of traditional scouts helped them get future stars Tim Hudson, Mark Mulder, Barry Zito, Eric Chavez, and more in the amateur draft—but by staying on the scientific tracks first laid by Eric Walker, the A's, despite one of the game's most paltry payrolls, reached the American League playoffs every season from 2000 through 2003.

DePodesta's role in this was no secret among baseball insiders, and he quickly became the major leagues' hottest general manager prospect. After the 2001 season, at the age of 28, he was offered the Toronto GM job but turned it down to stay with Beane.* The Blue Jays so wanted to tap into the Oakland philosophy, period, that they went one notch down the A's ladder to top scout J. P. Ricciardi. As soon as he took the Toronto job, Ricciardi knew he needed a numbers-based assistant for himself. He had to hire his own DePodesta. But where did you find that? Where did the brightest young statistics minds hang out? On the Internet, naturally. They wrote for a Web site called Baseball Prospectus.

For years, baseballprospectus.com had been the Internet's most influential sabermetric meeting room, the lodge for Bill James disciples. The forum allowed young professionals and college students to conduct complicated statistical analysis, write about their methods, and defend them against dissections by their peers. The community incubated many of today's cutting-edge statistical tools, all developed, as they have been for over a century, by baseball outsiders looking in for new ways to examine their favorite sport. These included:

*DePodesta was hired as GM of the Dodgers in early 2004, replacing Dan Evans.

- Equivalent Average (EqA): A Maryland meteorologist by day, Clay Davenport developed this metric to take everything a batter does (single, strikeout, caught stealing, home run, and so on) and mush it all together into one number that looks like batting average (.260 is ordinary, .300 is good) but measures far more. EqA goes the extra step in compensating for the size of the batter's ballpark, the overall strength of his league, and the position he plays.

- Pitcher Abuse Points (PAP): Invented by Rany Jazayerli while studying for his doctorate in dermatology at the University of Michigan, this statistic measures how often a starting pitcher throws enough pitches in a game to put himself at serious risk of injury. Later refinement by Keith Woolner, the Oracle software developer who also came up with the composite opposing pitcher statistic mentioned earlier, confirmed a correlation between starts above 100 pitches, particularly those above 120, and subsequent slumps and blown-out arms.

- Support Neutral Win-Loss (SNWL): Baseball fans have always known that a pitcher who pitched well (say, two runs in eight innings) could lose because of an incompetent reliever, and one who pitched poorly (five runs in six innings) could win, thanks to great offensive support. Michael Wolverton, a 29-year-old Stanford graduate student in computer science, developed SNWL in 1992 to figure out what each combination of innings and runs allowed was worth, on average, and assigned to it *fractions* of a win and loss, rather than one or the other. This produced a won-lost record that separated the pitcher's actual skill from the relief he did or did not receive.

- PECOTA: Nate Silver, a 24-year-old economics consultant in Chicago, came up with this method (the acronym stands for a convoluted phrase not worth knowing) in 2002 to project players' future equivalent averages and conventional statistics. By surveying the statistical career paths of every batter and pitcher in baseball history, noting when sluggers peaked and finesse pitchers declined, his system could predict current players' statistics for an upcoming season with alarming accuracy. Rotisserie fans rejoiced.

The Baseball Prospectus writers were occasionally incomprehensible, generally contemptuous of baseball's average front-office executive— most articles and chat-type posts were riddled with snide remarks about old-school, idiot GMs who *didn't get it*—but consistently provoked new ways of looking at the game, in the best Bill James tradition. The BP crew published an annual *Abstract*-type volume of sabermetrics and player evaluations every spring starting in 1996, enjoying modest sales, but really hit it big when ESPN.com began profiling their work and posting BP articles on the site. This exposed them to millions of readers—including two Oakland A's executives who liked keeping up with the newest sabermetrics, Billy Beane and Paul DePodesta.

When Ricciardi left to run the Blue Jays in November 2001, he wanted to bring a statistical analyst with him. DePodesta referred him to Keith Law, a BP writer who didn't necessarily invent any new statistics but was as adept with them as anyone. A Harvard grad with an M.B.A. from Carnegie Mellon, Law literally hadn't picked up a bat since he was eight years old—"unless to beat up a small appliance or something," he cracked—but sure picked up his eyebrows when Ricciardi phoned him out of nowhere, from the once unapproachable beyond of the baseball front office.

"We're trying to get ready for the Rule 5 draft here," Ricciardi said. "Any suggestions?"

Law tossed out the names of some fringe prospects the Jays could take a flyer on, and explained how their statistics gave them promise. The two bandied about various players and evaluation methods for ten minutes before Ricciardi popped the question.

"Would you come work for me?"

Law thought it over for about half a second.

"Absolutely."

By the time the Blue Jays brought in Law, most organizations in baseball were already integrated: They had hired a full-time employee, or an outside contractor like Eddie Epstein, to form their front office's statistical research division. Many of the in-house guys were assistant general managers out of the DePodesta mold: twentysomething kids from top schools (Harvard, Yale, Haverford, and others) with majors in political science and economics and minors in self-taught sabermetrics. They instinctively understood how to interpret a Double-A slugger's statistics to predict if he was ready for the big leagues. They knew how to use equivalent average and defense independent pitching stats. They programmed their own methods in Excel and Java. As older, more traditional executives have retired over the past decade, these kids took their place, transforming the landscape of front offices throughout the major leagues. In 2002, my survey of 50 baseball executives found that exactly half had learned the game in large part by playing Strat-O-Matic as kids. That portion will only grow.

The old are learning from the young, too. In that same survey, I asked each executive, who ranged in age from 24 to 75, "If you could choose only one conventional statistic to rate a hitter, which would it be?" The far-and-away winner was on-base percentage, with batting average pushed well to the side. Roger Jongewaard, a 66-year-old longtime scout for the Mariners, laughed when he realized his answer was OBP. "Ten years ago, I wouldn't have said that," he said. "I would have said batting average. But [OBP has] been proven to work. You'd be foolish not to take notice." Respect for on-base percentage has developed to the point where the A's, Dodgers, and Mets drill an on-base mentality into their minor league prospects by denying promotions to kids who don't reach certain OBP thresholds. In 2002, the Indians went straight from encouragement to outright bribery: any hitter who led his minor league team in on-base percentage won a $100 bonus.

Is on-base percentage the hippest stat around? Well, not quite. That honor goes to OPS, short for on-base *plus* slugging percentage. This number, first brought to public attention by Pete Palmer and the *New York Times* in the mid-1980s, merges baseball's two most significant official statistics into one übermeasure of hitting skill which is so easy to figure, and so intuitively reasonable, that it has graduated to the mainstream. Baseball's most popular journalist, ESPN's Peter Gammons, has used and evangelized it for years, with other writers and broadcasters following suit. Several major league stadiums have started putting the statistic on their giant scoreboards when batters stride to the plate. The ultimate triumph? Starting in 2004, OPS now appears on the backs of Topps baseball cards.

Twenty years after the on-base revolution began with Eric Walker and the A's, almost all of baseball has converted to this new understanding. Hard-core traditionalists may gasp as the OBP, OPS, and EqA gremlins invade their favorite sport. But more are coming. If Ron Antinoja and Bob Bowman have their way, if their 3-D cameras and other widgets work as expected, those quaint little statistics will soon have to make room for new measures the stat freaks have only dreamed of.

12

In God We Trust; All Others Must Have Data

That's the slickest fuckin' thing I've ever seen in my life."

Bob Bowman had just seen the future of baseball statistics, right there in his Manhattan conference room. It might as well have just reached out from the PowerPoint slideshow screen and grabbed him by the knot of his tie.

As CEO of mlb.com, Major League Baseball's mother Web site, Bowman has spent the past three years—and more than $70 million of baseball ownership's money—building a one-stop Internet portal that allows fans to connect with the game in ways unfathomable not long ago. They can listen to any radio broadcast in the country live. Follow every game at once through pitch-by-pitch box scores. Wake up in the morning, pop on the computer, and find customized video highlight reels of their Rotisserie league players waiting in their inbox. But one matter had stuck in Bowman's craw: his Web site's statistics section. For all the categories they'd added, all the sorting options, the thing just seemed so . . . twentieth century, dammit. Bowman wanted to blow fans away with statistics they've never seen before. New numbers that leave them entranced, slack-jawed—just like he was at that moment.

Two seats behind him, a bearded man before a laptop computer clicked his mouse, narrating giddily as he threw up yet another gorgeous graphic on the screen.

"You see, Bonds faced 1,266 pitches—70 were swinging strikes, 188 were looking strikes, and 304 were put into play . . . When he swings,

23.5 percent were strong contact, 33.1 percent were medium contact, 28.1 weak contact . . . If you click here, you can see that he hit only .263 against right-handed changeups."

Ron Antinoja kept on pressing PowerPoint keys in the business presentation of his life. Four years earlier Antinoja was a 50-year-old, burned-out software engineer wanting to try something new. So he developed the most futuristic stat-keeping system around, one so enticing that he was granted two hours to pitch the mlb.com bigwigs. With every mouse click Antinoja let loose a new statistic that might as well have skittered across the screen like one of those cymbal-clapping clowns, leaving his audience giggling in glee. Want to know which pitches Pedro Martinez is most likely to throw after a 1–0 fastball? No problem. Want to assess how Jason Giambi fares against sliders? You could look at his performance against each one he faced, where on the field he hit the ball, how hard, and his hot and cold areas within the strike zone. The coolest part came when Antinoja showed that the user could monkey with this last little feature all he or she pleased. "The hot and cold zones are calculated based on OPS," he said. "You can change that to slugging percentage, batting average, whatever you want." When Antinoja did just that, Giambi's red, yellow and green areas—*zip!*—adjusted accordingly. "Holy shit!" one executive blurted.

Bowman was slightly more restrained. He clunked his forehead on the desk in amazement. Moments later he lifted it up, laughing.

"We have to do this," he declared. "We haven't even scratched the surface of how interesting baseball statistics can be. We *have* to do this." He rose from his chair to remove his sport jacket and slipped his arms through the sleeves, never once taking his eyes off the screen.

As a kid in the late 1950s, Ron Antinoja was the best scorekeeper that the Ironwood, Michigan, adult softball league had ever seen. Perfect batting averages, typed out nice and neat. Keeping statistics was an escape for the little boy as he grew up on welfare (his father had been injured in a mining accident). In college, Antinoja studied the learning processes of dolphins and whales; he later caught the software-engineering bug, got a master's in computer science, and spent 20 years in Silicon Valley as a consultant on artificial intelligence. As the millennium turned, he was ready for something different. Something *fun*, as much fun as scoring those softball games as a kid. Antinoja was driving down I-280 outside San Francisco, en route to another dull workday, daydreaming about how he might merge his two passions: artificial intelligence and batting averages. The minute he thought of it, he got off the highway, quit his job, and began a new baseball statistics company.

The landscape was already quite crowded. STATS Inc. has been the industry leader for 15 years, servicing media outlets such as ESPN, the Associated Press, and Yahoo, as well as a majority of major league teams in packages worth $50,000 to $200,000. The Elias Sports Bureau, Sports-Ticker (a descendant of the old Howe Baseball Bureau), Inside Edge, and Baseball Info Solutions (the company founded by ex-STATS CEO John Dewan) have similar businesses. You can walk into the press box during any major league game—all 2,430 of them each season—and find at least four people sitting within ten yards of each other doing one and only one thing: keeping score. Many of them are recent college graduates dumb-founded at getting paid $75 for something they would do anyway. "My dad used to take me to Orioles games and taught me how to score when I was seven," one STATS Inc. scorer said in between pitches of a Mets-Expos game. "I never thought it would become a marketable skill."

Like the writers around them, each scorer's outlet asks for something different, trying to trump the competition with deeper information. Mlb.com scorers record where every pitch crosses the strike zone, the data instantly flashing across the Internet to surfers "watching" on their com-puters. (As the game tightens, viewers can instantly call up the statistics of every possible pinch hitter against any reliever.) STATS has started keeping what it calls "TVL" data—the type, velocity, and location of every pitch thrown in the big leagues, so that its clients (for this expen-sive product, mainly teams) can assess how hitters fare against fastballs and curveballs at different speeds. Antinoja is keeping TVL data as well, but most importantly, marrying it with his artificial-intelligence algo-rithms to make the information more usable than ever.

For now, Antinoja is on precarious financial ground. STATS has News Corporation as its corporate parent. BIS has Dewan's financial backing. Antinoja is basically going it alone. After convincing his wife, Margot, that he hadn't lost his mind with this statistics venture, the cou-ple sold their house in Redwood City, California, and moved to Bain-bridge Island, just across Elliot Bay from Seattle. Why such a remote outpost? One, it's a gorgeous, woodsy isle, a place anyone with eyes would love to call home. And two, in this day and age, you don't have to sit in the press box to keep baseball stats. You can be just about anywhere, keeping score off satellite.

This is just what Antinoja, and his staff of 17 former college and pro

Ron Antinoja (standing). (*John Clark*)

ballplayers, do for roughly 15 hours a day during the baseball season. The office is decidedly barebones: Fourteen cubicles each house one 13-inch DirecTV monitor, VCR, and TiVo digital recorder to allow scorers to pause and rewind live action. They watch and record each game's every conceivable detail: the type, velocity, and location of every pitch, even the degree of curve it experienced on the way to the plate; precisely where and how hard the ball was hit; and the results of every play. The work environment doesn't exactly scream big business—T-shirt and sneaker-clad scorers take breaks by playing Wiffle ball outside, and at night, when the drainage pond below the porch fills with frogs, their *ribbit*ing can get pretty distracting. That's not what Ryan Rongcal hates most, though. "It pisses me off when a commercial ends late and I miss a pitch," said the former junior-college shortstop, while scoring an A's-Twins game with Torii Hunter at the plate. With every pitch—even before Hunter swings for the first time—Rongcal made at least ten mouse clicks to record the action (or lack thereof). On a 2–2 count, Hunter slammed a high-and-outside curveball over the right-field fence for a home run. "What a stud," Rongcal said, before a dozen additional clicks stuffed ever more information into the database.

Making that data come alive is the hard part, and this is where Antinoja distinguishes himself among the STATS and BIS behemoths of the statistics world. His software interface, which can run on any PC connected to the Internet, is easy and intuitive enough for even tobacco-chewing coaches to master, allowing them to troll around the zillions of bits of information to find patterns in player performance that might provide a competitive edge. (This led Antinoja to name his company Tendu, for players' "tendencies to do things.") It's all well and good that Alex Rodriguez hits lefthanders at a .305 clip, with an 1.056 OPS—heck, Elias could have told you that kind of information in the mid-1970s—but what is the best pitch to throw him early? (A fastball: his slugging percentage against breaking stuff before 1–1 counts is 30 percent higher.) How does Curt Schilling alter his pitch patterns later in games? (After the seventh inning, he throws considerably more fastballs on the first pitch.) These types of statistics are accessible with the Tendu service, and complicated algorithms will soon extract the most significant patterns for coaches automatically. "In artificial intelligence, I studied how the memory works and how people retrieve the right experience and apply it," Antinoja said. "How do you present complex information to an expert so that someone can make decisions and do his job? That's the same thing I do now with the baseball data."

Two decades after STATS Inc.'s Edge 1.000 opened up front office executives to the power of new statistics, Tendu wants to indoctrinate on-field personnel. Tendu got its first two clients during 2003: The Mets, who paid $30,000 for the service, and the A's, who got it gratis because their then pitching coach, Rick Peterson, helped develop the software. "If we're looking at how to pitch a hitter, you can see that he's 2-for-42 against left-handed changeups down and away, and 10-for-20 against left-handed curveballs on the inside half. You're looking for predictability factors," Peterson said. "I have a philosophy: 'In God we trust; all others must have data.'" Peterson was hired away during the 2003–04 offseason by the Mets, whose hitting coach, Denny Walling, is also an avid Tendu user. "I can see what guys do with my eyes, but it's better to have proof," Walling said. "My hitters take it pretty seriously."

So do media outlets. ESPN has spoken with Antinoja about purchasing specialized stats for its network broadcasts and *Baseball Tonight* highlight show, to let fans get further inside crucial batter–pitcher confrontations. Does Manny Ramirez look for inside pitches late in counts? How does Barry Zito typically set up his curveball strikeouts? Said one ESPN executive, "This is the type of statistical information fans are going to come to expect." And not just at home. Antinoja has dreams for a wireless application that would allow fans in the stadium stands to predict pitches and other strategic decisions, using Tendu intelligence data, of course, through their cellphones or Palm devices.

These are expensive fantasies, though, and Antinoja just about ran out of money in 2003, falling behind on the data collection to the point where only about 60 percent of pitches were in his database. (Incompleteness can be a fatal failing for a stat company.) He pursued third-party investors with no luck, and started to hear the bloodhounds of bankruptcy scratching at Tendu's doors. Antinoja knew that he'd never survive 2004 without finding a major client or partner.

Then he met Bob Bowman. Antinoja's two-hour sales pitch at mlb.com's offices in December 2003, which I attended, so tantalized Bowman that he all but offered to underwrite Tendu's immediate future. "Don't worry about the collection costs. Don't worry about the feeds. We'll take care of that," Bowman bubbled across the table, sucking down his third Diet Coke of the meeting. "Just get me the data."

This was a perfect match, because little did Antinoja know, Bowman was seeking a partner himself. He was already on the lookout for someone with the software knowledge to design and process oodles of statistics no one had ever seen before. Bowman had his eye on far more than slugging percentages, or even tendency patterns. Getting his three-dimensional camera plan to work would blow the lid off fielding statistics.

In some ways, fielding is baseball statistics' holy grail. Few measures of it have ever carried much meaning. Fielding percentage—the percentage of plays made without an error—was the primary statistic used for more than a hundred years, even though Henry Chadwick, F. C. Lane, and others knew that it was laughably inaccurate. ("It is in the record of his *good plays* that we are to look for the most correct data for an estimate of skill," Chadwick wrote, way back in 1868.) No good-play stat ever developed, though, leaving most experts as confounded as Branch Rickey, who in his seminal 1954 *Life* article wrote, "There is nothing on earth anybody can do with fielding." Some liked to look at the total number of chances a fielder converted per game, a metric experimented with in 1872 and, a century later, dubbed Range Factor by Bill James. Pete Palmer devised a Defensive Linear Weights system, John Dewan and STATS Inc. tried to measure the percentage of plays a fielder made on balls hit in his area (Zone Rating), and James himself devised an incredibly comprehensive and complex übersystem called Win Shares in 2001. But none of these has gained any real currency, because they all basically derive from the same specious input: putouts, assists, and errors. To really assess the skill of a fielder, many more factors must be considered: How hard was the ball hit? Where was the fielder stationed at the moment of contact? How quickly was he able to close the gap between his glove and the ball? Would a stronger throw have beaten the runner, and how fast was the runner moving? Playing defense in baseball is a lot like playing pool: flashy maneuvers might get oohs and aahs, but the best are so deft that difficult-looking moves become unnecessary.

Because objective data is so scattershot, some of baseball's nastiest statistical debates concern fielding. The best example is that of Derek Jeter, the Yankee shortstop whose spectacular plays have become a staple of TV highlight shows. His detractors, most of them Internet statistical analysts from Baseball Prospectus and the like, maintain that for all the great plays Jeter turns, the numerical evidence suggests that he makes far fewer routine plays than scouts and fans realize. In making this point in a February 2001 column, ESPN.com's Rob Neyer trotted out several statistics: from range factor to Clay Davenport's Fielding Translations to Bill James's win shares. Jeter consistently rated among the worst shortstops in baseball. When a *New York Times* feature the next summer heralded how Jeter's already strong defense was improving, a flabbergasted Neyer made the same argument again, infuriating Jeter fans who are constitutionally unable to imagine the Yankee as anything less than great. "It got to the point where some e-mails were threatening to kick my ass if I set foot in New York," Neyer recalled. "Fielding is the last refuge of the idiots. People can say anything they want, because there aren't many statistics to refute it."

Back at mlb.com, Bowman sees an end to these arguments—through the lenses of his three-dimensional camera system. In six stadiums beginning in 2004, his company began installing three special video cameras that focused on the area in front of home plate. They will instantly capture the exact speed and trajectory of every pitch, down to a few inches or miles per hour, making the rather clunky television estimations on which Tendu, STATS, and other companies rely suddenly obsolete. (The technology is similar to the controversial QuesTec camera system the commissioner's office employs to monitor umpires' accuracy in calling balls and strikes.) This, however, is only the beginning. Bowman plans, within a year or two, to install several additional cameras to watch the entire field. These would become the ultimate set of scouting eyes: They would measure exactly how far a third baseman moved to his right to snare a line drive, and how fast that liner traveled; the time it took a runner to get from first to third; and how strong and accurate the throw from right field trying to nail him actually was. "Does Derek go to his left as fast as Nomar? Does he get to all the balls people say he does?" Bowman asked. "Now we can really find out."

These would be the ultimate fielding statistics, delivered in real time to fans over the Internet. And mlb.com could fold it into its growing subscription business, something that really gets Bowman excited. "I think we'll have one million subscribers to this product within three years," Bowman boasted. "Easily. *Easily.*" The trick is designing software that distills the zillions of bits of information the cameras capture into factoids and statistical categories a fan can understand. For that, all Bowman had to do was look a few seats behind him in the conference room in December, where Antinoja heard these grand ideas and smiled, knowing he was just the man for the job. The two companies quickly started negotiations on a six-figure contract. Bowman would get his backbone. Tendu would get its money. And the baseball public would get a whole new set of statistics in the works, estimated time of arrival: 2006.

When informed of the plan, one club's general manager couldn't help but start dreaming of the doors this mlb.com–Tendu alliance might open up. The cameras could record the trajectory of batted balls, identifying the hitters who consistently get the best "wood" on the ball. (Conventional statistics, from batting average all the way up to equivalent average, are contaminated with lucky bloop hits and give no credit for hot-shot lineouts.) Conversely, pitchers could be rated by the opposite measure of giving up the fewest solid shots. And of course, a full camera system could finally generate the first statistics that truly capture defensive skill. "It would answer a lot of questions that we have to just speculate and extrapolate on," the executive said. "We wouldn't have to do that anymore."

It's no surprise that this particular general manager gets jazzed by the notion of a whole new toolbox of sabermetric widgets at his disposal. He is Theo Epstein of the Boston Red Sox, running the most statistically so-phisticated operation in baseball history—complete with a billionaire Bill James disciple, Bill James himself, and a woman in orange sneakers.

To understand how the Red Sox use statistics, you must forget about Bill James. Ignore him. Even if the skeptics can't.

In November 2002, James was hired by the Red Sox as a senior adviser to baseball operations, ending a 14-year stretch in which, having sourly ended his bestselling *Abstract* series in 1988, he worked relatively removed from public attention. He wrote several more conventional baseball books, developed his win shares system, and was phoned by journalists for com-ment during the occasional statistical controversy, but he quite happily had stepped aside as his legion of young sabermetric followers marched on into the Internet Age. As for working for a team directly, he did a little part-time consulting for his beloved Kansas City Royals, but it appeared as if the door he had opened for the Craig Wrights and Eddie Epsteins was closed to him. But quite suddenly in the summer of 2002, the Red Sox called. The team was restructuring its front office with an eye toward incorporating more statistical analysis—owner John Henry was an early *Abstract* fan—so it naturally wanted the most respected sabermetrician of all time. James ac-cepted the position, affording him his first steady salary in almost 30 years, since guarding the Stokely bean plant back in Lawrence. Said Henry: "I don't understand how it took so long for somebody to hire this guy."

Problem was, New England's liberalism stops at the Fenway Park turnstiles; trying anything new with their beloved Red Sox without a town meeting was grounds for outright revolt. When James was hired, and as Epstein and others consulted with him on roster strategy throughout 2003, mortified press types and talkradio-whipped fans lampooned the Sox as an organization mesmerized by statistics, the entire club becoming a pack of number-mumbling zombies. Boston writers accused James of writing out lineup cards for manager Grady Little. Some portrayed Ep-stein as a teenager with a pack of Strat-O-Matic cards, literally rolling the dice on player moves. The Old Towne Team had become the Stat Geek Organization. Any team that would hire a symbol like James, after all, de-served to become a symbol itself.

For all the accusations that the Red Sox were blindly drinking the Kool-Aid of sabermetrics, their front office is far more complex than most understand, and could very well become baseball's model for the future. First, James is nowhere near Boston's sole statistical analyst, as several additional consultants and companies do numbers work for the team. Second, as robust as that side of the operation is, it does not come at the expense of traditional, sit-in-the-stands-with-a-stopwatch scouting. The club doesn't look through just one lens or the other. It looks through both, expecting the most accurate image to come into focus.

The mandate to trust statistics as highly as they do comes straight from the owner's office. Before heading the group that purchased the Red Sox in early 2002 for $700 million, John Henry had always been intrigued by the power of numbers. Born in 1949, and growing up on family farms in rural Illinois and Arkansas, Henry listened to Harry Caray's radio broadcasts of the St. Louis Cardinals so devoutly that he kept his own scorecards and statistics during them. He also played in an APBA tabletop league and learned to figure the stats in his head. When he grew up and became a commodities trader, he used his mathematical eye to devise a model by which a hundred years of price-trend data were used to predict the future; the formulas made him a billionaire, a genius regarded by *Money* magazine as "perhaps the world's foremost commodities broker." Through this, Henry never strayed too far from his baseball roots. He read Bill James's early *Abstracts* as well as Pete Palmer's and John Thorn's *The Hidden Game of Baseball*, looking to sabermetrics for concepts he could apply to the financial world. "I probably got into my business because of growing up with batting averages," Henry once said. "I think I excelled at knowing which statistics had meaning, and which didn't; what constituted a significant statistic in financial markets, and what didn't." The enduring lesson, Henry said, was that "actual data means more than individual perception or belief. It's true of baseball, just as it is in markets."*

Less than a year after buying the Red Sox, Henry went after the most sabermetric GM in the business, Oakland's Billy Beane, and actually bagged him before Beane changed his mind. Boston's next choice was Theo

---

*Sabermetrics and the stock market are becoming ever more intertwined. Morningstar fund analysts have been instructed to read James's old writings to learn how to question accepted truth through statistics, and to apply those lessons to handicapping mutual funds.

Epstein, already their assistant GM and, at 28, regarded by many industry insiders as the top GM prospect in baseball. Raised in nearby Brookline, Epstein (no relation to Eddie Epstein) was what New Englanders call "wicked smart": B.A. from Yale, law degree from the University of San Diego, and a top-notch young baseball mind. He was another prodigy out of the Paul DePodesta mold: no professional baseball experience, but a full spectrum of influences. Epstein was so young, he didn't play Strat-O-Matic; he was a whiz at Micro League Baseball, a computerized simulation game, in which he fiddled with different team structures (power, speed, and so on) to see what fared best. ("Ty Cobb at shortstop didn't work too well," he recalled.) Epstein got his start in baseball as an Orioles college intern and wound up in the baseball operations department of the San Diego Padres, his office literally between general manager Kevin Towers and Eddie Epstein. Towers had the traditional baseball scouting background, talking in tools; Eddie Epstein had the pure statistical bent toward numerical analysis. Theo listened to the two in stereo, picking up the best parts of both approaches. The combination became attractive enough that after Beane backed out, the Red Sox made Epstein the youngest GM in baseball history; he was so young that Jay Leno joked on *The Tonight Show* that Michael Jackson was seen dangling Epstein off his balcony.

Henry and Epstein are just the top of a vertically integrated sabermetric operation. Below them are assistant GM Josh Byrnes, another youngster (just 34) who had worked with Craig Wright in Cleveland and Colorado; Bill James; Vörös McCracken, he of the Defense Independent Pitching Stats; and Jed Hoyer, a 30-year-old assistant in baseball operations who coordinates the information-gathering from all these sources by e-mailing everyone up to 15 times a day. They all read Baseball Prospectus and similar Web sites. They all have access to specialized data from several statistics services, including STATS Inc. and Baseball Info Solutions. And if all these resources somehow don't provide enough statistical clarity, they can call on Susan Reynolds.

Reynolds, who has flown under the radar of even the rabid Boston press, lives and breathes baseball—when she isn't working as a systems engineer for Science Applications International Corporation (SAIC), a California-based defense contractor that does classified work for the U.S. Department of Defense and the CIA. The 39-year-old grew up in San Diego a passionate fan of the Padres, and after joining SAIC decided to merge her love for baseball and mathematical modeling. She developed an algorithm to predict the Padres' wins and losses each day, based on the team's recent performance, home-road splits, starting pitcher, and whatnot, that performed well enough to impress Padres president Larry Lucchino, who later left and became president of (you guessed it) the Red Sox. Lucchino assigns Reynolds projects left and right, most of them returning as gorgeous, three-dimensional graphs and analyses. Many concern Fenway Park's effects on the club. In one study, Reynolds examined a hundred years of Boston weather to see if there was any relationship between changing Boston atmospheric conditions and Fenway offense. "Boston historically has had phenomenal pitching in April and May, and then all of a sudden they fall off the cliff," said Reynolds, wearing a Red Sox jacket, chinos, and bright orange Converse sneakers, her short red hair leaving her a dead ringer for Shirley MacLaine. The weather analysis helped her identify the most suitable *summer* pitcher for Fenway Park. But she can not discuss it further; like her work for the government, that remains classified.*

The Red Sox have built the most comprehensive statistical gathering and analysis operation in major league history, with everyone from the owner to the GM to the front-office secretaries on board. It helped Boston reach the 2003 playoffs and come within one game of its first World Series since 1986. But then all these best-laid plans came toppling down, thanks to a misunderstanding over—of all things—a statistic.

Immediately after being made GM on November 25, 2002, Epstein used his mix of resources—Bill James's 100-page initial report to the club, the opinions of longtime scouts, and several stat services—to pull the trigger on a flurry of moves to improve the offense, all with an eye toward the numbers. He acquired Todd Walker, a good-hit, no-field second baseman; Jeremy Giambi, an on-base wizard best suited for DH; third baseman Bill Mueller, a cheap pickup whose statistics weren't much different than those of David Bell, who had gotten a shocking $17 million contract from the Phillies; another lumbering DH, David Ortiz, a promising hitter coming off injuries in Minnesota; and first baseman Kevin Millar. (All but Mueller

---

*Women are almost certainly the next untapped talent pool for baseball front offices. Executives claim they get outstanding résumés from women all the time. More will be coming: Across the Charles River from Fenway, in Carl Morris's QR32 statistics class at Harvard, two female students are doing their end-term projects on baseball—one assessing different relief statistics and the other examining the uses of Clay Davenport's equivalent average.

were offensive assets with little defensive value, straight out of the Eric Walker School of Roster Management.) The work of Vörös McCracken played a large role here. For each player, as well as dozens the Red Sox did not acquire, McCracken used his personal formulas to predict how they would perform while playing 81 games at Fenway Park, with each suggested stat line given a confidence interval (30 percent, 70 percent, and so on) depending on any injury history and playing time. These were mapped against projected player salaries so the Sox could identify bargains. And that's exactly what Boston got.

The lineup acquisitions hit the jackpot just like Henry's commodities funds. The Red Sox, with returning sluggers Manny Ramirez and Nomar Garciaparra, quickly emerged as one of the greatest offenses in the history of baseball—setting all-time records for extra-base hits (649) and slugging percentage (.491), the latter breaking the mark held by the fabled 1927 "Murderer's Row" Yankees—while scoring almost six runs per game. Mueller was a sensation, leading the American League with a .326 batting average and, in the categories that the Sox actually value, posted a .398 on-base percentage and .540 slugging percentage. Millar hit 25 homers and drove in 96 runs. The one pickup that backfired was that of Giambi: he struggled so badly the first two months, batting .191, that he lost his everyday lineup spot to Ortiz. (The stat men could have ascribed Giambi's falloff to luck—seven weeks was a small sample—but *traditional* scouting convinced the club that Giambi was swinging through so many easy fastballs that something more substantial had to be wrong.) Meanwhile, an early slump by Ortiz had no apparent cause, so Epstein felt comfortable chalking that up to simple bad luck. He was right: Ortiz soon caught fire and wound up batting .293 with 29 home runs and 82 RBIs the last two-thirds of the season, contending for the Most Valuable Player award.

The offensive moves worked beautifully; monkeying with the bullpen blew up in Boston's face. This was a gambit the stat buffs had long recommended. For three decades, managers had gradually come to use their top relievers exclusively in situations when they would receive a "save"—a statistic recording when a pitcher enters a late game with a one-, two-, or three-run lead, preserves the lead, and nails down the final out. (This is one case of baseball statistics actually changing strategy; the save rule was born in 1969, and starting with Chicago Cubs fireman Bruce Sutter in the late 1970s, closers soon were reserved for "save situations.") This approach was patently foolish to most followers of baseball statistics: Wasn't it better to deploy your top weapon when the game was most in doubt?

Eldon and Harlan Mills, way back in 1970, had proven that a reliever influences the outcome of games considerably more when the game is tied in the eighth than when his team leads by two in the ninth, so why save your best guy for a juncture when he matters less? Bill James took this view, as did Theo Epstein and his lieutenants, and even manager Grady Little said it sounded reasonable. So the Boston front office, justifiably proud of its gumption and bracing for public backlash, announced that in 2003 Boston relievers would be used according to logic, not legend.

It was a debacle from the start. Cruelly, on Opening Day, Boston relievers Alan Embree and Chad Fox squandered a 4–1, ninth-inning lead to Tampa Bay to lose 6–4. Several other similar disasters followed, quickly making Boston's bullpen strategy the laughingstock of baseball. (As Epstein's told me, "It Hindenburged.") It also became an indictment of sabermetrics in general, and raised Boston's inherent skepticism of the James-Epstein alliance to a fever pitch. Red Sox relievers finished the season with a 4.83 ERA, worse than all but the lowly Royals and Rangers. Were James and the Mills brothers proven wrong? Epstein doesn't think so: he believes that his 2003 relievers were simply not good enough to get hitters out, no matter when they were deployed. He defiantly promised to use his reconstituted relief staff the same way in 2004.

Through last summer's bullpen disaster, Boston survived well enough to post a 95-67 record, win the American League's wild-card playoff berth, beat Beane's A's in the Division Series, and move on to face the hated Yankees. Their Championship Series went back and forth until it reached a climactic Game Seven, when all of Boston was confident that the Sox would finally beat New York—mainly because their ace, Pedro Martinez, would be starting the game. This all but guaranteed Boston a late lead; Martinez rarely completed games because his fragile right shoulder tired at the end, but he was spectacularly effective if removed at the appropriate juncture. Needless to say, the Boston front office rendezvoused with Little to discuss when that juncture typically was. They delivered to him a comprehensive STATS Inc. report on Martinez's 2003 performance and specifically discussed these numbers, which illustrated how Martinez fell apart late in games:

Innings 1–6: .555 OPS

Innings 7–9: .758 OPS

Pitches 1–105: .574 OPS

Pitches 106 on: .845 OPS

Martinez quite clearly hit a wall around the seventh inning and 105 pitches, and Little, who met with Epstein before Game Seven to go over bullpen strategy, was made aware of this. Confident his manager understood Martinez's limitations, Epstein watched the game from his Yankee Stadium seat. What he witnessed went completely according to plan: Martinez mounted a 4–1 lead after six innings. In the seventh he appeared somewhat shaky, giving up a Jason Giambi home run and two singles. But after the Sox added a run in the top of the eighth to keep Boston's lead at three runs, Little stayed with Martinez, who was up to 100 pitches at that time. Martinez opened the eighth by getting Nick Johnson to pop to shortstop. Then all hell broke loose.

Derek Jeter worked a deep count before doubling to deep right field on pitch number 110. Bernie Williams singled him home on pitch number 115 to make the score 5–3. Little walked to the mound to check on Martinez, with almost everyone in the baseball world assuming he would remove him. But he didn't. Rather than go by the STATS Inc. report, which clearly suggested Martinez was through, Little gambled and kept him in. On pitch number 118, Hideki Matsui doubled to right, and then Jorge Posada doubled to center field, scoring Williams and Matsui to tie the game at 5–5. Boston's lead was gone. It was only then that Little emerged again and finally removed Martinez.

The Red Sox never led again. They lost the game in extra innings on an Aaron Boone home run that shattered New England's plans for a World Series. The irony was not that the Sox had lost again in horrifying fashion. (That was actually quite predictable.) It wasn't that they finished second to the despised Yankees yet again. It was that the most statistically prepared organization in baseball had been undermined by something so apparent in the stat sheets. A month later, Epstein saw Martinez's meltdown as a clog in the information pipeline the club had so carefully constructed. "It was just a failure of me to do my job well," he said. "I did not get through [to Little] what the front office wanted in clear enough terms on an issue that was obviously so important. I failed."

Epstein might have failed, but Little lost his job. The following week, the Red Sox announced that Little would not return as manager for 2004. They ultimately replaced him with Terry Francona, a younger, more tractable manager who expressed an openness to following the statistics—to having that information pipeline remain unclogged by something so flimsy and ephemeral as a manager's hunch. As Lucchino described it, the club wanted Francona to be more "synchronous" with the front office's trust in sabermetrics. He added, "We seek one unified organizational philosophy."

Soon after he uttered those words, though, the marketer in Lucchino pulled back. "This is not going to be a stat geek organization," he vowed. Such a label, of course, is the mortal fear of the modern front office. Respecting the numbers is fine. Explaining their importance to neophytes is fine. (It feeds the ego.) But being *identified* with statistics—courting any likeness to the oddball, laptop-toting propellerheads who populate SABR— is too great an indignity for a major league insider to risk. Lucchino isn't alone. Billy Beane, the patron saint of statistic-respecting general managers, was once asked if he might actually attend a SABR gathering, so that some of his biggest fans might get to meet him. Beane bristled at the idea. "That," he said, "would be like Captain Kirk going to a *Star Trek* convention."

In some ways, Beane wasn't that far off. Had he actually dropped by the 2003 SABR convention at the Denver Marriott, his image of the jamboree probably would have been confirmed. Particularly had he sat in on the meeting of SABR's Statistical Analysis Committee. The room attracted the nation's most passionate numbers buffs, a motley crew of fans downright pickled in their love of statistics. There were lots of beards, and even more thick, plastic glasses. Almost everyone wore some sort of baseball-logoed T-shirt, cap, or jacket, many with all three. An odd number of men spoke with a lisp, while another bore an eerie resemblance to, and sounded alarmingly like, the nerdy scientist from *The Simpsons*. But the annual convention affords these folks some safety in numbers—it is their one chance during the year to gather among themselves and talk about their new sabermetric theories. "I love developing new baseball statistics," confided one woman, in real life a University of Minnesota law professor. "But I can't talk about it with other faculty until I get tenure." Soon she broke off, rejoining her conversation with several men about optimal batting orders, clutch hitting, and other eternal questions.

When their hour was up, most members of the Statistical Analysis Committee remained in the room for the meeting that followed. Because any sabermetricians who want to look deep into baseball's past and determine what Babe Ruth batted with runners in scoring position, or figure out which all-time batter had the best leadoff on-base percentage, had better get to know the folks at Retrosheet.

Retrosheet is the brainchild of a University of Delaware biology professor (yes, he's tenured) who fell hopelessly in love with baseball in

July 1958, when he attended his first major league game. Ten-year-old
Dave Smith sat way up in the stands down the Los Angeles Coliseum left-
field line with his father, who, under the glow of the lights, taught him
how to score. Dave was hooked and became a lifelong fan, through college
and a successful biology career, keeping that scorebook forever to remind
him of the night it all began.

Many of his baseball-fan friends were jealous. They wished they
could look at a scorecard from their first game, to let the memories wash
over them anew. But nowhere—not at Major League Baseball, not in the
Baseball Encyclopedia file archives up in Cooperstown, not even at the
Elias Sports Bureau—did full accounts of games before 1975 exist. Distil-
lations in the form of box scores, yes, but not the narratives that play-by-
play provided. "This was a travesty," Smith recalled.

So in 1989, Smith founded a volunteer organization aimed to right
this grievous wrong—to, very simply, gather scoresheets from every major
league game, all the way back to 1871. The statistics those pages held!
What did Ty Cobb hit in the clutch? Did Ted Williams hit lefties as well
as he did righties? To what extent was Whitey Ford a groundball or flyball
pitcher, and (like Pedro Martinez) did he fall apart late in games? These
were the types of questions for which Elias had started its *Player Analysis*
printouts for teams in 1975, and inspired Bill James to found Project
Scoresheet in 1984. But play-by-play information from before those years
did not exist, because no outfit had bothered to warehouse the records.
Wanting to make up for that, Smith formed a group he called Retrosheet,
banding together fans like him who wanted to gather all those old play-
by-plays and romp in them like leaf piles.

Retrosheet's mission to piece together this long-discarded (and possibly irrecoverable) history into one integrated database is almost certainly
unrealistic; baseball historian Paul Dickson has likened it to "trying to recreate a puff of cigar smoke from William Howard Taft's mouth." But the
organization, which has grown to 100 members, has managed to gather
and computer-code almost 70,000 of the 116,000 major league games
that took place between 1901 and 1983, and adds new ones every day.
"Grains of sand don't have an end point," said the 56-year-old Smith.
"This has an end point. It's an awful lot of games, but an awful lot is not
forever."

Silver-bearded and delightfully bouncy, Smith first called individual
clubs and asked if he could copy their troves of scorebooks. Some, like the
Indians, had everything going back to 1947. Others, like the Braves, were

laughably lacking. But Smith approached other sources as well, mainly sportswriters. The widow of legendary New York baseball writer Dick Young donated all his scorebooks back to 1945. Bob Stevens, who covered the Giants for 30 years, almost cried when Smith called and offered to give his boxes of spiral notebooks a good home. "All these years I never knew why I saved my scorebooks," Stevens said. "I guess I was saving them for you."

Dozens of volunteers have joined Retrosheet's search for as many play-by-plays as possible. Some, like the first *Baseball Encyclopedia* team in the late 1960s, eyeball old newspaper microfilm to piece together game action. Jim Wolenhaus, a former government employee, scours eBay every day to locate old scorecards, contacts the sellers, and offers them $1 for a photocopy of the scoresheet page. Other people input the games into the computer. (One such volunteer has plenty of time on his hands. He lives at the South Pole—literally, he's an instrument repairman at South Pole Station—and stays connected via the Internet.) All the physical sheets wind up back in the wood-paneled basement of Smith's Newark, Delaware, home, the official Retrosheet repository. Five dusty, paint-chipped file cabinets house them all, next to a microfilm reader and the Retrosheet server, a homemade Linux computer whose LEDs blink every time someone around the world accesses data from a Retrosheet Web page. They flicker almost a thousand times a day.

The cost to fans? Absolutely nothing. Smith pays much of the expenses himself, including $200 a month for the server's high-speed Internet connection, and refuses to charge a penny to anyone, anytime, even when they guiltily beg him to accept. Why? Because Smith remembers how money, back in 1987, tore Bill James's old Project Scoresheet apart. Smith scored many Orioles and Phillies games for Project Scoresheet, and later served as the organization's president after John Dewan's acrimonious exit for STATS Inc. PS held on for a few years after that, but the infighting over finances proved too corrosive.* Wanting to avoid such

---

*In a wild twist, the heart of Project Scoresheet is still beating. Its computer scoring system, after some changes in ownership, was eventually sold to mlb.com, which now uses the algorithms to keep the statistics that get funneled to Elias to become official. How ironic that Bill James's group of renegade outsiders, formed to break the MLB-Elias statistics monopoly, now assists in the churning out of every official statistic.

arguments, Smith decided that all of Retrosheet's information would always be free, no matter what.

One of Smith's best friends was dumbfounded at this: *You're spending 50 hours a week on this stuff, and then giving it all away?* This was a guy who knew a thing or two about the baseball stat business, too. It was none other than Seymour Siwoff.

Believe it or not, Smith, whose goal is to make every statistic free, is buddies with the one lambasted for keeping them proprietary. The two crossed paths in the mid-1990s—they were bound to—and Smith was so friendly, his passion for baseball statistics so pure, that Siwoff immediately took a liking to him (particularly when Smith was smart enough never to ask for any data). In early 1999, the two got together up at Elias's New York offices one Saturday—even in his eighties Siwoff still tends to the business seven days a week—and shared an afternoon just talking baseball and family. When conversation turned to Retrosheet and Smith's charging nothing for his data, Siwoff was still befuddled.

"They'll take advantage of you," he warned.

"I can't be taken advantage of, Seymour," Smith said. "I want to give it all away to *everyone*."

Siwoff shook his head. Then he confided something that explained so much about the old man, about all the years he shut himself off from the growing statistics community.

"I'm terrified of you," he said.

Smith's generosity has indeed helped Retrosheet become the preferred resource for baseball researchers, and not just the stat fiends. For more than a century, ballplayers' rambling remembrances of so-and-so's seven straight strikeouts and a batter's 5-for-5 afternoon have been pure fiction, with no way to confirm them. Now there is. Following interviews for her recent biography of Sandy Koufax, Jane Leavy checked with Retrosheet 40 different anecdotes that old Dodgers players had told her, and found almost every one of them either off or entirely wrong. Billy Crystal's office called to confirm a scoreboard shot for the Mickey Mantle–Roger Maris movie *61**, while Spike Lee personally phoned Smith while researching a movie about Jackie Robinson.

Not surprisingly, Retrosheet's growing archives have unearthed more than a thousand mistakes in MLB's official statistics. Most are piddling little curiosities (even the most ardent SABRites don't lose sleep over the fact that in 1983 Cliff Johnson grounded into 11 double plays, not 10) but others are more serious. Smith is convinced beyond a doubt that Maris, in the 1961 season in which he broke the home run record, was assigned one RBI too many by the old Howe Baseball Bureau, and no one ever caught it. No huge deal, perhaps, but removing that RBI from Maris also takes away his outright RBI title and puts him into a tie with Jim Gentile at 141. A Retrosheet volunteer actually tracked down Gentile in Oklahoma to inform the 65-year-old of this development. "Who the hell is this?" Gentile barked, before getting increasingly intrigued. "Goddamn it, I had a $5,000 clause if I led the league in RBIs! You think I can get those bastards to give it to me?"

Retrosheet's Web site now houses full play-by-play of almost every single major league game dating back to 1967, and the complete seasons keep creeping backward. This allows sabermetricians to attack questions that until now had remained unanswerable. A perfect example came in 2001, when writers and fans were debating Jack Morris's candidacy for the Hall of Fame. Morris, an outstanding right-hander with three World Series rings (1984 Tigers, 1991 Twins, and 1992 Blue Jays), had a surprisingly high 3.90 career ERA, making some wonder if his 254 career wins derived as much from his teammates as his talent. A common response among Morris's defenders was that the pitcher bore down in close games, when it counted, but gave up meaningless runs in blowouts. (He "pitched to the score," in baseball parlance.) This alibi was impossible to examine until the play-by-play of every Morris start was available—in other words, until Retrosheet came along. Baseball Prospectus writer Joe Sheehan dove into the data, painstakingly measured the pitcher's performance in every score situation (up by one, tied, down by five, and so on) and discovered that, in fact, Morris was no more stingy in tight games than otherwise. It didn't matter what the pitcher, his teammates or baseball writers said; the statistics proved that this "pitching to the score" business was almost certainly hogwash.

In the end, Retrosheet has become a celebration of baseball built by fans for fans. Their sense of community and love for their favorite sport pulse through every Web page. Going through all the play-by-plays has allowed one researcher to gather the 190 known times a runner has fallen for the dreaded hidden-ball trick. Another list has all sorts of bizarre plays that time would otherwise forget, the crazy rundowns and other scoring oddities. (One day in 1970, a strikeout actually went down 7-6-7, with the left fielder throwing to the shortstop, who then threw back to the left fielder for the putout. Don't ask.) But at Retrosheet, the statistics are the stars. More than a hundred million digits are housed on the Web site, giving fans almost anything they could ever want—Hank Aaron's monthly splits to Bob Gibson's clutch pitching—all absolutely free. Back in Smith's basement, every blink of his computer lights testifies that someone, somewhere, is looking at Retrosheet's statistics, whether to relive their first game, to conduct some sabermetric study, or just to splash around.

Somewhere, Henry Chadwick is getting wired for broadband.

S mith doesn't spend as much time down in his cellar as he used to. Retrosheet has gathered enough momentum for him to step back a bit, and use his extra time to play catch outside with his 6-year-old, Graham.

Like so many others, father and son have devised a makeshift, backyard baseball game. Pop pitches while Graham, a brown-haired little kid about as skinny as his bat, tries to hit the ball toward the brick wall in front of a neighbor's garage. The post on the jungle gym is first base. The slide is second base. The two of them spend hour after hour out there in the yard, playing ball. Graham adores it even more than his father.

One afternoon, Graham took his place in the batter's box, hoisted his plastic bat above his shoulder, and awaited Pop's pitch. But just before play got under way, he stopped, dropped his bat and ran inside. Something was dreadfully wrong. His father ran after him.

Little did Smith know, but his son had inherited the same basic instinct that runs back through every generation of baseball fans, from John Dewan and Bill James, to George Lindsey and Allan Roth, all the way to Ernie Lanigan and Henry Chadwick, and the millions of others from which Graham's nascent love for baseball had descended. It was very simple: No ballgame could be complete without statistics, could it?

Smith opened the back door to find little Graham sitting happily at the kitchen table, pencil and paper in hand. He was scribbling out a scorecard.

Acknowledgments

O ne of the great pleasures of writing your first book, I have found, is the deep and pure satisfaction in getting to thank those who helped you along the way.

The generosity of members of the Society for American Baseball Research was simply staggering, and only underscored their passion for this subject. Pete Palmer and John Thorn donated their memories and libraries, and lent me research material without which the project might very well have stalled. The staff at the A. Bartlett Giamatti Research Center at the Hall of Fame in Cooperstown and *The Sporting News* archives in St. Louis were helpful as well. I shudder to think how I would have unearthed old articles, particularly those in *Baseball Magazine*, without the spectacular Baseball Index developed by SABR volunteers. Matthew Namee and Jim Meier provided research help, yet by no means can their contributions compare to those of my assistants, Jesse Spector and Eben Lasker, who in addition to a dozen library trips preserved my tenuous sanity by transcribing almost 100 hours of interview tapes.

As for those interviews, every one of the more than 150 people who took the time to speak with me deserves a thank you, but I tip my hat specifically to those who did so before the project gained any legitimacy: Carl Morris, David Neft, Jesse Poore, Bryson Cook, Eldon Mills, and George Lindsey. Counsel even before that came from Rick Wolff, Sam Vaughan, Greg Brown, Steve Marantz, and most of all my *New York Times Book Review* editor, Michael Anderson, who threatened to cut off all assignments until I wrote a damn book myself.

That book now exists in part because my *Newsweek* editor, David Kaplan, recommended me to his agent, Esther Newberg. (Esther, thanks for taking me on anyway.) Pete Wolverton at St. Martin's Press was a wonderful, reassuring editor. And I also must acknowledge my colleagues at *Baseball America*, who granted me the three-month sabbatical during which I formulated an early plan for the book, and who put up with my working on it throughout the 2003 baseball season.

Speaking of tolerance, no one offered more than my new and fantabulous wife, Laura, who not only put up with my eighteen months of preoccupation but even married me during them. Let the payback begin.

Alan Schwarz
New York, January 2004

 **Index**

Note: Page numbers containing illustrations are given in italics.